The United States in World History

In this short, accessible introductory survey of the history of the United States from 1790 to the present day, Edward J. Davies examines key themes in the evolution of America from colonial rule to international supremacy. Focusing particularly on those currents within U.S. history that have influenced the rest of the world, this study examines the key themes and concepts that have determined America's global influence. Offering a new way of examining the United States, this book reveals how concepts that originated in America's definition of itself as a nation – concepts such as capitalism, republicanism and race – have had supranational impact across the world.

Focusing on three areas, which examine the Atlantic world 1700–1800, the U.S. and the industrial world and the emergence of America as a global power, *The United States in World History* examines:

- the social and economic systems of the British Atlantic community
- the American Revolution and its international dimensions
- the impact of industrialization on U.S. trade and the emergence of the 'corporation' in the nineteenth century
- the expansion of U.S. consumer and cultural industries from the early twentieth century
- the Cold War and its implications for United States economic and political power throughout the globe.

This concise and readable text places the history of the United States in its broadest context and will be invaluable to those studying world history.

Edward J. Davies, II is an Associate Professor at the University of Utah. He has recently served on the Advisory Board for National Geographic's world history publication focusing on North America. He has also served on the Executive Committee for the World History Association.

Themes in World History
Series editor: Peter N. Stearns

The *Themes in World History* series offers focused treatment of a range of human experiences and institutions in the world history context. The purpose is to provide serious, if brief, discussions of important topics as additions to textbook coverage and document collections. The treatments will allow students to probe particular facets of the human story in greater depth than textbook coverage allows, and to gain a fuller sense of historians' analytical methods and debates in the process. Each topic is handled over time – allowing discussions of changes and continuities. Each topic is assessed in terms of a range of different societies and religions – allowing comparisons of relevant similarities and differences. Each book in the series helps readers deal with world history in action, evaluating global contexts as they work through some of the key components of human society and human life.

The United States in World History

Edward J. Davies, II

 Routledge
Taylor & Francis Group

NEW YORK AND LONDON

First published 2006 by Taylor & Francis Inc
270 Madison Ave, New York, NY 10016

Simultaneously published in the UK by Routledge
2 Park Square, Milton Park, Abingdon, Oxon OX14 4RN

Routledge is an imprint of the Taylor & Francis Group, an informa business

© 2006 Edward J. Davies, II

Typeset in Garamond 3 and Gills Sans by
Keystroke, Jacaranda Lodge, Wolverhampton
Printed and bound in Great Britain by
The Cromwell Press, Trowbridge, Wiltshire

Library of Congress Cataloging in Publication Data
Davies, Edward J., II, 1947–
The United States in world history / Edward J. Davies, II.
p. cm. – (Themes in world history)
Includes bibliographical references and index.
1. United States–History. 2. United States–Foreign relations. 3. World history.
I. Title. II. Series.
E178.D245 2006
973–dc22
2005036122

British Library Cataloguing in Publication Data
A catalogue record for this book is available from the British Library

ISBN10: 0–415–27529–6 (hbk)   ISBN13: 978–0–415–27529–3 (hbk)
ISBN10: 0–415–27530–X (pbk)   ISBN13: 978–0–415–27530–9 (pbk)
ISBN10: 0–203–08621–X (ebk)   ISBN13: 978–0–203–08621–6 (ebk)

To Lili, my sweet, sweet Love

And to my precious daughters, Erin and Mary Anne

Contents

Preface

In 1992 when I first introduced the United States in world history as a course, I never anticipated writing a book on the topic. Over the years as I read more and more in the various literatures that touched on the United States and its presence across the globe, I became ever more convinced of the worthiness of addressing the United States from a larger perspective. Several years ago Peter N. Stearns gave me the opportunity to write such a book for his series, Themes in World History. In researching and writing this book, I learned a great deal more about the participation of the United States in global processes such as migration and realized the need always to consider the ways what seem to be domestic issues are dramatically affected by distant locations and events.

I would like to thank my colleagues who helped me think through the topic of the United States in world history. Peter Von Sivers first encouraged me to participate in the World History group that introduced the field into our curriculum. Despite my initial misgivings on teaching world history, the decision to embrace it transformed my entire understanding of history as a discipline and certainly the place of the United States in the world. Anand Yang, now director of the Jackson School of International Studies at the University of Washington, remained a staunch supporter of my efforts to rethink United States history. He helped provide me with fiscal and material resources to learn world history and to develop the course, The United States in world history. He also included me in many trips to Asia that broadened my own perception of the world. Without his backing neither the course nor the book would have been possible. Eric Hinderaker, chair of the department, listened to many of my queries on the colonial period and provided many useful suggestions. Ray Gunn during his tenure as chair also gave financial support and flexibility in developing world history courses that created a very favourable atmosphere in which to write and teach. Of course what errors of fact or interpretation that exist in the book are solely mine.

On a more personal level, my daughters Mary Anne and Erin, contributed in many unseen ways to the completion of the book. Erin also proofread the entire manuscript. Both she and Mary Anne sustained me through some difficult moments. My mother, Mary, gave me her support and encouragement as she has throughout my academic life. Neither the book nor my career would have been possible without her. My only wish is that my late father could be here for my mother and to see this project reach completion. Last, in 2005 I met the love of my life, Liliana, who brought joy and happiness back into my life. This book is dedicated to her and to my precious daughters.

Chapter 1

Introduction

The United States and world history

My first encounter with 'world history' actually began as an undergraduate when I enrolled in a world history course in the winter of 1966. I was reminded of that experience when a colleague suggested that I join a group of faculty who wanted to introduce world history. From a professional standpoint it made little sense, given the huge commitment of time and energy. From an intellectual position it seemed exciting and full of possibilities. Intimidating from the start, world history demanded an incredible effort in mastering the details and themes that addressed different time periods, human communities, and multiple polities. While engaged in this daunting task, the United States seemed a distraction at best.

Of course, the United States existed as part of the larger human community. The Atlantic migrations of the late nineteenth and early twentieth centuries intimately connected the United States with Europeans. These migrations also joined other Atlantic states such as Argentina and Canada with Europe. The United States, then, relied on similar sources of inexpensive labor that fueled economic growth throughout the Western Hemisphere. United States corporations also created communities of professionals, managers and workers in states such as Mexico and Cuba. Clearly, the United States was intimately bound with larger human communities and processes.

United States' foreign policy also led to the establishment of financial protectorates in the Caribbean and Central America. In some ways, the British protectorate in Egypt inspired those who administered the United States' presence in the Caribbean. Yet, the United States also exported much. Its racial code moved with it to the Philippines, its one formal colony.

By the late twentieth century the United States had developed powerful economic and military institutions. These enabled the country to drive changes across the planet. The Cold War with the late Soviet Union signaled this new capacity, one that technology helped sustain and then expanded as the century came to close. United States corporations, including services companies such as McDonald's, appeared in every major region of the world. United States popular culture moved quickly through mass marketing, Hollywood movies and television programs.

The shift to a larger context in which the United States existed seems unavoidable. Yet, for many in the country, Exceptionalism remains its cornerstone. Its moral vision, its freedoms, its openness and its lack of fixed economic classes makes the United States the one nation in which all other states and peoples find inspiration. Scholarly work raised doubts about the claims to Exceptionalism. Arthur Schlesinger Sr. wrote pieces that called into question the Exceptionalist position. Others certainly followed his lead. Yet, the historical professional remained fixed on the United States until recently. Scholars such as Ian Tyrrell, John Dunlap, Lester Langley and others have revived Schlesinger's concerns. These historians have produced provocative pieces that cut across national boundaries. At the same time, world historians deliberately cast their nets across borders and even continents and oceans. They argue that national histories ignore the complexity of the past and often unmask what historians consider unique or even exceptional about their pasts. World historians have uncovered patterns of disease that proved fundamental in understanding the settlement of North and South America. Globalization, a new buzzword of the twenty-first century, describes the weakening of the nation and its borders as economic institutions, media, finance and a host of other transnational phenomena assume dominance in human affairs. The following chapters address the issue of the United States and its participation in larger human communities and processes that cut across national boundaries. The study argues that Exceptionalism masks patterns of human interaction that join the United States and its citizens to the world and its diverse peoples.

Chapter 2

The Pan-British world in the late eighteenth century

Introduction

By the early eighteenth century, the English had established a series of colonies along the Atlantic coast of North America. These stretched from what became Massachusetts in the north to Georgia in the south. The English claimed land emptied by disease, war, or treaty from the indigenous and then settled in increasingly greater numbers. By the mid- and late 1700s, North American colonies formed a critical part of the commercial empire British merchants built over the course of the seventeenth and eighteenth centuries.

The North American colonies contributed to the health of the British commercial system through the production of staple economies, the development of a vigorous shipbuilding industry and the fielding of an active fleet of ocean-going ships. The North American colonists also reaped important benefits from participating in this commercial empire. They drew the labor for their tobacco, rice and indigo plantations from Africa and they prospered by sustaining British sugar colonies in the Caribbean. They also depended on British laws to protect their economic interests and British warships for protection against hostile European ships. Of course the Atlantic Ocean and the rivers that flowed into it provided the means of moving people and goods across the great distances that separated departure points and destinations.

The British North American colonies joined other British holdings in this larger economic world. Ireland and Scotland exported textile, linen and/or food to England while purchasing manufactured goods. Ireland and Scotland also developed economic ties with the North American colonies. Similarly, the North American colonies engaged in a series of thriving commercial exchanges with British sugar colonies in the Caribbean. In turn, the sugar colonies sold their valuable commodity to the North American colonies and other parts of the British trading system.

Migration also brought together disparate regions of the Atlantic world. Migration pushed streams of individuals across borders, oceans and forests to seek out land and new economic opportunities. Involuntary migration also created African mini worlds in the western Atlantic, constantly reinforced as mortality or demand called for more and more shiploads of Africans destined for the slave pens of the Caribbean or North America. Few could escape the dependency on other regions and/or human communities to survive and prosper.

The North American colonists also existed as part of a broader social world. The leadership in North America looked to London and its fashionable style and behavior for their inspiration. They participated in a transatlantic literary culture anchored by the London publishing industry and the fashionable reading tastes of the city's upper strata. As part of a larger Atlantic world they shared many of the tastes and social distinctions that marked the gentry in Ireland and Scotland as well as England proper.

The middling sort occupied the middle ranks of North American colonial society. The members of the middling sort shared modest living standards and knew their place in the social hierarchy of the colonial world. Their counterparts in the British Isles also lived in modest conditions distinct from the upper strata.

The meaner sort, namely the slaves and the sailors, engaged in grueling and often dangerous labor. Sailors spent time in ports such as Boston and New York City that helped sustain the colonies along the western Atlantic shores. They provided the muscle that sustained the ships and moved the vital cargo that constituted the heart of commercial exchange. At the bottom of the social hierarchy, enslaved Africans or African Americans toiled away for white masters in the Carolinas and Chesapeake region and, especially, on the British sugar islands in the Caribbean. Few slaves lived in the British Isles yet their presence in the North American colonies and the Caribbean depended on the shipping, manufacturing and financial services provided by those in the eastern Atlantic. Interdependency marked all dimensions of the British North American colonies and the larger Pan-British world.

This chapter, then, focuses intensely on the economic, cultural, consumer, literary and labor connections that joined the British North American colonies to the Pan-British world. The chapter also compares the social dimensions of life in the North American colonies with Ireland, Scotland and England.

The dynamics of the Atlantic world: an overview

British colonists in the western Atlantic lived under a set of maritime policies established in London as early as the 1650s. Known as the Navigation Acts, these measures regulated the commercial world that determined so much of the material life in the British settlements in North America. Colonial merchants also depended on the Royal Navy that protected their commercial cargo and passengers alike. Under the umbrella of British protection and with access to distant markets, British settlers, including merchants, prospered in the decades before the revolution.

Colonial merchants relied on financial networks that sustained these Atlantic connections. Participants in these networks lent and borrowed money that sustained commercial exchanges, including the vast slave trade. Desperately short of money, British colonists relied on credit as the chief means of transferring goods from sellers to buyers. Once on land, goods moved inland via traders to smaller urban places. Auctions enabled merchants to sell off overstocked or slow-moving goods. For more distant locations not served by towns or local markets, peddlers brought the goods of the Atlantic world to farmers seemingly beyond its reach.

Merchants, whether in Boston or New York, relied on ships, the very heart of this vast mercantile system, to conduct this business. These ships moved products, information and people across the oceans to all ports. As the chief and most efficient means of transportation, ships stood at the top of the list of vital economic assets. Virtually nothing could be accomplished without them. They moved involuntary labor from the eastern Atlantic westward to plantations in North America and the Caribbean. They carried raw materials back from the Chesapeake to London, Glasgow, Liverpool and Bristol and took out finished products for colonial markets.

The ports in Britain's Northern American settlements stood as conduits that brought in the goods, services and personnel from the Atlantic world. They facilitated the introduction of European goods into colonial life and shipped out the exports that ultimately paid for these goods. The ports served as distributors for their large and, in some cases, dynamic hinterlands. Boston, Massachusetts, Newport, Rhode Island, Philadelphia, Pennsylvania, New York City, New York and Charleston, and South Carolina constituted the major seaports in the western Atlantic. The North American shipbuilding industry sustained both this commerce and a substantial maritime construction industry. Ships also turned to ports for maintenance and repairs.

Boston, New York City and other colonial ports looked to London, which stood at the center of the British Atlantic world. Straddling the River Thames, London housed extensive shipyards, numerable wet and dry docks, customs houses, and one of the largest communities of seamen and maritime workers in the world. The country's port facilities sustained fleets of British warships that constantly needed upgrading, and built new ships. The city's mercantile and financial people accumulated the huge amounts of currency to handle the enormous costs of maintaining these fleets. Its merchants ranked as the "most internationally minded traders" in the world. The city stood as the epicenter of the global British economy. As her fleets and merchants expanded so did London, where 25 percent of its large and ever-growing population engaged in some aspect of maritime commerce.

An explosion in population during the eighteenth century galvanized the developing Atlantic economy. The North American colonies saw a jump of almost two million people during the 1700s while Great Britain and Ireland both saw their own populations grow dramatically in these decades. Drops in mortality, increased life expectancy and the absence of famine accelerated the increasing numbers of people. Such widespread growth also accounted for the expanding markets in North America and across the Atlantic where colonial merchants conducted so much of their business.

The British North American settlements reaped tremendous benefits because of their connections with distant markets. In particular, New England ship owners joined the British slavers in the profitable, if inhumane, trafficking of humans from West Africa to the colonial south and the Caribbean. New England ships, principally from Newport, Rhode Island and Boston, Massachusetts, vigorously participated in the business of trafficking human cargo. Smaller ocean-side ports such as Savannah, Georgia depended on New England ships for their supply of Africans destined for rice and indigo plantations.

New England slave ships also picked up naval stores from North Carolina and shipped them along with molasses from the Caribbean to New England ports. There molasses served as the basis for rum making, a major export of New England, while naval stores supplied shipbuilders with essential products for ship construction, the central business in New England's maritime world. African slaves in the Caribbean produced the molasses so important for New England's economy. Ironically, Africans as human cargo gave New England ships a vital source of profits.

The slave trade greatly contributed to the health of the New England economy. By the late eighteenth century some 49 percent of the Africans shipped to the Western Atlantic shores rode in the New England-built ships that also accounted for almost 70 percent of the freight. New England ships also helped sustain the growing carrying trade between the northern colonies and the Caribbean sugar islands. New England slavers also picked up bills of exchange and hard currency that later helped pay for manufactured goods imported from Great Britain. New England ships actually imported food from the middle colonies to makeup for their own grain deficits, created by a growing population and unproductive farms.

The plantation settlements along the North American coast and in the Caribbean also capitalized on this waterborne trade. Tobacco, long a staple of the Chesapeake, had achieved mass consumption status in England by the end of the seventeenth century. By the 1750s it enjoyed a legion of buyers in the expanding markets of urban consumers in Europe and especially in France, the largest buyer of North American tobacco. Europeans preferred the scent of tobacco in snuff. Scottish users, mostly men, also embraced tobacco, and by the end of the eighteenth century Scottish working women also took up the habit. As European and Scottish demand for tobacco rose so did the pressure on tobacco producers. They faced the challenge of expanding the amount of land under cultivation and bringing more African Americans to be slave laborers on their plantations.

Rice, too, depended on water transport for its vitality. Rice emerged as a central export along the Carolina and Georgia coasts during the eighteenth century. Ships hauled rice to European and Caribbean markets and they brought African labor to the Carolina and Georgia coasts. The African labor provided the muscle for the rice plantations. Even more important, labor from West Africa incorporated their own rich knowledge of rice production into their management of the rice fields. Long experience in rice production gave these Africans a keen understanding of soil, rainfall needs, the employment of immersion in farming and the mechanics of using tidal water in rice production. West Africans also used their knowledge of processing rice for European and Caribbean markets. Planters knew which ethnic groups from West Africa held this knowledge and when possible they purchased men and women from Gambia and the Windward Coast where rice sustained dense human populations.

As much as the Chesapeake, the Caribbean depended on its connections to other parts of the Atlantic commercial empire to survive. The British islands in this sea embodied the singular dedication to one crop, sugar. This commitment made the Caribbean sugar islands critically dependent on the North American colonies for food and white-collar services and on Great Britain for investments, plantation managers and naval protection. The islands could have existed in no other way once they committed to sugar as their main export.

The sugar islands contributed to the growing prosperity of the British settlements in New York and Pennsylvania. Like their counterparts in New England, middle colony merchants, farmers and artisans, especially those from Philadelphia and its prosperous agricultural hinterland, provided the white-collar services, grains, mostly wheat, beef and pork as well as fish that maintained the caloric and protein needs of the Africans. The export of wheat from Pennsylvania also produced cash for local farmers who sold their grains to merchant mills. These produced high quality flour, some 40,000 barrels annually, for distant markets. Philadelphia made Southeastern Pennsylvania affluent with its huge demand for local services and food as well as the profits its overseas trade generated for merchants, farmers, agents and creditors.

Maryland and Virginia joined in capitalizing on the booming markets for foodstuffs. After 1750, Baltimore, Maryland developed into an important maritime stop because of the flourishing grain trade in the region and the major flour mills that appeared in the city to process the grains. These thrived for most of the eighteenth century because of their participation in the larger British commercial world. Norfolk, Virginia also grew into a substantial port because of its proximity to the Caribbean and the port's growing hinterland that produced goods for the Caribbean islands. Merchants in Maryland and Virginia also began to build their own ocean-going fleets after 1750. These carried grain and timber to the Caribbean.

Slave owners in North America were inextricably bound to the slave trade. Yet, the plantation operators simply lacked the funds to conduct long-term business operations. These funds remained in short supply in the Atlantic world. The colonials depended on British lenders in London to support the slave trade. Financial figures in the British capital provided the resources that held together the slaving enterprise so central in the economic life of planters in the western Atlantic. These lenders generously awarded credit to slave traders, such as those from New England, whose voyages took months before any profit appeared on the ledgers. Just collecting a full complement of slaves for their ships also took a significant amount of time. For the lender, such exchanges produced a steady profit, but only on a delayed basis. Slavers had to dedicate substantial amounts of time to purchasing Africans from indigenous sellers even before the long crossing and final sales. A financial bridge from England to the North American colonies sustained the capture and movement of human beings from Africa to the western Atlantic for sale.

The demand for slaves also had indirect consequences for polities in West Africa. The Dahomean, Oyo and Ashanti states fought bitter wars for control of the slave trade and access to European goods. In part, they relied on European weapons and gunpowder purchased via the slave trade to conduct these wars. European flintlocks and gunpowder flowed into these coastal states. By the eighteenth century, the Oyo state, situated along the Bight of Benin, gathered power and wealth because of its slaving activities. The state covered a substantial area including present-day western Nigeria and the inland Yoruba states in West Africa. Oyo slave dealers sold Africans captured in war and raids to North American buyers through Gold Coast ports such as Lagos and Porto Novo.

Scottish and Scottish-Irish migration

The British colonies in North America participated in a massive reordering of the populations on both sides of the Atlantic. By the mid- and late eighteenth century human ties and interaction greatly enhanced the cohesiveness of the British commercial empire and bound the thousands who migrated to North America with their families and friends resident in the British Isles. These ties facilitated further migration as well as a steady flow of information eastward across the Atlantic.

The British Isles sent thousands of migrants to North America. For example, Scotland and Ireland witnessed substantial loss of people, beginning in the 1750s. These migrants usually ended in North America. They left their homes for many reasons. Significant population growth placed great pressure on resources in the countryside, which made migration the only viable choice for thousands. More than just a growing population, changes in farm methods and new means of production transformed relationships between landowners and tenants and between artisans and the market. These changes diminished the need for rural and artisan labor.

In Ireland the booming port of Belfast created an avenue of escape for many caught in these economic and social changes. Thousands of Ulster Scots left for the British colonies in North America in the 1760s and 1770s. Many boarded ships that had just unloaded flax seed from the North American colonies, necessary to sustain the linen industry lodged chiefly in Ulster. The ships needed return cargo, which the Irish emigrants readily supplied. Hard pressed by rising land rents, these men and women sought cheap land, widely available in North America. A few even journeyed to the West Indies.

Yet, the Scottish-Irish sought out other destinations. By the 1790s a "permanent labor migration" back to western Scotland took root as Ulster Scots sought out new sources of income. This migration joined an older stream of skilled Ulster workers "recruited" for the Scottish linen industry.

The same pressures that made migration a necessity for many in Northern Ireland also appeared in Scotland. Farmers in the lowlands and the Highlands saw their rural worlds vanish under the weight of population growth and changes in production. Highlanders began to experience market-driven changes in agriculture as early as the 1720s and 1730s. These accelerated after the 1770s. Large landowners consolidated their holdings and replaced small-scale leaseholders with sheep intended for English urban markets to the south, a shift particularly acute after 1760. These changes sent many young people across the Atlantic to the British colonies where they hoped abundant land would revive their flagging economic fortunes. The colonies also promised ownership of land without an intrusive landlord.

In the Scottish lowlands, the number of small-scale farmers and renters dropped dramatically during the late eighteenth century. Ironically, the new agricultural system that developed actually demanded more labor yet the appeal of land and the economic independence in North America far out-weighed the advantages of staying in the lowlands. The healthy economies in the region's ports and towns also provided outlets for modest Scottish farmers who wanted to escape from a deteriorating agricultural world. At the same time, cattle and sheep began to replace the departing human populations throughout the region as the demand for their meat accelerated in the English markets.

Similarly, Scottish textile artisans faced technological changes in the work-place that greatly diminished the long-sought dream of craft independence in the confines of one's shop. Market pressures forced an emphasis on volume and speed, to the detriment of skilled workers. They sought to re-establish their skilled trades in North America. Broad economic and workplace changes precipitated a substantial stream of migrants to British settlements in the western Atlantic where less sophisticated means of production and a growing economy offered many opportunities.

Migration created bonds that joined populations in the British Isles with the dynamic British colonies in North America. These depended on familial and ethnic networks that maintained ties between families, persons and individual communities. The Highland Scots who settled in North Carolina kept these ties alive through correspondence, notices in Scottish newspapers and family letters. Scottish newspapers carried stories and depictions of life in the colonies. While these stories often proved harsh in their indictments of the unattractive features of slave colonies, they also gave more favorable accounts of the possibilities of success in these colonies, the very piece of information likely to catch the attention of short-stay migrants. Often newspapers included more personal stories about family life and the economic gains of Scottish emigrants who made their homes in the British colonies. These communication links that span the Atlantic facilitated migration and gave direction to those migrants once they landed in North America. They also transferred news about the migrants and their experiences to their family, friends and communities in Scotland.

Scottish sojourners developed an enclave strategy to exploit the resources of North America. These temporary visitors often consisted of businessmen who benefited from their lodging in a Scottish enclave. The residents who greeted these newcomers passed on information to and set up business leads for their fellow Scots. These sojourners employed the polish of their educational backgrounds, their professional skills and their new contacts with merchants and landholders to accumulate money and resources. Since they rotated back to Scotland, news traveled with them, as families of those who remained in North America desperately wanted news of their kin. The people who ran the commercial operations also wanted to keep informed about the performances of the men who ran their operations. A community of temporary residents in North America sustained a regular flow of personal and business information that informed both loved ones and business associates about affairs in Virginia and other locations where Scots conducted their commercial activities.

African migration

Involuntary migration also grew dramatically during these years in response to the developing staple economies in the British colonies in North America and the Caribbean. Beginning in the early eighteenth century, the sharp rise in the demand for sugar and production of other staples such as rice and tobacco accelerated the growth of the slave trade and pushed hundreds of thousands of Africans across the same ocean. In fact, the slave trade reached peaks during the 1760s and 1770s when some 65,000 Africans arrived annually in the western Atlantic. The slave trade re-Africanized the populations of the Chesapeake and the Carolinas. In the Caribbean the population remained chiefly African because of high mortality, the planters' preference for young men and the consequent inability to reproduce children. In contrast, the British settlements in North America drew substantially smaller numbers of slaves direct from Africa yet produced one of the largest slave populations in the world by the 1780s. The high fertility in North America, its healthier climate and the availability of adequate food accounted for this turn of events.

The social world of the British Atlantic

The British Atlantic consisted of highly specialized economies and societies with very different histories. Inevitably these produced different social worlds. True nobilities existed in Ireland, Scotland and England, while none appeared in the younger and far less sophisticated colonies in North America and the Caribbean. Below the true nobility in rank came the gentry, with fewer resources and less prestige. Still, these men and their families lived in grand country estates and enjoyed a sumptuous life in comparison with the ordinary people of the day. They acquired a quality education, wore stylish clothes and spoke elegantly. To their social inferiors, their position was unmistakable. In the cruder social worlds of the British colonies, the gentry in England provided the model for emulation.

The gentry

The upper strata in the North American and Caribbean colonies and the Eastern Atlantic shared the cultural practices of the British gentry. In North America the Better Sort, as contemporaries knew them, embraced the styles and fashion of the English gentry. The colonial leadership lacked the resources, the lineages and the ties to royalty even to approach the elegance of true English nobility. Yet, they could and did adopt the lifestyle of the English gentry and the latest London fashion. Behavior, possessions and elegant speech marked the Better Sort and separated them from the vast majority of colonial society. Education, a cosmopolitan view of the world and a sense of command and superiority bred into the Better Sort also distanced them from their social inferiors.

The appeal of grand country houses befitting the colonial gentry soon found expression in the Georgian-style houses and buildings that appeared in North America, particularly after the 1750s. Wealth and power embodied in an elegant house spoke volumes about one's social status. Elaborate staircases for display and fashionable parlors for polite conversation made the interior of these mansions suitable for the Better Sort. The elaborate houses also served as places of afternoon tea, a ritual that called for delicate porcelain tea ware imported from distant Imperial China, silverware, and, of course, the social grace of the hostess. The Better Sort entertained their friends and associates, with whom they engaged in polite conversation and sipped tea brought from East Asia and sweetened by sugar grown and processed by African labor in the Caribbean, and shipped north on Rhode Island cargo ships. For the North American elites, these houses also served as important signs of refinement and gentility, characteristics of the Better Sort. They also demonstrated the interaction of trade and commerce with the social world of colonial leadership.

The Better Sort also enjoyed the same literature, read identical law books and boasted the same history as their counterparts in the eastern Atlantic. The Better Sort drew their notions of society and behavior from such transatlantic readings. Prominent men in the North American colonies established libraries that catered to these reading interests. The Charles Town Library Society, the Library Company of Philadelphia, the New York Society Library, the Redwood Library Company of Newport, Rhode Island all opened their doors by the 1750s. Members saw London and its large and growing literary community as a source of sophistication and a civilizing influence. Close ties developed between the booksellers and the agents of the colonial consumers, including "churches, colleges, and gentlemen's societies."

A society built on status also relied on deference between betters and inferiors. To insure proper behavior on the part of the Better Sort, courtesy books appeared to help the uninitiated navigate through the maze of ranks. Courtesy books demonstrated the power of "European culture" to extend its reach to the very edges of the Pan-British world. These books originated hundreds of years earlier and grew in sophistication and appeal over the decades. While a young man, George Washington carried his courtesy book to guide him in social situations. Few could mistake the intentions of the courtesy books, to educate the young in social manners. These manners alerted everyone to your place in society and commanded respect and deferential responses from those beneath you on the social scale. Manners and behavior, even more than the flood of consumer goods, defined the Better Sort.

The elites in the Caribbean had always embraced London, its style, culture and ambience. The members of these elites thought of themselves as British regardless of birthplace, whether London or Jamaica, and always intended to return to what they perceived as their true homes in London. Parents in notable families reared their young to see England as their ultimate destination and, if the opportunity arose, sent their children to London for an education. Unlike the Better Sort on the mainland, who purchased English style and fashion and used these markers to demonstrate their importance to a white society, the Caribbean planters faced only a black society with few whites of any consequence. Status gave way to fear and created a "garrison mentality" among the upper strata that only reinforced their determination to take up residence in England.

The gentry in Scotland also embraced the sophisticated lifestyle that marked high social status throughout the British Atlantic world. The Scottish gentry, crude at best in the early eighteenth century, began to capitalize on the flow of British and Atlantic goods, especially after 1760. Tea and tea sets, pewter and fashionable cloths soon decorated the parlors and individuals in the gentry. As resources grew, the gentry also opted to build elaborate houses surrounded by "colonnaded" exteriors, with lavish grounds and carriage houses. They maintained "extensive libraries," a mark of high social status throughout the Atlantic world. Every aspect of their lives took on an air of civility and gentility. Private schools, tutors and etiquette guidebooks insured social awareness while separating them from their social inferiors. Few would go without these badges of status.

Academics who benefited from the notoriety of Scottish universities, and literary figures that capitalized on the vigorous Scottish intellectual life and a growing reading public, also held a social status comparable to the landed classes. The literary and legal output of Scottish scholars, mostly in the form of books, reached across the Atlantic world. Adam Smith, David Hume, John Locke and others developed enthusiastic audiences in the North American colonies, where their ideas inspired many of the colonial and later national leaders.

In Ireland the Anglo-Irish gentry made great efforts to distinguish themselves from their social inferiors. The members of the Quality, as locals knew them, built grand country houses and even grander public buildings in Dublin, the epicenter of Anglo-Irish cultural and political power. Using English models, Irish gentlemen with architectural training planned their own houses and edifices that were English in style, yet with a unique Anglo-Irish touch. Much like the mansions in rural Delaware of Pennsylvania, the country houses in Limerick or Londonderry embodied the wealth, social standing and power of the Anglo-Irish. Similarly, the Anglo-Irish counterparts placed great value in libraries as a sign of status and learning. Professionals, including doctors and lawyers, clergy and other prominent Anglo-Irish embraced a sophisticated literary world. They established historical societies and built their own private libraries often filled with books that circulated throughout the Anglo-American world. These demonstrated a substantial psychological investment in their books and distinguished the Anglo-Irish gentry from their social inferiors.

Surrounded by Irish Catholics, the Protestant gentry always experienced unease. Concern over their claims to gentry status enhanced this anxiety and compelled many to hire professional genealogists to trace and identify the distinguished origins of their families, even if their true ancestors came from questionable circumstances. Etiquette guides abound in Ireland as they did in Scotland and North America, and these defined all the dimensions of one's social world. Speech and manners, acquired through rearing and reinforced by these guides, marked the social boundaries that separated the Anglo-Irish from their less distinguished neighbors.

The Middling Sort

Below the gentry in the Atlantic world stood the Middling Sort. This group varied in size and character depending on location. In the British settlements of North America the Middling Sort dominated the population in the northern colonies, where it consisted largely of modest farmers, unlike its mostly urban-based counterparts in England. These men and their families toiled away on the land producing wheat and other products, often sold abroad or to urban populations. In North American cities, craftsmen, retailers, minor jobbers and innkeepers belonged to the Middling Sort. They provided services and goods to their fellow urban residents. Both farmers and artisans shared modest living standards and both worked to survive. Yet, they held respectable occupations and the reputations generated by these pursuits separated these men and their families from those at the very bottom of colonial society.

The growing prosperity of the North American colonies increasingly rewarded the Middling Sort. Producers in England manufactured products for the mass consumers. Often imitations of goods sold to the gentry, these goods may have lacked quality yet they fed eager appetites among the Middling Sort in North America. They saw their capacity to purchase from an increasing range and availability of consumer items as a mark of their rising status. In fact, manufacturers in the North American colonies adopted this strategy and deliberately copied the English products. Storeowners then invited ordinary people to participate in the world of the gentlemen and gentlewomen by purchasing these imitation goods. Soon, goods once reserved for the elite, often by law, now found their way into the homes of the Middling Sort.

For the Better Sort, these changes were worrisome as goods now seemed to threaten the hierarchy and deference upon which society was built and their position depended. In response, they intensified self-control and elegance as their defining characteristics. These grew out of childhood rearing practices and the free time to master every elite activity, from speech to dancing, beyond the reach of Middling Sort, who lacked the time and resources to develop such skills. Manners, grace, civility and breeding walled off the Middling Sort. Few could acquire the proper gait or the proper posture. Such markers created almost insurmountable barriers for most ordinary people.

In England, unlike the colonies, the Middling Sort recruited its members from the ranks of professionals, lawyers and doctors, as well as from artisans, innkeepers and others in respectable occupations. Mostly urban based, these individuals and their families vigorously imitated their superiors in style and fashion. When possible the Middling Sort spent their holidays in spas and towns dedicated to leisure. They purchased a host of consumer items that English small-scale manufacturers produced in large volume for the Middling Sort. Improved canals and roads moved these goods fairly inexpensively to the burgeoning urban markets, where substantial numbers of eager buyers from the modest backgrounds awaited their arrival.

The Middling Sort in Ireland appeared in the growing ports and inland cities, much like their counterparts in England. Unlike North America with its abundance of inexpensive land, Ireland possessed little of this resource. The scarcity of inexpensive land and the domination of landowning by the gentry and the nobility limited the number of Middling Sort who could operate their own farms. The urban based Middling Sort included tradesmen, tanners, innkeepers, teachers and other men in similar occupations. A modest income, physical labor and the visible lack of refinement marked the Middling Sort.

Members of the Middling Sort did aspire to the status of their social betters. They certainly pursued the consumer opportunities created by the emergence of a shopping culture and the new range of goods available. Those aspiring to the Quality made every effort for inclusion, from buying fashionable clothes to rubbing shoulders with those of the Anglo-Irish gentry in church. Much like their counterparts in North America, the Irish Middling Sort eagerly bought fancy linen and books, hoping to bridge the material gap that divided them from the Quality. Some even subscribed to newspapers when they were affordable.

Just as such goods never cleared a path for the once modest yet hard working farmer or artisan in North America so, too, in Ireland material objects never substituted for elegance and civility. Such actions also provoked sharp rebukes from the sophisticated. Few among the Quality in Ireland or the Better Sort in North America believed the people of common origins capable of refinement. It simply outstripped their abilities, their social origins and their crude ways.

The Middling Sort in Scotland drew its members from the ranks of businessmen and minor professionals whose income derived from activities other than manual labor. Men who engaged in domestic enterprises, such as transporting grain or shipping wool to buyers in England, belonged to Scotland's Middling Sort. Such dealings capitalized on Scotland's economic growth. School teachers, printers and other who drew comfortable incomes from Scotland's prosperity and the exploding demand for their services in a highly literate population also joined the ranks of the Middling Sort. Even self-employed skilled artisans occupied the middle ranks between the gentry and the laboring poor. As these occupations suggest, the Scottish Middling Sort lived in urban centers where their skills and products thrived on the dynamic Scottish economy.

The Meaner Sort

At the very bottom of Atlantic society stood sailors and maritime slaves identified by their harsh laboring conditions, in many cases their lack of freedom, and often by their racial identity. The sailors came from multi-ethnic and multi-racial backgrounds, including Irish, English, Scottish, African and African American men. Even Native Americans showed up on Anglo-American ships. They formed a critical part of the workforces of the British colonial ports in North America and made up the crews that sailed out of Boston and elsewhere in the British colonies. Despite their varied origins, they joined to make up the crews that worked the sails, repaired the ships and provided a host of other duties necessary to maintain ships. Ironically, to the respectable members of society in the British colonies of North America, the motley crew, both free and unfree, remained a rowdy and dangerous bunch, yet a necessity to make the engine of commerce move. Without these men and women neither merchants nor farmers could have prospered.

The institutions of the maritime workers contrasted with the social and economic establishment of the upper strata. The dockyards, the taverns and the inns along the waterfront acted as important mediums for moving information, organizing resistance or just enjoyment. Sailors met in dockside taverns in Boston and New York City, shared sleeping quarters in harbor inns, and fenced their stolen goods through the same agents.

In this world race played a lesser role than it did in the larger society. Captains often hired men for their abilities and endurance as opposed to their skin color, and those of African origins or descent found they could earn "equal pay" for the same jobs on the ship. Blacks in North American ports saw the ocean as a way to escape the limitations placed on them in the British plantations and settlements.

Plantation slaves also resided at the bottom of the status hierarchy. They provided the labor that proved as essential to the health of the commercial empire as the ocean-going counterparts. South Carolina demonstrates their worth. A small colony by the standards of Pennsylvania, its exports counted just two items, rice and indigo. Dominated by those of African origins or descent, it relied on the labor of these men and women for the profits that made the colony the wealthiest in North America.

Similarly, by the 1770s, St. Kitts, a tiny sugar-producing island in the Caribbean leeward chain stood out as the most valuable piece of real estate in the British commercial empire. Its wealth depended on its African workforce, without whom the island would never have produced a pound of sugar. The absentee slave owners enjoyed the good life in London and on their country estates because of the labor system that relentlessly drove their African workers to produce sugar.

Conclusion

The Pan-British world provided the larger economic context for the North American colonies. This world straddled the Atlantic Ocean and vitally depended on water transportation. Navigable rivers cut into the Atlantic shores of the North American colonies and gave merchants and their ships access to the interior. The economic well-being of each colony depended on water transportation essential in reaching distant markets. The staple economies of southern colonies such as Virginia and South Carolina used oceanic shipping to send their plantation products to London, Glasgow and elsewhere in the eastern Atlantic. Consumers in these ports, throughout Great Britain and in Europe valued Virginia's main export, tobacco, for its tastes and its rarity. Their demand drove the tobacco growers, the ships and their crews and the British government that depended on the annual harvests for profit and revenue. Ships and the Atlantic Ocean also provided the means to secure slave labor from Africa and carry Africans to the colonial plantations. Without the seemingly inexhaustible supply of African labor the plantation economies would never have survived.

Ports also played a crucial role for the North American colonies. They acted as key junctures in transiting goods in and out of the colonies. Of course London stood at the top of the economic hierarchy. It drew goods from all the colonies and from throughout the Pan-British world, and served as the economic focal point for the commercial system. North American ports such as Philadelphia and Boston also funneled goods and services from their hinterlands to the sugar colonies in the Caribbean that secured all their necessities in this exchange. Without this trade the monocrop economies of the Caribbean island simply could never achieve economic viability. Similarly, the ships built in Glasgow and operated by Glasgow merchants sustained the tobacco trade from Virginia and the Chesapeake in general, and Scottish merchants from Glasgow set up shop in the tobacco region to supply British manufactured goods to modest farmers. In both cases, long-distance connections rendered the North American colonies prosperous.

These ties also demonstrated the interdependence of the North American colonies on other regions in the Pan-British world. Virginia depended on Glasgow; Jamaica depended on southeastern Pennsylvania and New England. Each region had its own distinctive history yet they also shared a common history. The interdependence produced economic communities and exchanges that reached across the ocean and integrated the North American colonies into every facet of the Pan-British economy.

Migration, too, brought the North American colonies into long-term relationships with other parts of the Pan-British world. Innovations in farming, changing land use and population growth all combined to reorder the human communities on both sides of the Atlantic Ocean. Scotland and Ireland experienced these changes most acutely. Farm laborers, modest farmers and tenants all discovered they had no access to land, or land in sufficient quantity, to support their families. Some opted for additional employment outside of farming. A significant number chose to migrate to the North American colonies, bolstering their populations and claiming unsettled land distant from the Atlantic coast. These migrants moved into the backcountry in Pennsylvania and the Carolinas where they acquired land and established their own farming communities. Of course, they reached North America in one of the many ships that trafficked goods across the ocean and needed ballast on the return, a demand met by the migrants.

Importantly migrants carried memories of their homes, reinforced by family members and friends who stayed behind. The latter yearned for news of their relatives in North America. Soon, communications between the two distant parties developed. These networks passed news and stories from North America to Scotland. Letters also kept family and friendship ties alive and often led to further migration. These links created human communities that crossed the ocean to North America.

The social dimensions also integrated the North American colonies into the larger Pan-British world. The gentry in England, who took their cues from the nobility, provided the Better Sort in North America with their model for style, fashion, elegance and taste. The Better Sort also participated in the transatlantic literary world that created bonds among the upper strata from Charleston to Boston. London served as the epicenter of this reading culture and the source of publications that found their way into the libraries of the Better Sort. The gentry in Ireland and Scotland also looked to London and shared many of the same reading tastes as the Better Sort. They also copied the habits and social mores of the English. The Better Sort in North America, the Quality in Ireland and the Lairds in Scotland all knew their rank and their special place in the social order.

The Middling Sort also understood their rank and where they stood in this social order. In the North American colonies, despite divergent occupations, members shared modest living standards. Mostly modest farmers and a smaller proportion of artisans, the Middling Sort earned respect through the integrity of their occupations. The outburst of consumer goods in the late eighteenth century enabled many to acquire imitation goods that once marked the high social status of their betters. Yet, none could duplicate the refinement or the ambience of the Better Sort. In Ireland and Scotland the Middling Sort generally lived in the cities, and few pursued farming. They, too, sought goods that carried status, yet none could actually cross the line dividing them from their social superiors, certainly the case in North America. While the Middling Sort in North America differed in some important ways from their counterparts in the British Isles, all shared much the same social conditions and unrealized aspirations.

The Meaner Sort in North America held their unenviable positions because of their occupations, their race and their rejection of hierarchy. Sailors provide the energy to make the Pan-British world an economic reality. Sailors came from many ethnic and racial backgrounds. They labored in dangerous jobs and lived in the water world more than any other group. Ports across the Atlantic served as their temporary homes. They often joined in riots against authority from Boston to Jamaica. Enslaved Africans and slaves of African descent also occupied the bottom of the social hierarchy. They enjoyed no freedom, belonged to no legally recognized families and toiled away on harsh plantations. The slaves of the southern colonies in North America created wealth for their masters, much as their counterparts did in the British sugar islands in the Caribbean. Certainly the slave societies in the southern colonies differed in many ways from those in the Caribbean; yet they both represented a response to the plantation system and the drive for staple crops.

Overall, the North American colonies owed their economic vitality to the larger Pan-British economy. They drew much of their notions of social hierarchy from this world and they depended on it for migrants, who expanded settlement and increased the population growth. Few could exist outside of the Pan-British world, and almost none wished to do so.

Further reading

For an introduction to the British Empire, see C.A. Bayly, *Imperial Meridian: The British Empire and the World, 1780–1830* (New York, 1989) that covers the British Empire and its tensions from Ireland to India. See also Alan Taylor, *American Colonies* (New York, 2001) that focuses on all European colonies, including those in the Pacific, up to 1820. See also the articles in P.J. Marshal, ed., *The Oxford History of the British Empire. Volume II: The Eighteenth Century* (New York, 1998). These cover topics as diverse as the British sugar colonies in the Caribbean, the slave trade, the black experience, and the Irish, among others. They are also indispensable for developing an understanding of the diverse nature of peoples and settlements in the Atlantic world.

For a discussion of the British colonies in North America, see Gordon Wood, *The Radicalism of the American Revolution: How a Revolution Transformed a Monarchial Society into a Democratic One Unlike any That Had Ever Existed* (New York, 1992) and Richard Bushman, *The Refinement of America: Persons, Houses, Cities* (New York, 1993). To understand the communities and economies in Scotland, Ireland and Canada, see T.M. Devine, *Scotland's Empire and the Shaping of the Americas 1600–1815* (Washington, 2003); T.C. Smoot, *A History of the Scottish People 1560–1830* (Bungay, Scotland, 1972); R.H. Houston and W.J. Know, eds., *The New Penguin History of Scotland: From the Earliest Times to the Present Day* (London, 2001); David Allan, *Scotland in the Eighteenth Century* (London, 2002); Toby Barnard, *A New Anatomy of Ireland: The Irish Protestants, 1649–1770* (New Haven, 2003); R.H. Foster, ed., *The Oxford History of Ireland* (New York, 1985); R.F. Foster, *Modern Ireland 1660–1972* (London, 1988); Margaret Conrad, Alvin Finkel and Corneilius Joener, *History of the Canadian People, Beginning to 1867: Volume 1* (Toronto, 1993).

For a description of consumerism, consumer goods, consumer attitudes and the impact of consuming on the Atlantic world, see Cary Carson, Ronald Hoffman and Peter J. Albert, eds., *Of Consuming Interests: The Style of Life in the Eighteenth Century* (Charlottesville, 1994); John Brewer and Roy Porter, eds., *Consumption and the World Of Goods* (London, 1993); and T.H. Breen, *The Marketplace of Revolution: How Consumer Politics Shaped American Independence* (New York, 2004). For a description of the Atlantic Ocean merchants, see David Hancock, *Citizens of the World: London Merchants and the Integration of the British Atlantic Community, 1735–1785* (New York, 1995).

For an analysis of the impact of the slave trade on Africa, see Patrick Manning, *Slavery and African Life: Occidental, Oriental, and African Slave Trade* (New York, 1991), Jay Coughtry, *The Notorious Triangle: Rhode Island and the African Slave Trade, 1700–1807* (Philadelphia, 1981); Herbert Klein, *The Atlantic Slave Trade* (New York, 1996). For slavery in general, see Joseph E. Inikori, *Africans and the Industrial Revolution in England: A Study in International Trade and Economic Development* (New York, 2002); Jane Landers, *Black Society in Spanish Florida* (Urbana, Illinois, 1999); Ira Berlin, *Many Thousands Gone: The First Two Centuries of Slavery in North America* (Cambridge, Massachusetts, 1998); Barbara Solow, ed., *Slavery and the Rise of the Atlantic System* (New York, 1993); Judith A. Carney, *Black Rice: The African Origins of Rice Cultivation in the Americas* (Cambridge, Massachusetts, 2001).

For an exploration of the experiences of the men and women engaged in maritime life, see Marcus Rediker, *Between the Devil and the Deep Blue Sea: Merchant Seamen, Pirates and the Anglo-American World 1700–1750* (Cambridge, Massachusetts, 1987); Paul A. Gilje, *Liberty on the Waterfront: American Maritime Culture in the Age of*

Revolution (Philadelphia, 2004); W. Jeffrey Bolster, *Black Jacks: African American Seamen in the Age of Sail* (Cambridge, Massachusetts, 1997); Peter Linebaugh and Marcus Rediker, *Many Headed Hydra: The Hidden History of the Revolutionary Atlantic* (Boston, 2001).

For a broadscale analysis of migration, see Marilyn C. Baseler, *"Asylum for Mankind": America 1607–1800* (Ithaca, 1998).

Chapter 3

The Pan-British world in the age of revolution

Introduction

The Pan-British world depended on powerful economic ties to sustain its interdependence and to nourish its amazing prosperity. Beyond question, the British proved eminently successful in these twin tasks. Yet, the Pan-British world depended on more than its economic vitality for its persistence. At the very heart of the British success stood its notions of liberty and freedom. These ideals joined British subjects throughout the Pan-British Atlantic and gave them a powerful sense of belonging to a larger community.

Yet, the colonists in North America raised serious questions about British policies that seemed to threaten liberty and self-government, the very hallmarks of British rule. These questions arose when the British ministries began introducing new taxation and commercial regulatory policies as part of their efforts to concentrate power in London and resolve the pressing issue of the huge debt incurred in defeating the French in 1763. These new policies abandoned the partnership scheme that William Pitt had introduced during the struggle against the French. Pitt's innovative policies made the colonists brothers in arms against their common enemy, the Roman Catholic French. The new policies alienated them.

The post-1763 shift in attitudes toward the colonists ultimately led to revolution and an independent Creole state in North America, the United States, in 1783. At the same time, the departure of the former British colonies shattered the British Empire and deeply affected its various parts from Canada to Ireland. British subjects on both sides of the Atlantic certainly shared concerns over the official polices that angered colonists in North America. In the Caribbean, legislatures expressed dissatisfaction with the very policies that unsettled the colonists in British North America. The Anglo-Irish similarly reacted to the British policies of consolidating London's control over its holdings on both sides of the Atlantic. Yet these sentiments never overrode their commitment to London, nor the many advantages those in the Caribbean and Ireland believed resulted from their membership in the larger community of British subjects.

Africa, too, experienced the whirlwind of change that came out of the American Revolution. African American loyalists who fled to British lines in their quest for freedom ended up in Sierra Leone, founded by British abolitionists as a free colony. The presence of these loyalists changed the political face of Sierra Leone. In a bitter irony, these African American refugees carried with them many of the ideals of the United States revolution embraced by their former owners yet denied to their slaves. Calls for more effective representation, and oppoisition to what these loyalists perceived as abuses of power by the Sierra Leone administrators, shook the colony's very foundation.

Of course, Great Britain also experienced significant change. After all, the core of its holdings in the western Atlantic bolted from the empire to embrace independence. The British also faced old enemies, who capitalized on the British predicament by joining the British colonists in their fight against London. The war moved beyond a colonial struggle for independence in North America into a worldwide conflict that affected British subjects from the Irish shores to the islands of the Caribbean. The revolution upset and then dissolved Pan-British world's economic, political and emotional interdependence.

The Empire of Liberty and Great Britain's history

Before the turbulent revolution, a transatlantic identity took hold of the British subjects throughout Great Britain's Atlantic settlements. Liberty stood at the center of this emerging identity. Representative government protected the liberty of British subjects and limited the power of the monarch. At the same time, British Common Law safeguarded their lives and their property. The British system of governing distinguished Great Britain from the other European states.

To legitimize these notions the British invented an historical memory that reached back to Norman and Anglo-Saxon England for the origins of their liberty and representative government. This story featured Magna Carta, the fabled document signed by King John that guaranteed representation for his subjects. Over the centuries measures such the Bill of Rights (1689) and the Act of Settlement (1701) reinforced British freedoms. Such acts served as the basis for what the British labeled their "Matchless Constitution." The phrase "Free-born Briton" incorporated the rights and legal protections that marked an emerging imperial identity from New England to the Caribbean.

The Empire of Liberty and the British Atlantic

The traditions of liberty and representative government followed British settlers wherever they migrated. In fact, British commentators hardly considered a settlement "fully colonized" until it had a legislature. Assemblies personified "the essence of the British constitution." Using Parliament as their example, British subjects established colonial legislatures very early in their histories. By the mid-eighteenth century, these assemblies had developed rich traditions of representing white people.

The right of representation demanded constant vigilance throughout the colonies, as it had in England. The assemblies in North America struggled with crown officials over issues of jurisdiction, the right to control finances and the limits of royal prerogatives. The General Court in Massachusetts and the House of Burgess in Virginia stood as pioneers in speaking for their constituencies. The North American colonies long contested power with royal officials and expanded their decision making vis-à-vis these officials whenever possible.

British pioneers also set up legislative bodies in the Caribbean. These demonstrated the same expansionist tendencies of their North American counterparts as they successfully gathered more and more power over the daily affairs of their colonies. The capacities of these assemblies always kept the rapt attention of the colonists, since these institutions safeguarded the freedoms and rights basic to English tradition. An assembly compromised in any fashion by British royal officials, therefore, threatened the British settlers.

British legislative institutions also appeared in Ireland, where the Anglo-Irish ruled. The institutions traced their origins to the migration of English settlers during the seventeenth century. By the 1690s these settlers firmly established their political power, marked by the the emergence of the modern Irish Parliament in 1692. Throughout the 1700s the Anglo-Irish constantly sought to expand the powers of the Dublin Parliament and even imagined the possibility of an autonomous institution equal in power to the British Parliament in London. The Irish Parliament constantly engaged in battles with the Viceroy, the Crown's emissary, over jurisdiction in matters such as public finance. These fights echoed the struggles in the western Atlantic between Crown official and colonial legislatures. For the Anglo-Irish, their resentment over the English presence was manifest in the patriot ideology that articulated the goals and interests of the Anglo-Irish for greater autonomy.

In Canada, the most recent of all the British eighteenth-century acquisitions, representative government grew slowly. As the British established tighter control over all of Nova Scotia during the Seven Years War, officials worried over the unwillingness of British settlers to move to this daunting region. The colony's reputation for tyrannical government also scared many in the British colonies to the south. Finally, the Commissioners on the Board of Trade and Plantations responsible for the British colonies took drastic steps to make the region appealing to these very people. British administrators ordered their officials in Nova Scotia to adopt an elective assembly. In 1759 another proclamation outlined the structure of the assembly, articulated a judicial system familiar to all British subjects and guaranteed freedom of religious affiliation to all, excluding Roman Catholics.

These measures, along with the offer of free land and a moratorium on taxes, precipitated the migration of some 8,000 New Englanders to Nova Scotia, where they set up permanent homes and began to build a representative system common to all British communities. The transplanted New Englanders also brought their dissenting religious views, close-knit families, a penchant for trading, and a fierce individualism. They continued to rely on Boston as a market for farm goods and fish products. These connections kept the ties between New England and newer British colonies in Canada alive and vigorous.

Political protest, revolution and the end of the Empire of Liberty

The protests of British settlers in North America over post-1763 British policies began in the 1760s. In that decade, imperial ministries abandoned the partnership approach Prime Minister William Pitt had used when prosecuting the war against the French. Pitt's idea of a federated empire gave way to a consolidated empire in which the British colonies in North America and, in fact, British holdings throughout the Pan-British world lived under tighter direction from Westminster in London. Colonists began to experience British rule as subjects rather than as equals in a larger British community. The task of resolving the difficulties of the huge wartime debt and the new populations under British rule led to such a seismic shift in attitudes and policies toward British colonists.

In the wake of the victorious and expensive war against the French, the British government faced the new charge of ruling expanded populations – French Canadian Catholics, French Caribbean Catholics and indigenous peoples. These alien populations stood outside the mainstream of British and British colonial societies. Few throughout the Anglo-American world believed it even remotely possible to integrate these peoples into a British world built on liberty and representation, perceived as foreign to the Gallic temper and beyond the capabilites of native peoples.

British policies first addressed the place of indigenous peoples in the newly reconfigured empire. The British stationed troops in the territory beyond the Appalachians to preserve order among their new subjects and keep out settlers from the British colonies to the east. The British also changed the nature of the relationship with the Ottawa, Delaware, Miami and other native peoples in the region that had flourished under the French. British administrators ended the French practice of gift-giving and mediation of disputes among these populations that had cemented the relationship between the French and the indigenous people in the past. Many among the indigenous expressed anger and dismay over this change. At the same time, these peoples were in the midst of a spiritual and anti-European revival that argued for a return to native ways and a rejection of European goods and social exchanges.

Capitalizing on these sentiments an Ottawa leader, Pontiac, preached a Pan-Indian vision that he believed provided the only means of stopping the advance of British settlers and preserving the indigenous peoples and their lands. Having watched the Cherokee fight a losing war against the South Carolinians without the aid of neighboring polities such as the Creek Confederation, Pontiac realized the consequences of a divided peoples. By 1763 these sentiments led to an uprising among the native peoples that challenged British rule. After two years of fighting, the British restored order and ended Pontiac's hopes for a Pan-Indian Confederation.

As the insurgency diminished, the British still faced the problem of settlers east of the Appalachians pouring into the region. The London-based ministry kept British troops in the region to insure peace and keep order. The troops also acted as a means of restraining squatters from occupying indigenous lands. Still, clashes between the indigeneous and the settlers occurred and violence seemed to escalate by the year.

Colonials, of course, saw this affair very differently. To them the migration into these newly conquered lands extended the boundaries of empire, a move that should benefit everyone. Their personal ambitions and their understanding of empire collided directly with British policies and only inflamed the turmoil that engulfed the region. The colonial anger over the British refusal to lift the ban on migration to the west intensified when it became apparent by the 1770s that the British had no intention of reversing this policy. The new demands of a racially and ethnically mixed and territorially expanded empire vexed British policy makers and inflamed colonials.

The British also faced another daunting problem – reducing the enormous debt incurred winning the French and Indian war in North America. The London ministry enacted commercial measures deigned to rationalize imperial administration, make the collection of custom revenues more efficient and generate more money from the colonies. Laws such as the Currency and Sugar Acts of 1764 marked new directions in imperial regulation. The Currency Act attempted to end the colonial practice of issuing quickly depreciating paper currency. This practice upset British merchants owed debts by colonial buyers. The Sugar Duty acted as a revenue generator and demanded that importers pay fees in gold or silver, both in very short supply in North America.

The Stamp Act of 1765 seemed more intrusive than these early measures and even appeared to menace colonial representative institutions. These very institutions embodied the meaning of being British in a world of autocracy, and threats to them endangered the very notion of liberty. The colonists saw the Stamp Tax as a violation of their own right to self-government since it bypassed the colonist legislatures and imposed the tax directly on the colonists. Without representation in the London Parliament, the colonists had no recourse in the measure. The Stamp Act also empowered the imperial vice-admiralty courts to try those who ignored the tax. In the process it removed the long-held right to a trial by jury. The unduly high rates placed on newspapers also threatened those venues of free expression, so important in the British world. The Stamp Act even demanded payment in specie (i.e. gold or silver), which intensified the economic stress of the colonists who notoriously conducted their economic affairs without precious metals. The intent to use the revenue generated by the Stamp Tax to support British regulars in the colonies only inflamed an already angry colonial population that increasingly saw British troops as an occupying army enforcing unpopular parliamentary measures.

British policies continued to frustrate colonials. The Townshend Duties of 1767 again assaulted the colonial tradition of self-government. London used the measure to generate revenue to free royal officials from reliance on colonial legislatures for their salaries. For colonials, the Townshend Duties again threatened their representative institutions and appeared to colonists to form part of a larger conspiracy to undermine their very liberties. Without representation in Parliament the colonials had no one to speak for their interests. The colonials struck back through a non-importation movement designed to cripple British commerce, which had come to depend on colonial consumers for its prosperity. Eventually the British ministry repealed all the duties except for that on tea.

The political crisis culminated in 1773 with the passage of the Tea Act. It kept the original Townshend duty on tea and awarded a monopoly on its distribution and sales in the colonies to the financially troubled East India Company. This proviso removed colonial merchants as middlemen in the profitable tea trade. To the colonists conditioned by more than a decade of menacing British Parliamentary acts, the measure reeked of privilege and conspiracy that benefited the interests of the few to the detriment of the many. The affair ended with the Boston Tea Party and the destruction of East India Company tea. In response the British passed the Coercive Acts that closed the port of Boston, reduced the power of the town meetings and made the colony's council an appointed body. The two sides now stood perilously close to war.

In the midst of the fury, Parliament passed the Quebec Act. It greatly enhanced the status of the French Catholics in the province of Quebec, the boundaries of which were extended to include the Ohio Valley. It sustained an accommodationist policy of the British toward the resident French population. Under benign British governors official policies tolerated Catholicism, enabled the French to participate in the English legal system and allowed French colonial society to operate to its own norms. The Quebec Act recognized French civil law that ended trial by jury. The act also replaced the British installed legislature with the older Gallic "appointed council," one that stood in sharp contrast to the defiant assemblies in British North America.

For the British the Quebec Act removed any possible tensions with the French Canadians, whose religious freedoms were guaranteed. The British settlers in North America believed the gestures toward the French were a betrayal and part of a larger conspiracy to restrict their rights. In fact, the settlers linked the Quebec Act and the Coercive Acts.

For the British the measures of the 1760s and 1770s represented a response to fiscal crisis and the need to preserve the Empire's frontiers. The British argued that millions in Great Britain lived under Parliamentary rule despite lacking the direct representation the colonists demanded. These millions conducted their daily lives under Parliamentary measures because they shared a "common nationality," as did the colonists in North America. The notion of a transatlantic identity promoted on both sides of the ocean opened up an avenue that supported Parliamentary acts without the representation the colonists demanded.

Revolution and the North American colonies

Angered by Parliamentary measures that seemed to violate their rights, British colonists took up arms against the British in April 1775. This decision, and the ensuing war and victory, sharply divided the Pan-British world. The revolution rearranged populations, transformed the rebellious colonies and created a new set of relationships among the British holdings that remained under British rule.

In the North American colonies this victory destroyed the social world of the mid-eighteenth century with its ordered ranks, its gentry, its nobility and its titles and distinctions. The Patriots, as the Revolutionaries styled themselves, declared the colonies a self-governing republic. This form of government was manifested in state constitutions written during the American Revolution, and the Articles of Confederation, drawn up in 1777, that enshrined representation and liberty and severely limited the power of the central government. No longer would citizens live at the behest of his/her betters since in a republic all were equal. Reflecting the new ideals, citizenship took a new meaning, one filled with political and legal freedoms and the right to choose who would carry out the functions of government.

Public office no longer gave holders opportunities for personal advancement. Now it rendered obligations upon those chosen by their fellow citizens to fulfill the duties of the office in a fair and impartial fashion. They served the people and not themselves. In accordance with this new ethos, political leaders dramatically expanded suffrage. As the electorate broadened so did the social origins of office-holders, who even came from the ranks of artisans. Jefferson best summed up these new hopes and aspirations when he wrote of a future republic peopled by free and virtuous citizens. The United States and not Great Britain, the former colonials believed, provided a model society for all peoples to imitate.

The revolution, slavery and race

Yet, the new face of the republic remained deceptively disingenuous. It was, after all, still a republic built, in part, on slavery. The war, on one hand, gave the institution new life. On the other, the revolution unhinged the social and racial hierarchies of the thirteen colonies. The British army acted as one of the chief agents precipitating this change. It served as a magnet, attracting slaves wherever it marched. African Americans joined the British army as soldiers and as laborers to assist British arms. Other African Americans saw British promises and protection as a means to achieve the freedom denied them by the Patriots.

The departure of so many African Americans obviously created severe labor shortages, which affected the staple economies of the southern states. South Carolina saw its rice and indigo production drop off considerably during the revolution. Indigo never recovered, while rice did reach pre-revolutionary output by the 1790s. Another crop, cotton, promised a new beginning for southern states. Cotton took off as a major source of economic growth in the 1790s when the cotton gin and short-staple cotton began to fuel economic growth. Cotton quickly replaced the older staples and promised decades of prosperity if an adequate supply of labor could be found.

The resolution of the labor shortage came in two parts. By the 1790s plantation owners in the tidewater region of the Chesapeake discovered they had a surplus of slaves. Natural fertility accounted for this surplus. Some plantation owners chose to migrate with their property in search of new opportunities readily available in the developing cotton economy. A substantial interregional slave trade also developed as slave owners sold off their "surplus" to buyers in the cotton region of the lower South. Next, with the full resumption of the slave trade in 1803, South Carolinians purchased tens of thousands of slaves from Africa and the Caribbean. Equipped with an adequate supply of labor, whites moved inland to develop cotton plantations around communities such as Columbia, South Carolina. Cotton replaced the dependence on rice and indigo and renewed the state's economy. In the process it revived slavery, which became as vital to cotton production as it had been to the region's staple economy in the colonial period.

Georgia also encouraged the inland migration of slaves through its bounty program. It awarded land and slaves to men who had served in the state militia or the Continental army. Some 9,000 veterans claimed millions of acres of land in the backcountry and substantial numbers of slaves, who moved to the interior with their new masters. Cotton plantations grew up around Augusta and other inland communities that thrived on cotton and newly emerging markets in Great Britain and later the European continent. Cotton and slavery reconnected the South with the Atlantic economy.

The Chesapeake, too, witnessed economic change accelerated by the revolution. Slave owners often joined the stream of refugees that fled from the British armies operating in eastern Virginia. They moved to the uncultivated western lands in the state where the population of Euroamericans and African Americans grew at a lively rate during the revolution and afterward. In these areas slaves and new tobacco fields helped offset the decline of tobacco production in the tidewater region. In northern Virginia and on the eastern shore of Maryland landowners began to shift out of tobacco into grains, especially wheat, on the eve of the revolution. The more prosperous markets in Europe and the Caribbean persuaded tobacco growers to make such a radical adjustment. The most visible example of this change was George Washington, who completely abandoned tobacco in favor of wheat, hoping to reap profits from the new markets.

In Maryland landowners gave up their once prosperous tobacco crop, freed substantial numbers of slaves and then leased back the land to the manumitted African Americans. They, too, joined the shift to grain production and away from tobacco. As a result the number of free blacks jumped from under 5 percent of the state population in 1776 to 20 percent by the 1790s. Grains now powered much of Maryland's economy and ex-slaves as much as whites enjoyed the benefits of the new crops. The Atlantic economy continued to make these states economically successful, much as it had their colonial predecessors. Yet, a combination of slave and free African Americans as well as Euroamericans provided the labor for this new, vibrant economy.

In the South the Declaration of Independence and the success of the revolution clearly carried a very different meaning for African Americans. Race had always marked colonial society and it remained so in the new republic. Economic change in South Carolina, Georgia and Virginia secured slavery's future while in Maryland the shift to grains resulted in a growing free population of African Americans who could make decisions about what they would farm and how they would run their own personal lives. Politically, the constitutions in the southern states recognized slavery, as did the Federal Constitution of 1788. The latter also extended the slave trade until 1808. Slavery remained an intimate part of society and the foundation of the economy in the South. Economically slavery remained the central institution, reconnecting the region to the Atlantic economy and its British and European markets.

Revolution and the Caribbean in the Pan-British world

The consequences of the revolution and its outcome extended far beyond the North American colonies. The elites in Ireland, the Caribbean, Canada and Scotland could hardly ignore the mounting fury in North America or the implications of the revolution for their societies. In the Caribbean the leadership vigorously opposed the imperial reforms that had aroused the ire of the mainland colonists. They strenuously objected to the Stamp Tax and other subsequent measures because they saw the acts as encroaching on the rights guaranteed in their charters. The Sons of Liberty on St. Kitts and Nevis islands openly demonstrated against the Stamp Act during the crisis that engulfed the North American colonies. The Caribbean leaders, too, worried over the expanding power of the London Parliament in light of many past battles with Crown officials. The islands, the main target of the Stamp Tax, actually contributed the greatest share of the revenue collected by imperial officials.

The Patriot Declaration of Independence in 1776 undermined the support the Caribbean islands had given their counterparts in the thirteen North American colonies. The revolution now jeopardized the British communities in the Caribbean in a profound way. The sugar islands vitally depended on their close economic ties with their northern neighbors. Colonial ships, farms and merchants provided the very foodstuffs, white-collar services and slaves that sustained the Caribbean plantations and their exports. Yet, the perpetual unease over the large slave populations placed limits on the planters' ire over British policies. As important, the Caribbean planters and their families looked to England as their intended destination, an attitude mainland colonists never embraced.

Once the revolutionary war erupted in North America, the island elites looked with dismay as British military resources were deployed northward to meet the challenge of the mainland revolutionaries. Planters in Barbados, Jamaica and elsewhere in the region correctly saw the departure of troops and ships as diminishing Britain's ability to protect the Caribbean from internal slave rebellions. The constant worry over French and Spanish assaults intensified once these traditional enemies declared their support for the revolutionaries in North America. The island colonies also saw their anxieties over food shortages realized when hostilities interrupted the very trade with the mainland that made the sole dedication to sugar production a viable strategy. Disease, combined with diminished diets, reduced populations throughout the British Caribbean during the years of conflict. Only the British redirection of martial resources to the islands once the French entered the war calmed the nerves of white societies in the region.

Despite the abiding fear of slave revolt, the Jamaican leaders reacted to the new French threat by raising several regiments of blacks and free coloreds. In fact, Jamaica recruited men of color even from Charleston, South Carolina where they had taken refuge under British protection. Service in either the British army or navy carried the guarantee of freedom and persuaded those of African descent to join in defense of the plantations where they labored as slaves. The British also enlisted people of color, both free and unfree, to build forts and dig protctive trenches in preparation for a French invasion. Ironically, the people of color built these defensive works to secure the sources of wealth and power of the slave owners, plantations and slavery. The British integration of men of color into the ranks represented a broader trend underway among all the participants in the revolution.

After the conflict, the British stationed uniformed African Americans on the sugar islands. The model unit, the Black Carolina Corps raised in South Carolina in 1779, arrived in 1783. These troops provided the template for other British officers to organize black units in the sugar islands. Veterans of the revolutionary battles, these officers understood the value of African Americans as a fighting force. Contradictions that beset Jefferson and Washington in Virginia hardly touched their counterparts in the Caribbean. The revolution both secured slavery in North America and the Caribbean while creating European military forces increasingly dependent on people of color to fill their ranks.

The end of the revolution brought important demographic and economic changes to an unexpected location, the Caribbean coast of Central America. Loyalist slave owners joined the exodus of British supporters from the United States in the wake of the 1783 peace treaty. Many chose to settle along the Moskito Coast of present-day Nicaragua and Honduras. Pro-British slaveholders and their property also departed from East Florida, ceded to Spain, and joined the loyalists along the Moskito Coast. By the mid-1780s hundreds of white slave-owning families and their property, almost 2,000 Africans and African Americans in number, worked new coastal plantations.

An even greater number of slave owners and slaves relocated from the United States to the Bahamas in the wake of the British defeat. By the late 1780s, hundreds of slave owners and thousands of slaves had altered the population of the Bahaman islands, many of which came under settlement for the first time. These refugees, free and unfree, revived a plantation system struggling to survive. The soil was ideal for cotton production and the slave owners quickly put African Americans to work planting and preparing a crop for export. Owners also compelled slaves to harvest salt, in great demand by the sailing ships in the Atlantic.

Bermuda, to the north of the Caribbean, also experienced a demographic and economic revolution as a result of loyalist refugees. The large numbers of loyalist slaveholders with their attachment to cash crops, plantations and slave labor soon transformed Bermuda into a cotton-producing island feeding the same growing British textile markets. The Caribbean, in fact, supplied the lion's share of cotton to British mills before the emergence of the cotton economy in the United States South.

The revolution, Canada and Africa in the Pan-British world

Canada, too, experienced the consequences of the revolution. The Patriots held high hopes for Canada and even reserved a place for them in the new nation. Yet, Canadians disappointed the American revolutionaries. The British holdings to the north either depended too greatly on Great Britain for trade to declare for independence or consisted of populations hostile to the Patriots' interests. Obviously the French showed no sympathy for the Patriot cause. Empathy for the revolution existed among the New England population in Canada, yet few proved willing to sacrifice property, livelihood and even life for a cause so distant from the daily life of rural Nova Scotia. The revolutionaries' practice of raiding maritime Canada only steeled the determination of most coastal Canadians to support the British.

Given its proximity and pro-British position, Canada became a safe haven for thousands of refugees. Their arrival significantly affected the populations of Upper, Lower and Maritime Canada. Some 3,000 African American supporters of the Crown made the surprising choice of Nova Scotia. They had served with British arms and took advantage of the British guarantees of freedom in the wake of Great Britain's defeat in 1783. Few resident Nova Scotians welcomed these newcomers and soon racial tensions flared up. The African American Loyalists desperately wanted land, as did other refugees. Unfortunately, the black Loyalists stood at the bottom of every waiting list. A minority received small parcels of land while the majority joined the ranks of transient laborers who constantly searched for work.

Similarly, hundreds of freed slaves encountered racial discrimination and hostility upon arriving in London. British attitudes proved no more enlightened than those held by their counterparts in Nova Scotia or the new republic of the United States. These men and women then joined a larger group of Africans heading for the west cost of Africa, where British abolitionists intended to establish a colony for freed people of color. Administered by the Sierra Leone Company, the first wave of settlers founded the colony of Sierra Leone in 1787.

A second wave, fleeing the unremitting hostility of the white population in Nova Scotia, arrived in 1792. Some 1,200 former slaves hoped to find a more accommodating environment. Instead they encountered a disease-ridden land and an oppressive climate. They also faced raids conducted by local slavers and tribal leaders, and some unfortunates again ended up in chains. Despite such challenges, the black Loyalists, with the aid of British abolitionists, did establish Freetown, the new capital of Sierra Leone.

Those who came from the former British colonies in North America carried with them their own brand of republicanism. The men and women of African descent, too, wanted freedom for themselves and their families as well as land to farm. Land insured their economic independence. They also saw themselves as heirs of the revolution and its promise of freedom and equality. Imbued with the notion of representative government that so profoundly shaped the revolution, these former Nova Scotians participated in political protests in Sierra Leone over what they deemed as the excessive powers of the governor. The Nova Scotians and others objected to the power of the governor and his council to make laws and impose criminal punishments without considering the opinions of Sierra Leone's people. To the dismay and often regret of these men, the governor and his supporters crushed the opposition, exiled some and ended all debate.

White Loyalists also made their way to Nova Scotia. These men, women and their families settled permanently in the maritme province. Largely New Yorkers, the 40,000 refugees immediately created a more diverse population. Most of these Loyalists came from modest circumstances. Some even came from the ranks of ex-soldiers and slave owners in the rebellious colonies. The newcomers complained about the distance of their settlements from Halifax, the capital and seat of government. They called for a division of Nova Scotia. The Loyalists also expressed unhappiness over political affairs in Nova Scotia, which were dominated by the older New England population. The British responded by establishing New Brunswick and giving the new arrivals greater access to the newly created provincial government. For the British, the Loyalists acted as a counter to the resident New England population and diminished the fear of a repetition of the disaster that occurred in New England in 1775 when the revolution broke out.

By the early 1790s continued pressure from Loyalists compelled the British to write the Canadian Constitution of 1791. This document grew out of Loyalists' calls for representative government. The Constitution divided Quebec into Upper and Lower Canada. The Upper Canadian political system incorporated a legislative institution that realized Loyalist demands for some measure of self-government as they understood it from their experiences in the former British colonies. Painfully aware of the poor decision making that led to the American Revolution, the British carefully avoided levying direct taxes on the Canadians until their assembly agreed to such measures. In addition, the loyalists realized their calls for an assembly in French Canada despite serious reservations from elements in the French-speaking population. Yet, despite these reservations, the French did continue to dominate Lower Canada. At the same time, the French population were a Catholic majority besieged by a Protestant minority, much as existed in Ireland.

Ireland and the eastern Atlantic

The eastern Atlantic also reacted to British efforts to shore up control over territories as they had in North America. The arrival of George Townshend in 1767 as Lord Lieutenant of Ireland marked the beginning of the effort to reduce the influence of the Anglo-Irish in governing Ireland. He faced the powerful "caretakers," Anglo-Irish leaders who used patronage and their own influence to run the Dublin Parliament and local boroughs. Unlike his predecessors, Townshend also took up permanent residence in Dublin, as a sign of his determination to enhance the authority of London. He and his successors diminished the influence of the "caretakers" and expanded the power of the metropolitan center over the periphery. Yet, Townshend's reach had limits. He could make appointments to the Revenue Board and similar agencies under his powers; yet local politics remained under the guiding hand of the caretakers.

Even before Townshend's arrival, the Anglo-Irish expressed concerns over London's policies, especially those directed toward the North American colonies. Anglo-Irish leaders worried over Parliament's imposition of measures such as the Stamp Tax. They feared that if Parliament forced their counterparts in North America to pay the duties and taxes demanded by Parliamentary measures, then Ireland would soon be subjected to such harsh treatment. Parliament's use of the 1720 Declaratory Act that articulated its supremacy over Ireland to fashion the 1766 Declaratory Act reminded the Irish leaders of their own vulnerability. Ben Franklin made this very point in 1771 when he told a Dublin audience that the trampling of constitutional rights the British colonies endured would also be the fate of the Irish. The growing crisis in North America intersected with the political crisis in Ireland.

As might be expected, the leading Anglo-Irish political faction, the Patriots, sympathized with the colonial cause. As a show of encouragement they lent their support to the factions out of power in London that openly opposed British policies in North America. In the private realm, support for the colonial cause appeared most visibly in the praise the Anglo-Irish gave to George Washington, who symbolized the colonial cause. Sympathizers placed his bust on the mantlepiece of the most celebrated mansion in Ireland, the Castletown House in Dublin. Washington also carried on a lively correspondence with Irish Patriots and sent his warmest regards to them when they achieved legislative autonomy for the Dublin Parliament in 1782.

The Anglo-Irish retained sufficient power to exploit the British inability to achieve a decisive victory in the North American colonies and the new danger posed by the French alliance with the North American revolutionaries. The Anglo-Irish successfully pressed for commercial concessions, which opened British domestic and colonial markets to Irish goods and merchants. In 1782 the Irish also won major political concessions that gave the Dublin Parliament independence in drawing up and enacting their own legislation. The British Privy Council still retained its power to review Irish legislation, yet rarely exercised it. This victory realized the long-held ambitions under British rule. The Anglo-Irish also won the repeal of the 1720 Declaratory Act and changes in Poynings' Law that had placed the Irish Parliament under the English monarch. The Irish admittedly shared sympathies with the North American revolutionaries, yet autonomy marked the extent of their political ambitions, not independence.

At the same time as these developments were taking place, a powerful pro-American lobby among dissenter Scottish-Irish Presbyterians emerged in Belfast. Scottish-Irish Presbyterians in North America kept close ties, both individual and economic, with their countrymen in Ireland during these years. The flood of Scottish-Irish, whose migration to North America peaked in the 1770s, reinforced and refreshed these ties. The tales of harsh British policies and actions rang true for the Scottish-Irish Presbyterians who lived as a minority in Northern Ireland and suffered under the rule of the Anglo-Irish. The colonials also keenly understood this relationship, and attempted to capitalize on the existing tension. In the various boycotts the colonials conducted in North America during the latter half of the 1760s, they deliberately continued to buy Irish goods, a decision meant to exploit Scottish-Irish Presbyterian sentiment in Ireland.

The entry of the French and the Spanish on the side of the revolutionaries in North America immediately affected the situation in Ireland. Once the Catholic French joined the war against the British, new concerns arose over the loyalty of the Irish Catholics. To defend Ireland against French invasion, the Anglo-Irish took the lead in creating militias that donned uniforms and marched under their own banners. The Volunteer movement, as it was known, eventually incorporated Catholics who joined in defense of Ireland.

The Volunteers used this occasion to advocate political and economic ends that benefited both the Anglo-Irish and the Irish Catholics. Their representatives called for free trade, adding one more voice to a chorus of demands for an end to commercial restictions. They also petitioned the British government to remove discriminatory measures such as Poynings' Law, which placed severe hardships on Irish Catholics. Such proposals sustained the cohesiveness of the Volunteer movement in the defense of Ireland and built its force for political and economic change.

Great Britain and the revolution

Great Britain, too, experienced significant changes resulting from its participation in the American Revolution. As the enemy and loser in the first major colonial war, Great Britain came away wounded but still convinced of its moral and political supremacy. The long years of fighting, the casualties suffered and the mounting fiscal costs compelled British officials to justify their position in prosecuting the war. They attempted to build a moral stance by painting as bleak a picture as possible of colonial rebels. The British repeatedly criticized the American revolutionaries for their harsh treatment of loyalists. Vulnerable, the innocents suffered grievously at the hands of the rebels and often lost their property and occasionally their lives. British officials also reminded their people that slavery remained an essential part of colonial society and the revolutionaries showed no inclination to end the practice. In fact, many prominent revolutionary leaders, Jefferson and Washington among them, depended vitally on slavery to sustain their fortunes. Few could commend such behavior.

The British reacted to the allies of the Americans, namely the French and Spanish. By 1780, British public opinion asserted that only the British Crown, Parliament and people remained the sole defenders of freedom and liberty in the western world. The Americans had taken league with the most despotic regimes in the west, regimes under absolute monarchies and aristocracies that fed off the labors of ordinary people. Neither law nor representative bodies protected the common people in France or Spain from the predations of their rulers. Yet, the American Revolutionaries sought aid from these very regimes to win their war for freedom. By the early 1780s the British stood alone in fighting for the ideals of liberty, rule of law and freedom enshrined in the British Constitution that secured rights and freedom for every citizen.

The British actions spoke as loudly as their declarations. London liberalized laws toward Catholics both in Great Britain and in Ireland through relief measures aimed at improving their lives. Ironically, British officials and the Anglican Church continued to harbor deep suspicions toward Scottish-Irish dissenters whose close ties and occasionally open sympathies with the rebellious colonists raised doubts about their loyalties. In 1784 Scottish-Irish writer, Richard Price, published *Observations on the Importance of the American Revolution*. He argued for religious tolerance on the United States model, the very thing the Anglican Church was determined to block. Dissenters, in fact, would endure another four-plus decades of religious restrictions before Parliament granted them full liberties.

Conclusion

The revolution precipitated changing relationships throughout the Pan-British world. The United States, home of the former rebellious colonies, broke its ties with Great Britain and the revolutionary leadership created a new governing system built on republicanism and egalitarianism. All men, or most men, generally enjoyed equal status – the triumph of 1783 swept away the rhetoric of rank and hierarchy. An egalitarian ethos prevailed in the United States' political language.

After 1783, the United States operated as an independent economic power, pursuing its own economic interests. Once a supplier of goods and services, the middle states, for example, shifted their trade toward Europe, where growing populations needed more and more food. Even tidewater tobacco producers in Virginia and Maryland moved out of the old staple and into grains destined for these same continental markets. Of couse, grain production commanded more skills, and often depended on family farms and free labor. In Maryland, landowners freed many of their slaves and leased the land back to its former cultivators, who benefited from the change in their status. The landowners relieved themselves of the financial burden of manitaining their slaves and reaped the profits of their labor as freedmen.

The South in the United States faced a serious crisis, since the rice and indigo plantations of the Carolina and Georgia coasts collapsed during the war. The war significantly diminished these markets. Rice would recover and begin to equal and then to exceed pre-wartime levels only in the 1790s. Indigo never returned as a staple export. Desperate planters serached for new crops. Seaside cotton, relatively easy to harvest, provided an adequate substitute but suffered from ecological limitations, since it only grew along the coast. Short-staple cotton held great promise, realized once Eli Whitney introduced the cotton gin. It made separating the cotton seed from the fibers quick and inexpesnive. Now short-staple cotton had a future and South Carolina and Georgia re-connected with British and later European markets with a new crop that was in great demand by British textile manufacturers. A staple economy re-emerged, and it drove the southern economy during the nineteenth century. As important, cotton revived a flagging slave system that had diminished under the pressures of British promises of freedom to slaves and the temporary disruption to the slave trade. Cotton rejuvenated slavery and extended its life for decades.

For the British, the loss of their North American colonies produced major changes in their empire. The resulting version proved even more diverse in its ethnic and racial makeup than in 1763. The loss of the most British and most Protestant part of the British empire immediately highlighted its other constituencies. At the same time, liberty and representative institutions that had once served as the hallmarks of the British commercial empire faded in the wake of the departure of Britain's thirteen colonies. The 100,000 indigenous peoples who came under Britain's paternalistic rule remained outside the imagination of British policy makers, none of whom could even conceive of representative bodies for these peoples. The revolution that produced the United States transformed the British Empire.

Yet, the revolution resulted in a more cautious imperial policy toward Ireland and Canada. The Anglo-Irish took advantage of London's quagmire in North America to achieve autonomy, which diminished London's guiding hand. Ironically, this achievement stood in contrast to the original intentions of Westminster to re-establish tighter control over its territories, a goal sought in the 1760s and 1770s and temporarily lost in the 1780s. The Anglo-Irish capitalized on the military pressures of the revolution in North America to alter its relationship with London. The Dublin Parliament won the autonomy it had sought for decades and the Anglo-Irish ruled Ireland with little interference from London.

The Ministry in London also addressed the political position of the Irish Catholics. It granted them more political rights, in part, by suspending Poynings' Law. For the Scottish-Irish, the outcome proved less sanguine. They sympathized with the plight of their fellow countrymen in North America who suffered at the hands of British officials. These officials refused to lift the legal measures that penalized the Scottish-Irish for their religious beliefs and rituals. Scottish-Irish Presbyterians correctly saw the Anglo-Irish as the main cause of their plight. Backed by London, the Anglo-Irish marginalized the Scottish-Irish minority, who felt the sting of restrictive measures.

Ireland, too, reconfigured its relationship with Great Britain. Seething under British rule and efforts to tighten up imperial administration, the Anglo-Irish capitalized on the revolution and the wartime pressures to alter their political and economic relationships with Westminster. They achieved their goals of free trade, once restricted by Westminster, and, most importantly, the Anglo-Irish persuaded the British Ministry to grant the Dublin Parliament the autonomy they had long pursued. As Irish enjoying English rights, the Anglo-Irish now had political equality with England yet they continued to maintain their profitable economic relationship and access to British military and naval resources. As a Protestant minority in a country dominated by Roman Catholics and a small but vocal Presbyterian dissenter population, the Anglo-Irish had no taste for the independence embraced by the North American revolutionaries. With a different history, demography and goals, the Anglo-Irish remained within London's orbit, a relationship that would persist into the twentieth century.

The Caribbean planters, too, found themselves in a new world. Their dependence on the British colonists in North America for essential resources virtually ended during the revolutionary war. They faced food shortages and disease during the wartime years and saw their populations diminsh. They also faced an Africanization of their militia and British regular units safeguarding the islands. Once the French and Spanish entered the war against Great Britain, the British responded by sending military resources to guard the extremely valuable sugar islands.

The migration of peoples because of the revolutionary war also changed the face of the Pan-British world. The revolution led to the re-creation of new human communities that claimed membership in what remained of the Pan-British world. The Loyalists who fled the United States for Canada dramatically changed the politics and demography of their new homeland. Sensitivity to protests from their territories gave these new Canadians a constitution in 1791. It adopted many of the notions first articulated in the United States Constitution of 1788. Above all, Parliament refrained from passing taxation measures until English-speaking representatives had studied and given their assent to the bills. Canada and its new population replaced the thirteen colonies as Great Britain's largest holding in the western Atlantic. It also assumed the role of sending raw materials to British ports.

Black Loyalists chose Nova Scotia as their new home. Frustrated by racial attitudes they then moved to West Africa, where they settled in Sierra Leone, founded by supporters of the new abolitionist movement. The Loyalists brought with them many of the ideals of the revolution, and in attempting to realize these they challenged the administrators of the colony. At the same time, their presence in Sierra Leone gave substance to the new abolitionist movement that would grow into one of the major reform movements of the nineteenth century.

The Atlantic world experienced a seismic shift because of the revolution in North America. The United States did reconnect with Great Britain through the emerging cotton economy, which was dependent on distant markets and slave labor. In some ways, the new cotton-driven economy of the southern states was reminiscent of the colonial era. The British also regained their access to United States markets, where cotton products sold well.

The revolution led to changes in the population in Canada, where Loyalists flocked by the tens of thousands. It temporarily diminished London's grip on Ireland and sustained a dissatisfied Scottish-Irish minority in Ireland. Believing the Anglo-Irish and British Ministry conspiracy, the Scottish-Irish remained a disgruntled and truly marginalized people. Yet, they looked to the United States as an inspiration in the struggle against what they perceived as the tyranny of British rule. The revolution ushered in a new era in every sense of the word, from demographic, economic and political dimensions.

Further reading

For an understanding of the British position during the revolution, see Eliga Gould, *The Persistence of Empire: British Political Culture in the Age of the American Revolution* (Chapel Hill, 2000); C.A. Bayly, *Imperial Meridian: The British Empire and the World, 1780–1830* (New York, 1989); P.J. Marshal, ed., *The Oxford History of the British Empire. Volume II: The Eighteenth Century* (New York, 1998); Stephen Conway, *The British Isles and the War for American Independence* (New York, 2000).

For the United States' position, see Gordon Wood, *The Radicalism of the American Revolution: How a Revolution Transformed a Monarchial Society into a Democratic One Unlike any That Had Ever Existed* (New York, 1992); Jack P. Greene, *Peripheries and Center: Constitutional Development in the Extended Politics of the British Empire and the United States* (New York, 1986) and *The Quest for Power: The Lower House of the Assembly in the Southern Royal Colonies, 1689–1776* (Chapel Hill, 1963).

For a discussion of the impact of political protest and the revolution on the British Caribbean colonies, see Andrew J. O'Shaughnessy, *An Empire Divided: The American Revolution and the British Caribbean* (Philadelphia, 2000).

For the reaction of the Irish, Scots and Canadians, see T.M. Devine, *Scotland's Empire and the Shaping of the Americas 1600–1815* (Washington, 2003); T.C. Smoot, *A History of the Scottish People 1560–1830* (Bungay, Scotland, 1972); R.H. Houston and W.J. Know, eds., *The New Penguin History of Scotland: From the Earliest Times to the Present Day* (London, 2001); David Allan, *Scotland in the Eighteenth Century* (London, 2002); Toby Barnard, *A New Anatomy of Ireland: The Irish Protestants, 1649–1770* (New Haven, 2003); R.H. Foster, ed., *The Oxford History of Ireland* (New York, 1992); R.F. Foster, *Modern Ireland 1660–1972* (London, 1988); Margaret Conrad, Alvin Finkel and Corneilius Joener, *History of the Canadian People Beginning to 1867: Volume 1* (Toronto, 1993); J.M. Bumstead, *The Peoples of Canada: A Pre-Confederation History* (Toronto, 1992). For a discussion of Ireland and its relationship to the broader Atlantic world from the American Revolution to the French Revolution, see Kevin Whelan, "The Green Atlantic: Radical reciprocities between Ireland and America in the long eighteenth century," in Kathleen Wilson, ed., *A New Imperial History: Culture, Identity and Modernity in Britain and the Empire, 1660–1840* (New York, 2004), pp. 216–238.

For the impact of consumerism on shaping attitudes of the revolutionaries in British colonial North America, see T.H. Breen, *The Marketplace of Revolution: How Consumer Politics Shaped American Independence* (New York, 2004).

For analysis of the role of people of color in the revolution, see Sylvia Fry, *Water from the Rock: Black Resistance in a Revolutionary Age* (Princeton, 1991); Ira Berlin, *Many Thousands Gone: The First Two Centuries of Slavery in North America* (Cambridge,

Massachusetts, 1998). For a discussion of the black Loyalists and abolitionists in west Africa, see Lamen Sanneh, *Abolitionists Abroad: American Blacks and the Making of Modern West Africa* (Cambridge, Massachusetts, 1999).

For the experiences of maritime men and women engaged in revolutionary activity, see Paul A. Gilje, *Liberty on the Waterfront: American Maritime Culture in the Age of Revolution* (Philadelphia, 2004); W. Jeffrey Bolster, *Black Jacks: African American Seamen in the Age of Sail* (Cambridge, Massachusetts, 1997); Peter Linebaugh and Marcus Rediker, *Many Headed Hydra: The Hidden History of the Revolutionary Atlantic* (Boston, 2001).

For a broadscale analysis of migration, see Marilyn C. Baseler, *"Asylum for Mankind": America 1607–1800* (Ithaca, 1998).

Chapter 4

Industrialization and the remaking of the world, 1750–1900

Introduction

The revolutions of the late eighteenth and early nineteenth centuries produced representative governments and new national identities in the Atlantic world. In the midst of these revolutions, economic change occurred that equaled the political transformations in scope and intensity, first in Great Britain and then spreading across the western world. By 1900 Great Britain, the United States and a unified Germany ranked as the three most economically powerful states in the world.

Entrepreneurs and inventors in these states developed new technologies, mechanized production and built up new forms of transportation and communication. These changes transformed pre-industrial economies once bound by human and/or animal power. Novel technologies produced new means of production. These also enabled entrepreneurs to deploy steam-powered ships, railroads built with iron, and new forms of communication such as the telegraph and the submarine cable that transcended the barrier of distance across oceans and continents.

The new economic world continued to depend on water transportation and even water power, much as the pre-industrial age had. However, new technologies greatly enhanced the use of water both for transportation and manufacturing. Ships equipped with steam power and iron hulls moved with great speed across the oceans and waterways, while new oceanic cables provided immediate communication across the Atlantic and later the Pacific Ocean. Speed, safety and volume of cargo all increased dramatically, while the ability to co-ordinate voyages and cargo appeared for the first time in history. The ocean no long served as a barrier to rapid communication.

The mechanization of manufacturing also depended on water power. New machinery capitalized on new hydraulic technology to transform textile manufacturing. These enabled textile factories to draw power for their machinery. Entrepreneurs also used coal to generate steam power for locomotives, mining equipment and other industrial uses. The rail and shipping industries created huge demands for iron and iron products, and their demands rippled throughout industrializing economies and accelerated the transition from pre-industrial forms of manufacturing.

Ironically, industrial economies continued to draw staples, such as cotton, from distant agricultural sites. The British textile economy reinvigorated the plantation complex in the United States South and its slave labor regime. Rooted in an early commercial system, plantations and slaves now played a central role in the emerging industrial economies. Industrialization freed many men from the struggle of hard physical labor while demanding that others remained enslaved and engaged in grueling laborious tasks for generations.

Industrial technology also launched rails and locomotives powered by coal and steam. The rail lines increased the total freight hauled and the speed with which it moved to its destination. Rail lines transformed the meaning of distance and time on land as ships had done on water. It demanded more and more energy, namely coal. Rail, mining, textiles, heavy manufacturing and other related activities transformed the economies in Western Europe and North America. This change had tremendous implications for the rest of the world, where industrialization had yet to take root. Innovative communication proved as crucial to industrialization. The telegraph provided rapid communication between any two locations on land. The telegraph complimented the railroad and joined the submarine cable to move information across the globe.

By the late nineteenth century, Great Britain, the United States and the German states led by Prussia built industrial economies based on these innovative technologies, new industries and older forms of rural production and labor. These three each pursued different strategies to achieve this economic preeminence. Great Britain relied on textiles and services, the United States on consumer, light and heavy industries. Germany relentlessly built an industrial economy based on heavy industry. For the United States and Germany, the British technology and industrial knowledge enabled both states to begin building their industrial economies. By the late nineteenth century, competing states across the globe understood the vast power of industrialization.

Great Britain and early industrialization

The foundation of British industrialization stretched back to the eighteenth century, when British entrepreneurs began to reconstruct the country's transportation system. They improved roads to complement coastal and river transportation. Roads, where they existed, often traced their origins to the Roman period, which made shipping or traveling a dangerous, expensive and uncomfortable proposition. In the last few decades of the eighteenth century, engineering methods borrowed from the French enabled the British to make significant improvements to their road system.

The country also developed a network of canals that could effectively and cheaply move goods and people to urban centers and markets. This network integrated northern industrial cities, including Birmingham and Manchester, with major British ports such as London and Liverpool. It also tied together the four major rivers in England, the Trent, the Mersey, the Thames, and the Severn. The road system reinforced these links. Together these innovations proved essential in creating a viable national market, notably absent on the continent. These changes greatly enhanced early British efforts in developing a textile industry, which would power the British economy throughout the nineteenth century. The introduction of rail lines in the 1830s would only enhance an already effective transportation system.

British manufacturers counted on new, productive technologies to meet the demands of rapidly growing domestic and overseas markets. Innovations such as the spinning jenny and the water frame enabled Britain's emerging textile industry to make cheaper and higher quality goods that appealed to consumers. Of course British manufacturers needed cotton, the basic material for their products, in huge volume. Here, they looked overseas, much as British traders had in an earlier era.

British industrialization and the United States South

North America provided the cotton and the Atlantic Ocean supplied the means of shipping the cotton to British textile factories. At first, British mills purchased sea-island, or long-staple, cotton from Barbados and the Bahamas. Separating the seed from the cotton by hand was relatively easy and inexpensive. Soon coastal South Carolina began to grow the long-staple cotton, which was eagerly purchased by agents of British mills.

Long-staple cotton created a serious problem. It only grew in swampy coastal environments, and there was no possibility for expansion. The rapidly expanding British cotton industry would face shortages of its basic raw material. Short-staple cotton did thrive in the interior of the United States South, yet the difficulty of separating cotton from the seed made it very costly. There seemed no way to change these conditions.

Eli Whitney's invention of the cotton gin in 1792 resolved this quandary. It enabled cotton producers to adopt new strains of cotton suited to the untapped inland and precipitated a revolution in cotton production. In the process it assured English textile manufacturers of an abundant supply of quality cotton. The gin separated the cotton balls from their seeds. Fortunately it performed this crucial task for the short-staple cotton that would thrive in the climate and soil of the state's interior.

Soon cotton appeared in regions around the inland cities of Columbia, South Carolina and Augusta, Georgia. These cities stood astride rivers that connected them with the ports of Charleston and Savannah, which in turn housed the businessmen, merchants, and shippers that linked the emerging cotton economy of the South with distant markets.

Within a short time cotton reached the Mississippi, where it underwent a transformation. Plantation owners in Natchez, Mississippi developed a hybrid of Mexican and local cotton that resisted known diseases, produced greater yields and proved undemanding to harvest. Ultimately, this strain of cotton served as the standard for the entire cotton complex in the United States South.

Steamboats facilitated the development of the Lower South and regions that bordered the Mississippi. The steamboat owed its power source to James Watt and his steam engine first developed in Great Britain. Once deployed in the United States South, it dramatically reduced transportation costs and increased the volume of cotton shipped to river and coastal ports and then to Great Britain via New York City. The capacity of steamboats to use even the shallowest of rivers encouraged the spread of the cotton crop throughout the South and made it an extremely profitable enterprise.

The expansion of cotton production called for an equally large boost in the labor supply. The resumption of slave imports into South Carolina in 1803 marked the reconnection of the South with African slave markets. The migration of planters and their "property" (i.e. African American slaves) from the Upper South to the newly developing cotton regions also contributed to the growing population of African Americans who would make the cotton plantation an economic success.

The men who owned these slaves lived in the broader Atlantic world where, in fact, the cotton industry existed. The planters of Natchez, for example, sold most of their cotton to buyers in Liverpool via the New York auction system. They bought their quality wines from sellers on the Atlantic coast of France or in London. They purchased what contemporaries labeled Negro Cotton from New England textile manufacturers to clothe their slaves.

Businessmen and professionals from mid-Atlantic and New England states provided financial, medical, commercial, shipping and other crucial services that helped sustain the cotton world. In general, the United States South bought the majority of its manufactures from northern producers and distributors. These northerners also represented New York City interests that auctioned off cotton to British buyers. In every sense of the word, the United States South sustained early industrialization in Great Britain by dedicating its efforts to staple production and using distant manufacturers and sellers to meet many of its needs.

It also drew the energies of many outside of the South and made businessmen in the eastern United States part of the British overseas network that accounted for the flow of cotton to British mills. Great Britain's industrialization owed much of its success to the steady supply of quality cotton from the western Atlantic and the capacity of New York City to provide the white-collar services that made the commercial relationship possible. Great Britain and the United States developed a highly interdependent relationship.

Great Britain and technological creativity

Domestically, the British also benefited from an entrepreneurial environment that encouraged technological creativity. Constructing a new piece of machinery merely started a long process of continual improvements. For example, James Watt patented his famous separate-condenser steam engine in 1769. Subsequently, Watt and scores of skilled workers began to experiment with minor and major changes in the design to improve efficiency and productivity. Speed, tool design and materials all came under the imaginative eye of British artisans who worked constantly to enhance the manufacturing process.

British skilled workers discovered that machines that sped up one part of production created bottlenecks down the line. The mere volume produced by mechanization often overwhelmed a subsequent task unequipped with comparable machinery. The mechanization of weaving in manufacturing cotton textiles created an intense demand for spun cotton only met once entrepreneurs introduced the carding machine. This provided spun cotton in volume and inexpensively. An expanding consumer market drove these changes and the absolute need to increase production. This mechanization also enabled cotton to replace wool as the leading industry in the British economy by 1800. This "technological creativity" marked all aspects of Great Britain's industrial transformation.

The British developed the factory, a new workplace to house this machinery and the new industrial workforce. This concentration yielded important advantages for the entrepreneur. The workers who once labored in their own cottages out of the owner's purview now came under his direct supervision. The entrepreneur and his small staff controlled the pace of work and monitored the quality of production on a minute-by-minute basis, if needed. The factory also made possible uniform production, so critical for the large volume markets.

Factories and their machines required flexible and sustainable power. The steam engine provided this. Developed to draw water from copper- and coal-mines, the steam engine quickly moved into textiles and, once in place, reshaped the entire industry. The steam engine depended on the abundant supply of coal in Great Britain. From the first decade of the nineteenth century coal and the steam engine increasingly met the growing demands for large-scale power to drive the country's manufacturing base. Steam power compensated for Great Britain's lack of adequate water power and enabled her to meet the rising demands for manufactured products.

Technology and the industrial community

Steam power also reshaped urban economies. Glasgow, Scotland provides an ideal example of this change. Glasgow combined an old business, shipping, with the new technology to ascend to prominence in Britain's industrial urban world. The port city prospered in the eighteenth century, based on the trade with the British colonies in the western Atlantic and the Caribbean. As a result, its merchants invested their capital in shipbuilding to sustain the urban economy. The development of Watt's steam engine dramatically affected manufacturing and transport technology. Watt's invention called for iron cylinders and other iron-based parts, and this new demand sustained a rapidly expanding iron industry in the Glasgow region.

By the 1820s entrepreneurs had adapted the steam engine to power steamboats and this demand accelerated the expansion of Glasgow's shipbuilding industry. Regional iron makers produced boilers for the steamboats and soon began to manufacture parts for iron boats that sailed in local waters. Finally, Glasgow manufacturers began to build ocean-going iron ships that would transform seaborne transportation. The city would later develop into a worldwide leader in the shipping industry.

Glasgow relied on improved water transport, which gave it a powerful "connection" with the rest of Great Britain, until the 1840s when a rail line reached the Scottish port. Of course, the steamboats, the ocean-going ships and the railroads all carried the cotton textiles manufactured by the 300 textile factories in Glasgow that relied on the steam engine. Watt's engine enabled Glasgow to combine an old industry, shipbuilding, and a new, revolutionary industry, cotton manufacturing, to create a new economy.

The United States, transport innovation and industrialization

Unlike Great Britain, the United States faced a continental geography. Distances in the United States stretched into unimaginable lengths and often incorporated natural barriers, most notably mountain ranges. Nothing comparable existed in Great Britain, served well by water and roads by 1800. The United States first turned to the same alternative chosen in Great Britain, roads and turnpikes. In New England and the middle Atlantic States entrepreneurial and public interests built these from the 1790s onward. Roads and turnpikes proved especially important in regions that lacked river systems. In fact, the Philadelphia-Lancaster turnpike marked the United States' first major highway. Turnpikes provided the first effective means of transportation to farmers and entrepreneurs who lacked inexpensive coastal transport or nearby markets.

The United States developed canals on a massive scale appropriate to the huge distances between geographic regions. By their very construction, the length of the canals and their great number overshadowed the far smaller network of Great Britain. When combined with the Great Lakes and huge inland rivers such as the Mississippi and the Susquehanna, canals held the potential to create a national system of transportation that would benefit the national economy. Completed in 1825, New York State's Erie Canal greatly enriched New York City and the communities along its path. It connected the eastern manufacturers with the growing farm communities in the Midwestern states on its route from the Hudson River near Albany to Buffalo on Lake Erie. The Erie Canal provided inexpensive and quick transportation to passengers heading for territories in the Midwest and greatly hastened the settlement of Ohio, Indiana, Illinois and elsewhere in the region. An engineering triumph, it later added spokes that joined it with Lake Champlain, the Finger Lakes region in upstate New York, and the Susquehanna River.

The Erie Canal precipitated a canal building craze. In an effort to capture the trade of the Ohio Valley, Pennsylvania built the Main Line Canal that joined the eastern and western parts of the state. Pennsylvania also built an impressive canal system that connected the coal-producing region in northeastern Pennsylvania with Philadelphia and New Jersey–New York markets via the Morris and the Delaware and Raritan Canals. In the Midwest canal links joined Chicago with the Illinois River by the 1840s. The Mississippi gave farmers and manufacturers access to New Orleans and other southern markets. Canals also linked the region with the Great Lakes and via the Erie Canal with the rich east coast markets. Together these provided the United States with a national system of transportation by the 1840s. Nothing comparable in scale or size existed in Great Britain.

Steamboats proved central to the northern development. New York and Philadelphia incorporated the steamboat as part of their transportation complexes. Steamboats also provided service to New Haven, Providence, Boston and Baltimore as well as other key ports along the east coast of the United States. By the 1820s, steamboat companies scheduled regular services between New Orleans and the east coast. Pittsburgh emerged as a major steamboat port as these vessels moved up and down the Ohio River to Cincinnati, Louisville and to St. Louis on the Mississippi River. Combined with canals, roads and turnpikes, the steamboat created a truly national system of transportation.

New England and technology

As entrepreneurs and state governments began to construct a new transportation system, many in the new republic also turned their attention to Britain's technology. National leaders, notably Alexander Hamilton, promoted industrial activities designed to emulate what Great Britain's entrepreneurs had achieved. A well-known Philadelphian, Tench Cox, eagerly sought British inventors and artisans who knew the secrets of the new technology and the new workplace, namely the factory.

One such individual, Samuel Slater, arrived in New York City in 1789 after finishing his apprenticeship in cotton textiles. He came equipped with knowledge of and experience in the British textile factory. On his departure Slater actually disguised himself to avoid detection by British authorities, who were worried over the loss of such talent and the advantages it gave to competitors. Eventually, Slater teamed up with the Brown brothers, Providence, Rhode Island merchants, who supplied the capital to set up textile operations in Pawtucket, Rhode Island. From this small beginning, Slater and those recruited and trained by him, provided a stream of entrepreneurs who helped start the textile industry in rural and small town New England. Armed with Slater's knowledge, these eager young entrepreneurs constantly worked to improve the machinery and better organize production.

In 1810, just over twenty years after Slater's arrival, a prominent New Englander, Francis Cabot Lowell, began an extended two-year stay in England to see first hand the way the English ran their textile operations. He returned to the United States with this knowledge. Backed by wealthy friends, Lowell established the first successfully planned industrial community in the United States, across the Charles River from Boston, in Waltham, Massachusetts. The textile community relied on nearby water power for its energy. New England benefited directly from men such as Lowell and Slater and their abilities to organize factory production.

Yet, United States entrepreneurs developed their own machines and improved those shipped across the ocean. Francis Cabot Lowell developed a power loom in 1813 to enhance the manufacturing capacity of his factory and to compensate for the chronic labor shortages that plagued the United States. The demand for machines also created the first machine shops in New England, as extensions of the textile plants. Soon, these shops developed into separate companies prospering on healthy textile production. Much like Slater, Lowell then combined the Atlantic orientation with a focus on the continental United States to produce a successful textile operation.

Lowell's associates used the Waltham scheme as the basis for a series of planned industrial communities along the Merrimack River in Massachusetts. These consisted of Manchester, Lawrence and most notably Lowell, established in the 1820s. Lowell ranked as the most impressive of the three communities. By the 1840s, Lowell stood as the most technologically advanced site in the world. Like Waltham, its predecessor and inspiration, Lowell was a planned industrial community designed to exploit the water power resources of the Merrimack River on a scale not seen in the United States, Great Britain or the European continent. Established in 1822, it marked the largest concentration of textile factories in the United States, and by 1845 it symbolized American technological creativity and sophistication in hydraulic engineering. It demanded a major investment of private capital to pay for startup and maintenance costs and managerial skills to handle the huge volume of power generated by the waterfalls and in constant demand by the large-scale factories astride the Merrimack River. Since the industrial operations depended on a steady flow and certain volume in the water supply, the builders constructed smaller canals, dams, reservoirs and millponds and controlled lakes further north along the river, all in an effort to regulate the available water power on a year-round basis. These efforts represented a response by the managers of the vast water system to the constant demands of textile manufacturers for more water power. Last, entrepreneurs set up machine tool works to produce the equipment needed in the textile mills and to operate the water and power facility resources. Lowell quickly became the model for industrial communities dependent on water power. The knowledge of Lowell's engineers and managers proved indispensable to these industrial cities.

Lowell and Glasgow

Lowell's reliance on water power provided a contrast with Glasgow. The Scottish city's industrial prominence depended on a complex of steam power, coal mines, shipyards, ships, machine tool sites and cotton factories. British entrepreneurs deployed steam power most frequently in mining operations that produced the coal used in steam engines. Steam power enabled Glasgow to maintain its position in the Atlantic trade both as a producer of ships and as a shipper of cotton textiles.

Lowell built its prosperity on a hydraulic network that integrated a natural resource, water, multiple construction sites from plants to dams, streams and runoffs from the Merrimack basin. The continued use of timber in much of the industrializing United States, rather than coal, showed the persistence of pre-industrial approaches to manufacturing. Lowell also benefited from the expanding domestic market, unlike Glasgow that still maintained its waterborne trade. Both communities continued to depend on raw cotton grown and harvested in the United States South by African American slave labor. Both of these forward-looking communities existed only on the supplies produced by a slave regime. Last, the immensely complicated task of managing an industrial operation on Lowell's scale called for skilled managers. They ran a delicately balanced system that extended up and down the river and involved many distinct tasks, from control of lakes to maintaining small-scale canals for the transit of goods. Lowell's fame spread throughout the North Atlantic world and drew visitors from its every corner. It "dazzled" guests, such as Charles Dickens, who made their way to its factories and waterways during the nineteenth century, much as it continues to attract tourists to see these reconstituted sites in the twenty-first century.

Water power and steam power

In the United States, the widespread availability of fast-moving streams and rivers and the abundance of waterfalls made water power an appropriate choice for New England manufacturers. Water power cost far less per unit than steam power, enhancing its appeal to price-conscious manufacturers. Water power would prevail as the main source of power for United States industry until the 1860s and 1870s, before yielding to steam power.

Lacking comparable natural resources, British entrepreneurs relied on their most abundant resource, coal, to fuel the steam engines and secure their power needs. The steam engine gave British manufacturers the freedom to expand their operations and to relocate them closer to the urban markets of the very ports that facilitated overseas exports. The value of Watts' steam engine continued to enrich the British economy decades after its development. The steam engine made economic sense for the British, just as water power accommodated the United States' needs.

Steam power and railroads

From the 1840s onward railroads and heavy industry moved industrial economies in new directions. In the case of an already developed Great Britain, railroads and heavy industry significantly broadened the industrial base, while in the United States and Germany they increasingly recast the economic base and transformed the national economies on a wider scale than was possible in light industry. Railroads and their complex technology owed their existence to British inventors and entrepreneurs. By the early 1830s British railway entrepreneurs had built about one thousand miles of track in Great Britain, and over 6,000 miles by the late 1850s. The earliest railroads, such as the Liverpool–Manchester line, replaced canals as a more effective means of carrying goods to coastal ports. By mid-century, railroad companies connected Great Britain's major urban markets. The railroad industry in Great Britain employed in excess of 300,000 men and accounted for a significant share of the gross national product. The railroads also capitalized on the existing British iron industry, which had developed alongside coal mining, textiles and engineering. To meet the demands of the rail companies, iron producers increased their output 200 percent. Later, railroad construction needs precipitated a rapid expansion of the steel industry, once the Bessemer process made steel inexpensive enough for rail companies to purchase. Steel also fueled capital goods production, the engineering industry, machines and shipbuilding in the later nineteenth century. Railroads completed the transportation system, complemented the steamboats that appeared at roughly the same time and broadened the industrial base beyond textiles.

The United States and British railroad and mining technology

As early as the late 1820s the British began to export the new rail technology. Eager for an alternative to canals, eastern investors in the United States bought a version of the first locomotive, the Stephenson *Rocket*, to haul goods to and from the mouth of the Susquehanna River to Baltimore. As locomotives were an unproven technology in the 1820s, most risk takers in the United States preferred the canals. These would soon prove inadequate when compared to the railroad. British construction techniques, British locomotives and British iron rails suited the British economic landscape and Britain's geography. British engineers and construction personnel, for instance, spent a good deal of money per mile in building track. Since rail lines ran short distances and endured heavy use, quality construction made good economic sense. In the United States long distances made British methods cost-prohibitive for major United States companies. The Baltimore & Ohio Railroad used English techniques in its early construction but soon abandoned these in favor of the designs and approaches developed by its engineers.

At the same time, United States manufacturing was unable to produce locomotives and forced rail companies to import these from Great Britain. By the 1840s the United States railroad companies developed the skills to manufacture their own equipment. Domestically produced locomotives soon pulled rail cars for United States rail lines. Manufacturers also made Iron T-rails, specialized carriers such as boxcars and cattle cars, and the hundreds of complicated tools and parts demanded by railroads.

Railroads eventually demonstrated their superiority over canals. Railroads operated year round and without environmental restraints, unlike canals that froze in winter or were blocked by debris. Their speed, punctuality and huge carrying capacity greatly benefited manufacturers and shippers. The railroads opened up markets across the North American continent and placed the insatiable demands of metropolitan consumers within easy reach of any producer. For the United States, with its great distances and imposing terrain from mountains to large rivers, these assets accelerated industrialization.

The rapidly growing rail industry soon affected the coal mining and iron making industries, lodged mostly in eastern Pennsylvania. Here, too, the migration of talent and knowledge proved essential. British mining technology and techniques began moving to the United States in the 1790s. At this time, the bituminous coal fields around Richmond, Virginia dominated the infant mining industry in the United States. Virginia colliers such as Henry Heth used their connections with British miners to acquire technology and knowledge from their British counterparts. Heth, for instance, confronted the problem of removing water in his mines. In 1814, while the United States and Great Britain were actually at war, he made a trip to England where mining engineers advised him on the skills and machinery needed to resolve his problem. As a result, he recruited experienced Scottish miners who knew how to cope with the removal of water. Heth then purchased from British manufacturers the steam engine pump system that actually removed water from the mines. The Scottish miners provided the practical knowledge to maintain the pumps once they were in place.

The Virginia bituminous fields kept their leadership in the mining industry until the 1830s and 1840s, when the anthracite coal in Pennsylvania began to take control of domestic markets. Anthracite coal also combined with iron manufacturing to expand the United States' industrial capacity Here, too, the flow of talent and technology from Great Britain proved decisive.

Coal miners and highly skilled iron workers from all over Great Britain flooded into the state from the late 1820s. Welsh coal miners brought their knowledge of working anthracite coal veins to the anthracite mines in northeastern Pennsylvania. Entrepreneurs in Catasauqua, located in this region, solicited a Welsh skilled iron maker from Swansea, Wales to build the very first blast furnace that used anthracite coal, a task he completed to their satisfaction. By the early 1840s railroad purchases accounted for 33 percent of all iron production in the United States, a figure comparable to the British iron industry. Anthracite coal fueled the iron industry and the rail industry.

Philadelphia increasingly saw its future in the rail industry. Entrepreneurs financed the rail lines that connected the city with the anthracite and iron industries to the north by the 1840s and 1850s. These men also supplied the capital for the mining and iron making operation in north-eastern Pennsylvania. Major commission agents located in Philadelphia sold iron and iron-based goods manufactured in or near the anthracite coalfields to customers throughout the United States. By mid-century, Philadelphia also housed one of the country's major manufacturers of locomotives, a mark of the United States' diminishing reliance on British industry. This region would increasingly rely on steam power, since it lacked the rivers of New England yet had the key raw materials, coal and iron, to produce and use steam engines.

The rail lines into states such as Indiana and Illinois connected these rich agricultural regions with the prosperous urban markets in the east. The production of wheat, corn and other farm products soared in the wake of rail connections. With an effective means of shipping an almost unlimited volume of farm produce to market, agricultural implement manufacturers, notably John Deere and Cyrus McCormick, accelerated their production of plows, reapers and other farm machines. These enabled farmers to produce the needed volume. The rail industry provided the foundation for an economy that would eventually surpass the British economy.

Railroads also desperately needed current information on the operation of their trains. Here, the telegraph and its new code, developed by Samuel Morse, provided the answer. The telegraph lines enabled the managerial ranks that directed the railroads to keep close track on the arrival and departure of locomotives in their system as well as the freight and passengers the trains carried from station to station.

By 1840 the United States surpassed Great Britain in rail track. By the 1850s United States rail companies had laid track across the Appalachians and began to reach the Mississippi and beyond. In large measure, these achievements began with British technology. United States manufacturers and skilled rail workers adapted this technology to the rigorous demands of the geography of the United States. By the mid-1850s the rail lines had built the major trunk lines that linked the east coast and the developing west, where rich agricultural lands benefited from this effective form of transportation. Large rail corporations such as the Erie, the Baltimore & Ohio, the Pennsylvania and the New York Central Railroads provided the best transportation available. By the 1860s thousands of miles of rail lines covered these states. Soon, United States rail companies and their workers had built more than 20,000 miles of track, giving the United States the largest rail system in the world. The rail lines created the physical basis for a carrying capacity able to sustain the growing economy and population of the United States. The railroads also represented a new and dynamic force that would drive an industrial economy for the next century.

Germany, railroads and industrialization

The states that would comprise Germany embarked on their drive to industrialize a full generation after the United States. The wars of the French Revolution and the Napoleonic conflicts forced their energies into military campaigns. Once these wars finally ended in 1815 the German states turned their attention to economic issues. Unlike Great Britain and the United States, Germany's disunity produced divided markets that appeared most strikingly when German states raised tariffs in the wake of Napoleon's defeat in 1815. The high duties slowed commerce by adding significantly to costs of transportation and threatened economic interests in central Europe. As a result, by the mid- and late 1820s many leaders were compelled to agitate for the free movement of goods.

In 1834, the states in north Germany, led by Prussia, established the *Zollverein*. This union removed tariffs and encouraged the free flow of goods to the benefit of all the participants. Raw materials moved to manufacturers and finished goods moved to consumers with ease and with far less expense than before the trade agreement. A free market proved crucial for economic progress, a fact confirmed by the experiences of the United States and Great Britain where goods and services flowed uninterrupted from one market to another. The *Zollverein* also created a uniform currency that facilitated commerce. The German states had begun the slow process of economic unification. Over the next few decades, the German states would continue to reduce tariffs, simplify currencies, and free traffic along the Rhine and Scheldt Rivers from duties and fees.

German states faced the same problem the United States encountered in 1790s and early 1800s of how to acquire the knowledge of industrial production. Of course, the solution proved identical, and Germans persuaded the British to share their precious knowledge. Governments intervened in this process since it served their own interests in building a strong economy on the basis of the latest technology. Officials made available to entrepreneurs, every resource possible from financial subsidies to practical advice on technical matters. They even allowed these men to import industrial machinery free of customs. For the Germans, these strategies represented a massive effort to equal the British in industrial capacity.

Soon British technology and entrepreneurs began to make their way to Prussia, Bavaria, Saxony and other German states, all determined to develop their own industrial economies. At first, Germans adopted textile machinery to produce cotton products. In fact, even in the 1850s after the rail industry had made its appearance the only standardized machines produced in the German states were those involved in textile production. Major engineering houses such as Borsig and Egells manufactured a broad range of goods to customer specification. None chose to specialize in a particular product.

By the 1830s a handful of British-made locomotives steamed throughout the German states carrying freight and passengers to their destinations. British capital, industrial goods and personnel accounted for much of this early success. From the late 1840s onward, the rail industry increasingly claimed a larger and larger share of German efforts. Slowly Germans began to take over the construction and maintenance of the railroad industry and greatly expanded it. Rail and heavy industry grew dramatically from 1850 through the 1870s. Railroads and railroad construction accounted for 75 percent of capital invested in Prussian joint stock companies. Railroads also pushed the expansion in machine shops vital to the operation of rail lines. Mining, iron manufacturing and metallurgical industries all benefited directly from the growth of railroads.

The developing rail connections and the *Zollverein* made possible a market unobstructed by duties, distance or terrain. Entrepreneurs in the German states dedicated their efforts to building rail lines capable of handling and even increasing the volume of industrially produced goods. At first constructed by individual businessmen and private companies, railroads began to crisscross the German states in an unsystematic fashion, often connecting with rail lines from non-German states. By the 1850s, these companies built the outlines of a more orderly rail network that came under the control of the Prussian government and its bureaucrats. They used their experience in running the *Zollverein* to manage the rail system. The demands of the railroad moved rapidly throughout the German economy. Rail construction, locomotives, steam engines, car axles and other components of a railroad called for a dramatic increase in iron production.

These demands fueled a growing and dynamic economy that bound the states in the *Zollverein*. Iron-making sites appeared in the Ruhr, the Saar basin and even in remote Upper Silesia. The almost unlimited capacity of railroads to carry consumer goods to markets precipitated a major investment in industries which produced these goods. The railroad achieved preeminence as the main source of industrialization in Europe.

The construction of the rail system sparked a significant jump in coal production. From the 1840s on mining entrepreneurs in Upper Silesia, the Ruhr Valley and the Saar Basin accelerated their coal production to meet the rising demand of railroads and heavy industry. Coal production also depended on the completion of rail lines to the coalfields, which reduced the transportation costs and created effective ties with markets throughout the

German states. The coalfields in distant Silesia in eastern Prussia benefited from the rail lines.

In the west, railroads, a local railroad passenger service and a River Rhine cleared for navigation provided a superb transportation system to sustain industrial growth in dynamic regions such as the Ruhr Valley. The Ruhr developed into the hub of the emerging industrial economy in Prussia and later a unified Germany. It capitalized on local coal and ore deposits to produce iron and later steel, once the Bessemer process made it inexpensive to manufacture. By 1870 the main urban industrial centers such as Essen, Dortmund and Bonn that housed major iron and steel operations fueled the Ruhr Valley and made it the leading industrial site in Europe. By 1860 the Ruhr had assumed the lead in pig iron and steel production on the continent. Without the rail lines, the Ruhr, Prussia and later a unified Germany would have realized little of their economic potential.

By the 1870s Germany began to threaten British dominance in Europe and by 1900 she moved ahead of Great Britain. The United States' industrial economy grew at a significant rate during the rest of the nineteenth century and also overtook Great Britain by 1900. In fact, the United States achieved unquestioned economic leadership among the western economies.

Conclusion

Industrialization remains one of the most powerful engines of economic change in world history. It grew out of innovative technologies in manufacturing, mining, transportation and communications. These transformed the way humans made products and the volume they were able to produce. British textile mills pioneered the mechanization of making clothing. British mills that integrated new technologies turned out finished products in tremendous volume, in a quality that ranged from modest to high end and on a scale unimaginable in the pre-industrial era. Novel transportation depended on steam power and iron manufacturing. The United States and Germany depended vitally on railroads to industrialize. Great Britain, already an industrialized economy when British entrepreneurs introduced the first steam powered locomotive, still relied heavily on the railroad to move goods and people. Technology also changed dramatically the way information was moved and its speed. The telegraph and the submarine cable coupled with the railroad and the new steam powered ships produced a startling new economic environment. Together these changed the meaning of time and distance.

The industrialized states of Great Britain, the United States and the German states (Imperial Germany in 1871) all incorporated the assets of technology, novel transportation and communication and manufacturing to create the most powerful economies in the world. Yet, none of them accomplished this feat based solely on their own resources. Great Britain, the leader for most technological changes in the first stages of industrialization, depended vitally on the southern United States for raw cotton. Unless British textile manufacturers had access to quality cotton on a sustained basis, mills in Lancashire and Glasgow would have been silent.

The reliance on cotton from plantations in the southern United States ultimately depended on business agents throughout southern coastal ports, shipping companies that made the journey from southern ports to New York City or British ports. The mercantile community in New York captured the cotton trade and controlled it through the auction system. Buyers, whether from Great Britain or the United States, participated in the fierce bidding for cotton conducted in New York City. Businessmen and merchants made the auction system a successful mechanism for moving one of the most valuable raw materials in the world to the first industrial economy on the globe. Once sold, British ships then carried the cargo to ports in England or Scotland. At the same time, it greatly enriched New York City. Cotton, United States merchants and businessmen, New York auctioneers and British industrialists and ship owners all combined to make cotton a global product.

As important, Britain stood as the main source for novel technologies, its entrepreneurs pioneering in textiles, transportation, iron making and mining. Numerous inventions, from carding machines to steam-powered locomotives, came from British innovators.

Beginning in the 1790s the United States faced the task of developing an industrial economy. Leaders such as Alexander Hamilton understood the importance of industrial activity for the future. It, too, relied on a broader economic world than merely the national economy to promote industrialization. The United States invited and/or attracted many craftsmen skilled in manufacturing textiles and iron, coal miners who knew the demands of deep mining, and those versed in the complexities of locomotives. United States merchants and businessmen also simply bought British technology or toured the country's industrial landscape. They brought back valuable information on the organization of work and machinery, and the construction and design of cotton mills. Some United States entrepreneurs also visited British engineers for advice and then recruited skilled workmen to solve specific problems. Whole industries, from textiles to iron manufacturing and coal mining, owed a great deal to the British precedents.

The German states, too, looked to Great Britain for their technology and skilled workers. The Germans developed a strategy of promoting railroads and heavy industry. With British models, knowledge and workmen, they were able to move quickly to industrialize parts of their economies.

States that borrowed technology also improved upon it and adapted it to their landscapes and environments. The United States certainly relied on British locomotives and rail knowledge to build and operate the first railroads. Entrepreneurs in the United States also faced huge distance and required inexpensive rates. They built rail track cheaply, which enabled their companies to lay the rail lines between cities as distant as New York and Chicago. The one company that adopted the British emphasis on quality track failed. The costs of maintenance and construction overrode profits. In textiles, United States entrepreneurs exceeded their British counterparts in the construction of the largest textile manufacturing site in the world in Lowell, Massachusetts. The United States relied on abundant and inexpensive water power, and in Lowell hydraulic engineers operated the most sophisticated system of water power on the globe. The British, with scarce water power, depended on the steam engine and steam power. Such adaptations and improvements made the United States a powerful economic force by the 1870s.

By this time, all three countries enjoyed growing industrial economies. Each chose its own path to industrialization and capitalized on their particular assets. The British determined the future with the birth of industrialization. The United States and Germany followed suit. By the 1880s, the scale of United States companies had exceeded anything previously known in the industrializing western economies. The United States would take the lead in developing sophisticated organization and new industries dependent on innovations in science. Power now rested with technology, knowledge and industry. Industrialization had transformed the United States and its place in the ranks of nations.

Further reading

For a general discussion of industrialization, see David Landes, *The Unbound Prometheus: Technological Change and Industrial Development in Western Europe* (New York, 1999) and *The Wealth and Poverty of Nations: Why Some are So Rich and Some So Poor* (New York, 1998); and Eric Hobsbawm, *Industry and Empire: The Birth of the Industrial Revolution* (New York, 1999).

For industrialization in specific states, see, for the United States, Stuart Bruchey, *Enterprise: The Dynamic Economy of a Free People* (Cambridge, Massachusetts, 1990); Walter Licht, *Industrializing America: The Nineteenth Century* (Baltimore, 1995); Alfred D. Chandler, Jr., *The Visible Hand: The Managerial Revolution in American Business* (Cambridge, Massachusetts, 1977); Louis Hunter, *A History of Industrial Power in the United States, 1780–1830. Volume 1: Water power* (Charlottesville, 1985) and *A History of Industrial Power in the United States, 1780–1830. Volume 2: Steam Power* (Charlottesville, 1989); D.W. Menig, *The Shaping of Transcontinental America, Volume 3* (New Haven, 1998) and *The Shaping of Continental America, Volume 2* (New Haven, 1993). For the impact on societies, see Peter Hall, *Cities in Civilization: Culture – Cultural Innovation* (New York, 1999); Joel Mokyr, ed., *The British Industrialization: An Economic Perspective* (Boulder, Colorado, 1998); T.C.W. Blanning, ed. *The Oxford History of Modern Europe* (New York, 2001); William Otto Henderson, *The Rise of German Industrial Power, 1834–1914* (Berkeley, 1976).

For a series of essays covering several major industrial powers, see Thomas K. McCraw, ed., *Creating Modern Capitalism: How Entrepreneurs, Companies, and Countries Triumphed in Three Industrial Revolutions* (Cambridge, Massachusetts, 1991). For a specifically comparative work, see Mansel G. Blackford, *The Rise of Modern Business in Great Britain, The United States, and Japan* (Chapel Hill, 1998).

For the transfer of technology and industrial skills, see Sean Patrick Adams, *Old Dominion Coal, Politics, and Economy in Antebellum America* (Baltimore, 2004) and Grace R. Cooper, Rita J. Adrosko, and John H. White, Jr. "Importing a Revolution: Machines, railroads, and immigrants," in Carl J. Guarnei, ed., *America Compared: American History in International Perspective* (Boston, 2005), pp. 270–285.

Chapter 5

The global rise of corporations

Introduction

The industrial economies of the world had earned a reputation for their technological achievement and their rising levels of prosperity. By the late nineteenth century these economies also began to develop organizational and scientific capacities that would enable them to move far beyond their earlier productive abilities of the first part of the century. Matched with increasing technical proficiency, these economies would reach out beyond their borders both for markets and for raw materials. The emergence of the corporation that would amass capital and produce goods on a scale yet seen stood as the major organizational innovation of these industrial economies. This economic institution quickly developed into a powerful agency transforming business, individual lives and human societies across the globe. The United States would take the lead in this phase of industrialization, followed closely by a united German state. Great Britain would maintain its economic presence, yet rarely duplicate the achievements of either of its competitors. By the outbreak of World War I, the basis for an interdependent global economy had materialized through the activities of the modern corporation.

Railroads, organization and managers: the United States

The beginnings of the corporation in the United States appeared in the railroad industry. The railroad first confronted the problem of scale, distance and time previously not encountered by other industries. To meet these demands, the men who ran the railroads developed new organizational capabilities and in the process developed into the very first generation of managers.

The railroad industry in the United States faced a domestic market continental in size and with one of the most rapidly growing populations in the world. By the 1850s several companies operated large-scale rail systems that linked numerous metropolitan centers, scores of medium-sized industrial cities and hundreds of towns. A company directing an operation of this size and scope faced severe organizational problems as the number and variety of goods multiplied, namely how to coordinate and track its many activities and expanding workforce.

The answers to these problems emerged over the course of years, usually via trial and error. Large-scale railroads such as the Pennsylvania and the Baltimore & Ohio established central offices that monitored operations throughout the entire company. Company leaders then subdivided the railroad into geographic divisions. Within these, corporate officers separated tasks by function, such as freight, transportation or maintenance. The men who handled these tasks formed the core of the new managerial hierarchies able to coordinate the daily activities of thousands of employees over hundreds and even thousands of miles. These hierarchies marked a major innovation in the United States business community, one unparalleled elsewhere in the industrial world.

At the same time, the upper levels of management, including the general superintendent, the president of the company and, often, the chairmen of the board of directors, formed the finance committee. This group made key strategic decisions that affected the company's position in the industry, its investment strategies, and the adoption of new technology or integration of new markets. The teams of managers, both upper and middle, increasingly operated free from family ownership, which gradually lost the capacity to run such complex organizations. For managers, their life's work became the company and its business.

Railroad managers understood the importance of keeping costs low to insure the highest volume of business. The capacity to shape every transaction throughout the railroad enabled these managers to determine the prices charged to customers in ways simply unavailable to small-scale companies. Few wished to operate throughout a business cycle with little idea as to volume of business, availability of raw materials and price range in the consumer markets. The invisible hand, so widely praised by Adam Smith and his disciples, menaced the large-scale companies and they would open any path to diminish the unpredictable nature of a market. The sheer size and managerial efficiency of large-scale railroads allowed them to dominate markets by forcing out less competitive, smaller companies. The visible hand of the manager now began to determine the prices of products and the shape of the market.

The huge railroad industry also provided an almost insatiable market for steel, machines, machine tool steam engines and other parts needed to build and maintain rail lines, locomotives and rail cars. These drove much of the United States industrial development from the 1840s onward.

As important, the rail industry along with the emerging telegraph industry created the basis for a truly national market where information, services and goods moved quickly, with regularity and predictability. These innovations resolved the issue of shipping grain, meat and many other products on a scale and distance unimaginable just twenty years earlier.

Heavy industry

The crucial organizational innovations that resolved these challenges for the rail companies soon moved into other industries. Railroad men who pioneered such innovations often introduced them to steel, urban transportation and other capital-intensive industries where scale and scope shaped their production schemes and markets. Unlike textiles, lumber, printing or other early industries where economies of scale and scope proved ineffective, the new industries depended on sophisticated technology, coordination of complex activities, and an extremely high ratio of capital to labor for the vast increase in production and proportionate drop in unit cost.

Andrew Carnegie provides a clear example of the new, capital-intensive industrial operations that followed in the wake of the railroads. Carnegie mastered the managerial challenge in the rail industry when he worked as divisional chief for the Pennsylvania railroad under its president, Tom Scott. He took this experience as he moved into bridge building and then steel in the 1870s. Carnegie knew the advantage of economies of scale and new methods of production. These he incorporated in the huge blast furnaces that stood at the center of his steel operations. He acquired other tools of modern steel manufacturing, including barges sufficiently large and sophisticated enough to haul coal to his mills and huge ladles to handle the molten steel central to production. He also integrated industrial activities and raw materials necessary to produce steel. For instance, he acquired coke smelters needed to transform coal into coke, a vital ingredient in manufacturing steel.

Alert to his market, Carnegie introduced Henry Bessemer's steel-making process, which reduced costs and turned out price-effective steel rails. The rail market remained his largest consumer until the 1890s when the plate steel market began to replace it. At that point, he adopted an open-hearth technique that produced first-rate plate steel. These capital-intensive industries depended much more on technical information than older industries such as textile manufacturing had, where science and technology played a small or no role in manufacturing, and labor-intensive operations prevailed over capital-intensive ones.

Carnegie also brought with him the new managerial schemes that had proven so successful in the rail industry. He installed a cost-conscious mentality acquired from railroad managers to organize and run the steel mills. The visible hands of the many managers determined the costs of Carnegie's products. By establishing prices through his cost mentality and through control of all phases of steel from ore mining to production, Carnegie significantly diminished the invisible hand of the market. In fact Carnegie so dominated steel, his company out-produced the whole of Great Britain. Then, in 1901, Carnegie sold out to financier J.P. Morgan, who made the company the centerpiece of his United States Steel Corporation. It stood as the first billion-dollar company and the largest single operation in the world, and gave the United States immense global economic power.

Carnegie also recruited the best and the brightest of the engineers, chemists and other professionals to staff his technical ranks. These men brought the mathematical, scientific and engineering skills and knowledge necessary to improve steel and to produce superior plant design. Contemporaries considered Alexander L. Holley, Carnegie's top engineer, as the best in the business. He also hired a leading German chemist trained in a German university system deemed the most sophisticated in the industrial world. Carnegie understood the growing need for such university-trained individuals.

Unlike Carnegie, who relied on vertical integration to build his corporation, Rockefeller used horizontal combination, or, simply, buying out the competitors in the oil industry through some persuasive means. Using Cleveland as his base, Rockefeller moved into the fledgling oil industry in the 1860s and 1870s. His refineries soon made him a powerful force in the industry. In the 1870s he began to move to minimize the dramatic swings in the industry that grew out of its fiercely competitive nature. Unable to stabilize the industry, he turned to a cartel strategy to diminish the impact of this competition. Members of the oil cartel agreed to set prices, restrict competition and operate in distinct markets. Menaced by uncooperative oil refiners and legal attacks on measures that violated the free market, Rockefeller eventually set up the Standard Oil Trust that gave him control of the industry. Rockefeller used the immense economic leverage of his huge operations to persuade other companies in the refining industry to surrender their stocks in exchange for trust certificates, a move that gave Rockefeller control of almost all oil refining. The trust enabled him to bring order to the oil industry and to coordinate its various enterprises from a central office. He also reduced the number of refineries and concentrated production in a handful of operations. These actions lowered the price of kerosene and gave Rockefeller control of the oil industry.

Science-based industries

New capital-intensive industries also incorporated scientific and technical knowledge into their production. Of these the electrical industry proved one of the most far reaching. It provided a new form of energy to business and individuals on a scale and with a consistency unimaginable with early forms of energy. It also powered motors for urban transportation and remade production, factories and individual homes. Electricity demanded men educated in a variety of disciplines, from physics to chemistry. General Electric and Westinghouse Companies, for instance, depended on professionally trained electrical engineers who brought the latest knowledge and most sophisticated theory demanded in the construction and maintenance of electrical systems and powerhouses. Virtually no companies could operate in the business without these highly educated professionals.

Companies such as General Electric, Westinghouse and Allis Chambers also manufactured complex equipment. Costly, these products demanded that plant managers worked closely with the professionals who designed the products and with the sales people who moved electrical equipment to consumers. The investment in managers and in economies of scale created tremendous market advantages for these companies. The managers also adopted the strategy of scope, the ability to manufacture different commercial goods with just minor adjustments to the production, to enhance their competitive edge. They developed teams of marketers to promote their products. These characteristics marked the most crucial dimensions in the rise of the modern industrial enterprise.

Consumer industries

Consumer industries developed and maintained mass markets for their products. Companies as diverse as James Duke's American Tobacco, John Campbell's canned soup and Proctor and Gamble's soap operation all depended on scale and scope. These companies sold their products to individual consumers and, as a result, invested most of their resources in developing marketing and sales branches. These men invested in plants of sufficient scale to meet the purchasing power of hundreds of thousands of individuals. These big companies also developed marketing organizations to persuade consumers into adopting new habits that depended on the consumption of these products. Of course, they also recruited managers in numbers adequate to insure the flow of raw materials to production sites and products to consumer markets.

These same companies capitalized on market advantages inherent in scale and scope. As in the electrical industry, scale obviously enabled manufacturers to reduce costs per product, assets small-scale producers lacked. Corporate operations also invested capital in scope manufacturing similar products with minor adjustment to production. This tactic allowed a company to exploit different mass markets. Campbell's Soup, Heinz Catsup and Borden's Milk, for example, adopted this strategy.

Both strategies depended on adequate investment in marketing. To sell the volume of products manufactured, corporations also had to set up marketing systems designed for each of their products. These networks enabled the companies to reach distinct mass markets for each of their commercial goods. Last, the managers who handled the many distinct activities of big companies continued to regulate operating costs and therefore were able to determine prices for their goods independent of the market.

Gustavus Swift, the leader in the meat industry, demonstrated the convergence of new technology, managerial efficiency and marketing acumen. He developed and incorporated refrigerated technology that enabled his company to reach consumers across the continent. He resolved the vexatious problems of delivering unspoiled meat over long distances by developing refrigerated rail cars. Swift then used his huge disassembling and packing plants to process large numbers of cattle purchased from western ranchers. From these cows,

Swift's workers produced a variety of meat products that met the diverse tastes of his consumers. Swift also relied on teams of managers to administer these increasingly complex operations.

Introducing a new product, Swift first had to assure the multitudes that eating refrigerated meat shipped over hundreds of miles in no way endangered the customer. He relied on advertising and marketing departments to convince his initially suspicious consumers that frozen meat posed no danger and then to persuade them of the superiority of his products. Sophisticated and relentless advertising won the day for Swift. Competitors lacking the capital and financial resources of these corporations and their capacities for production simply proved unable to challenge them.

Mass consumer corporations such as Swift depended on brand and packaging schemes to promote their products. Consumers began to recognize the design of the Campbell's canned soup or the Heinz ketchup bottled products. As a result, manufacturers grew to depend on national advertising agencies or their own departments that promoted their products across the country's diverse markets. Corporations such as Coca Cola incorporated new mechanized bottling technology to produce and make their products ready for markets.

Financing corporations

Financing the growth of these companies and their merger activities demanded capital on a scale never seen before in the United States. Railroads demanded enormous sums of capital in the 1890s. Even in their early years during the decades after 1850 railroads called for capital beyond any previous industry. Investment houses grew up in New York City, where the stock market also operated to fund railroad and other "closely allied" securities. This concentration made the city the "money market" for the entire country, and second in the world only to London. Their participation in the railroad industry gave the bankers in New York City a financial sophistication and expertise that made them useful to industry. These banks negotiated and discussed and urged rationalization upon the companies to reduce the poison of competition. Yet, corporations that depended on "individual investors" and/or "retained earnings" for their capital never developed long-term ties with these banks. Companies looked to the stock markets and to retained earnings as the means to support their operations. Corporations did need the services of investment banks for such activities as "international monetary exchanges" or for "transfers of stock."

Investments in the large railroads also came from overseas, with the money handled by New York City financiers. Bankers in New York and London worked closely enough to integrate their fiscal markets, more so than any other financial centers across the globe. Both Great Britain and the United States also embraced the gold standard that secured exchanges while the new steam-powered iron and, later, steel ships and the oceanic cables tightened the connection. British and, to a lesser extent, continental investors bought significant amounts of railroad bonds. This money proved essential to meeting the capital demands of these large-scale enterprises. In fact, London investors relied on the railroad bond market to the degree that bond investors formed the English Association of American Bondholders in the late 1880s. The group dedicated all its energies to handling the fiscal activities surrounding the investment its members made in the United States. As bondholders, foreign investors lacked the intrusive potential of stockholders. Financial institutions on the east coast facilitated the movement of manufactured products and capital between this region and the larger Atlantic economy. Last, despite the large volume of capital supplied by the British and European investors, United States companies relied on domestic investors for 75 percent of their capital needs.

Germany and the impact of large-scale enterprise

The success of corporate enterprise in the United States also accounted for the rise of a united Germany (1871) as the second leading industrial power in the world by 1900. Two characteristics acted as the basis for this startling achievement. First, German industry developed a close and intimate relationship with the unique German financial institution, the universal bank. Second, Germany developed her scientific and technical dimensions to a level unsurpassed in the industrial world. She used these assets to build superior chemical, electrical and other industries that depended on scientific theory, scientific research and advanced technical knowledge and experts. The manager, the banker and the scientist all played key roles in the emergence of Germany as the second leading industrial state in the world by the outbreak of World War I.

German successes in the capital-intensive, knowledge-dependent industries of the late nineteenth and early twentieth centuries depended in part on the strength of the country's universities. These institutions put an emphasis on research in the developing sciences such as physics and chemistry. They also stressed mathematics. German universities included graduate training for engineers at a time when British universities had none. By the 1870s graduate research chemists at the University of Munich alone outnumbered their counterparts in all of England. In fact, enrollment in the German schools jumped by 170 percent in the decade after 1890 while the population of Germany grew at just 10 percent. Engineers trained at universities also achieved prominence in leading German companies, demonstrating the central role of education in advancing German industrial interests.

Germany's ability to link her universities and their powerful programs in the natural sciences and engineering with the private sector gave her an edge over the British. Britain's educational programs languished, and could never overcome the German lead. In the United States, research-driven universities developed in the late nineteenth century and slowly began to integrate new fields in their curricula. The Americans made a pragmatic choice and sent their best and brightest students to Germany for graduate training.

The Germans were also the first to set up research laboratories dedicated to basic exploration of "theoretical" challenges in the sciences. The German research teams, for example, pioneered "artificial indigo," a discovery of immense commercial importance. German research teams often moved the discoveries of scientists in other countries from the laboratory to production. Professional and technical associations such as the Association of German Engineers systematically disseminated this scientific information and its application to manufacturing throughout German industry. The Imperial Institute of Physics and Technology (1887) preceded The National Physical Laboratory in Britain (1900) and the National Bureau of Standards in the United States (1901) by over a decade. Germany, in fact, provided the template copied by their competitors. German institutes had established links with the other key institutions of the German economic landscape, namely the universities and corporations, as well as schools that emphasised technical training.

German railroads, first, and then other capital-intensive industries, developed a relationship with German banks very different from those in the United States. As the rail industry accelerated expansion in the 1840s and 1850s it discovered a desperate need for capital on a scale unavailable from private sources. The first of what Germans labeled *Grossbanken*, or great banks, appeared in Cologne. There, Abraham Schaafhausen organized a bank to fund railroads and other industrial operations situated in the lower Rhine. The driving force in the bank's expansion, Gustav Mevissen, eagerly purchased shares in recently established industrial and commercial undertakings and so encouraged the economic expansion of Cologne and the Rhineland. Soon, the bank's tentacles reached into railroad, mining, textiles and other industrial companies.

It was the spectacular success of the *Credit Mobilier*, a French financial institution, rather than the Schaafhausen institution, that caught the attention of German bankers. The *Credit Mobilier* organized all financial functions from those of a commercial to an investment bank. Its notoriety spread to the German states. Soon banks in Darmstadt, Berlin and Hamburg adopted the practices of the *Credit Mobilier*. In fact the Darmstadt Bank gathered much of its initial capital from the *Credit Mobilier* and soon placed its financial resources at the disposal of a number of German railroads. It even invested money in the Austrian state railways. These banks acquired capital on a scale commensurate with the needs of the railroads and soon engaged in financing the construction of the rapidly expanding German rail network and then the transportation system throughout the continent. *Grossbanken* such as the Deutsche Bank of Berlin and the Commerz-und-Disconto Bank of Hamburg made possible the second burst of railroad construction in the 1870s.

The Deutsche Bank understood the value of German companies, and its directors lent money to prominent corporations such as the steel tubing company, Mannesmann, and Siemens & Halske, a major operation the electrical industry. A Deutsche representative held a seat on the board of Siemen & Halske and the bank also owned a significant share of its stock. In this way the bank remained a powerful presence in the affairs of one of Germany's most profitable enterprises. The Deutsche Bank made available the capital that enabled Mannesmann to make the critical investment in economies of scale, recruiting talented managers and promoting and selling their products. These decisions propelled the company to leadership in steel tubing. Before World War I, Mannesmann had built plants in Austria, Silesia, Italy, Bohemia and Great Britain. Deutsche Bank representatives held seats on the boards of 186 companies.

As universal banks, German financial institution required a large number of staff, and experts in the many areas where the banks operated. The Deutsche Bank invested in companies in a number of key industries and hired specialists to handle their financial operations in these arenas. The practice of holding seats on the boards of railroads transferred to other industries. As board members equipped with detailed knowledge and understanding, the bank representatives played a major role in the short- and long-term policies of a company. Of course their presence in the financial affairs of a company proved decisive and unassailable. In fact, banks focused their efforts on the financial affairs of corporations. Often banks forced improved accounting measures on a corporation and urged restructuring when market conditions demanded such changes. By the twentieth century, the *Grossbanken* began to influence the decision making of major corporations.

Great Britain and large-scale corporations

The British led the world in industrial production for decades. By the twentieth century, her lead had vanished under fierce competition from the United States and a resurgent and united Germany. The British still exercised a good deal of economic muscle throughout the globe, primarily through services such as banking and secondarily through her leading industry, textiles. Yet, British entrepreneurs chose not to develop complex organizational structures comparable to General Electric. Instead they remained wedded to older, first-generation industries. Even more important for their overseas presence, British businessmen developed sophisticated financial institutions that moved capital around the globe and gave the British a major presence from South American to the United States.

For British entrepreneurs who operated in a fairly small geographic market in Great Britain and who remained tied to industries of the first era of industrialization, organizational schemes such as those developed in the United States never emerged. British officials also chose not to nurture an educational system capable turning out graduates with first-rate training in the sciences or mathematics. The British also lacked an emphasis on the pragmatic side of education, the "how to" once a graduate leaves a university and enters the world of business and manufacturing. Given these weaknesses, the British both chose not to and lacked the capacity to compete with either the Americans or the Germans in the new capital-intensive industries.

Great Britain's success as the first industrial country on earth carried liabilities that limited her performance in the late 1800s. She achieved her industrial status before the age of the railroad and, as a result, the rail industry was far less dramatic in remodeling her economic institutions than it was in the United States or Germany. The geography of Great Britain also severely limited the impact of the railroad on British industry, and especially on her organizational abilities. British lines, the first in the world, faced a small, compact urban market bounded by London, Cardiff, Glasgow and Edinburgh, totaling 10 million people by 1850. It would remain the largest and richest consumer market in the world. This quadrangle also enjoyed superb pre-railroad transportation. The companies that served this region developed into highly specialized operations focused on a single product and run by the company's owners. The compact markets serviced by several means of transportation never provided the demand for organizational innovation that characterized United States railroads. Water transportation effectively continued to serve the region where urban markets and industrial centers were rarely more than 100 miles from each other. A superior road system and mild weather, which made water transportation possible for most of the year, minimized the impact of the railroad. In Great Britain, the invisible hand of the market still ruled in an era when the visible hand of the manager drove markets in the United States and Germany. What occurred in the United States and Germany simply had no place in Great Britain.

British railroads did emerge as the largest enterprises in Great Britain during the nineteenth century. British railroads developed thin managerial hierarchies that handled the dense traffic that used the compact rail network serving the consumer quadrangle. This small area made limited demands on the organizational capacity of British rail lines. The London North Western Railroad ran three geographic divisions yet its total track mileage, 800 miles, hardly compared with the Pennsylvania Railroad in the United States. The British never encountered large, multiple geographic divisions, the rule in the United States and to a lesser extent in Germany. British railroad managers had no reason to construct the sophisticated managerial hierarchies that ran the United States railroads over vast distances and employed thousands and thousands of men. A United States railroad company would operate 6,000 to 10,000 miles of track while a British counterpart would handle only 600 to 1,000 miles. Railroads did not act as the pioneering industry for large-scale hierarchies. Railroads in Great Britain gathered their capital from local sources, while United States rail corporations went to New York City with its investment bankers and huge capital markets for capital. Their needs surpassed whatever local sources could provide.

British entrepreneurs serviced a domestic market which, while rich and large, grew at slower rates than its counterpart in the United States. Large-scale markets that existed on a continental scale created the important conditions for scale and scope. In Britain's smaller, single market economies of scale in production and distribution carried fewer marketing advantages than in the United States.

Chemical, electrical engineering, heavy machinery and transportation equipment companies that thrived in the United States and Germany played a small role in the British economy. In fact, corporations of the United States and Germany flooded the British market with their manufactured wares. The British corporations that stood at the top of the national economy drew their strength from the first generation of industrial manufacturing industries, such as textiles and food. Rooted in older technologies, these industries depended on labor-intensive operations to manufacture their products. For example, the largest British manufacturing firm in 1900, J. & P. Coats, a sewing-thread manufacturer, employed 5,000 people – only a third of the number employed in the largest German corporation at that time.

British management culture

The culture of the managers that emerged in Great Britain contrasted sharply with that in the United States. Personal capitalism, as one noted scholar has labeled it, dominated management culture in Great Britain. Family-owned companies persisted and single-product, small-scale operations dominated the British economic landscape. Very few major British companies operated on a centralized managerial hierarchy or relied on managers recruited from outside the ranks of the founders and their heirs to run these operations.

The founders, their sons and grandsons continued to remain a major voice in company affairs. Unlike the management culture in the United States, executives in major British companies interacted daily with the management below them. They even made decisions on manufacturing and selling their products. Promotion to top positions in British companies reflected one's individual relationship with the owners as much as talent. These types of companies thrived in labor-intensive industries where the technological demands proved simple and uncomplicated when compared with the scientific theories that drove the electrical and other new industries. They lacked the resources to compete effectively in the new, often science-driven and capital-intensive industries. Corporations that housed several business ventures operated as coalitions of companies controlled by individual families.

The British-owned Imperial Tobacco Company and American-owned Duke's American Tobacco Company provide a sharp contrast in organizational approach. Imperial consisted of a number of family companies that operated relatively free of central direction. Virtually no teams of managers directed these companies, and family members of those who set them up continued to shape their operations and future. Duke's operation did business under a well-defined managerial structure and line of authority ascending from the shop floor to the company executive. These managers handled every aspect of production and marketing. From Carolina to Turkey, the company collected tobacco and then moved it to curing, then to manufacturing and finally to sales, from where a global distribution system marketed Duke's cigarettes across the world. The charge, as in any large-scale organization, remained maintaining the movement of raw materials and cigarettes at a steady pace throughout the year. Driven by the visible hand of the manager, Duke contrasted with Imperial, where a coalition of companies set policies in the interests of all the participating companies.

Since British firms operated with less capital and found their money from sources other than the major London banks, no investment bankers worked closely with these companies. British companies relied on profits as sources of capital as well as income derived from sale of stock and even "from the families and managers" involved in the companies.

Great Britain: domestic and overseas markets

The activities of corporations in the United States, Great Britain and Germany in domestic and overseas markets demonstrated their assets and liabilities. In products dependent on simple processing of imported raw materials, notably tobacco, sugar and cocoa, brand-named companies in the United Kingdom still thrived in their home markets. These producers also benefited from the well-established British distribution system that served her domestic consumers and obviated the need for these food manufacturers to set up their own outlets. In this sense, the invisible market of Adam Smith effectively served British manufacturers and provided them with their strength.

These British companies also developed a major overseas presence. Cadbury Chocolate prospered in commonwealth countries where large British populations dominated. Some manufacturers, notably Lever Brothers, set up overseas plants as distant as Australia and Japan. Their plants also operated independently of each other and never developed systematic strategies for influencing markets. The nature of British industries also compelled the British to invest in plantations and commercial companies located overseas. These guaranteed supplies mostly of raw materials. Such investments proved very different from those in the capital-intensive industries that drew United States and German capital. British overseas operations also worked under less direction from a central office than did either German or United States branches.

The British also dominated oceanic communication, a crucial asset in moving information. Until these cables successfully appeared in 1866, the passage of information between Great Britain and her colonies, the sources of many of her raw materials and often her markets, took months. Needless to say, this time gap restricted the flow of trade and information. At the same time, Great Britain also engaged in a lively trade with the Western Hemisphere, where markets and raw material regions abounded. While steam power reduced the time length of the journey from London to the Americas, information moved only at the pace of transportation. Once the telegraph transformed land communication, businessmen and inventors looked for ways to use the telegraph underwater to bridge the oceans and seas.

If successful, electronic communication would provide instantaneous communication to any part of the world and reduced the impact of distance. Entrepreneurs eventually discovered an adequate insulation for the copper wire, namely gutta-perch, that protected the cable under water. Cable soon stretched from Great Britain to Newfoundland and then to the United States. Within a few decades a combination of land and ocean wires and cables connected Great Britain with her major colonies and markets. The British possessed the best technology and cable ships. For some time the *Great Eastern* remained the only cable ship able to carry loads of thousands of pounds from one end of the Atlantic to the other end. The *Great Eastern* actually laid the cable to the United States and to India. Cable ships such as the *Great Eastern* also had to carry brakes sufficient to manipulate the cable as it reached the ocean bottom. The British would subsequently drop cables across the Pacific to provide communications among its regional holdings from Canada to Australia. The Americans would also lay cable lines across this vast ocean to reach Hawai'i, where sugar producers eagerly waited for electronic connections with the mainland. These cables would enhance the United States' presence in the Pacific as her hold expanded dramatically in the wake of the Spanish-American War in 1898. United States cables, for instance, reached the Philippines in 1904. The United States colony demanded rapid communications for the new rulers, much as such holdings did of the British.

By 1904, when some forty-one cable ships operated, almost 75 percent of them remained in British ownership. The British submarine cable companies relied on the mutual ties with manufacturers, banks, import and export firms, and shipping lines to expand their business. Since the vast majority of these named London as their headquarters, the city developed into the center of world trade. The British, then, used their dominance in controlling international communications, which enhanced their abilities to communicate with their colonies and their markets.

The British successes overseas also grew out of her financial and service sectors. Here, she capitalized on existing assets and the move to large-scale banking. Great Britain had numerous small-scale and medium-sized banks in the nineteenth century. By the end of the 1800s, large-scale banks emerged in London and came to dominate the finance industry. Joint stock operations displaced the older, personal-style banks and ranked among the largest financial institutions in the world by the outbreak of World War I in 1914. These banks funded overseas ventures; Great Britain vigorously exported her venture capital to fund operations in other countries and accounted for over 40 percent of such investment by the outbreak of World War I. The British also set up financial companies to handle their overseas investments. Companies dedicated their energies to specific markets in one region, such as South America or East Asia.

These greatly enhanced the scale of British overseas activities both in number and volume of capital. Here, again the invisible market of middlemen, including trading companies, commission agents, wholesale and factoring houses and consultants worked to the immense advantage of the British. Great Britain employed a far greater proportion of its workforce in services than any major industrialized states except the Netherlands. The invisible market stands in sharp contrast to the visible hand of United States and German industry. Ironically, British finance, which had adapted to the world of large-scale production and distribution ushered in by the United States and Germany, sustained British business that traced its origins to the first phase of the industrial revolution. The sophisticated communications system that the British installed across the oceans and seas facilitated the deployment of the state's services across the globe.

The British also accounted for 40 percent of all capital exported across the globe. Much of this money actually funded industrial and other activities in the British settler colonies, namely Australia, New Zealand, Canada and South Africa. These colonies paid for this capital by sending wheat, gold, wool and dairy products to England, in much the same way as British colonies had a century or more earlier. Canada, for instance, drew heavily on British capital to fund railroad construction across her western provinces. The rail line also shipped out wheat ultimately heading for British families. Australia depended in part on the huge volume of wool sent to Great Britain to sustain its woolen industry. Britain also depended on Australia, and to a lesser extent on New Zealand and Canada, for gold to help shore up her finances. Australian banks searching for capital inevitably went to London, where they borrowed significant sums of money from city-based financial institutions. Neither the United States nor Germany had large-scale settler colonies to exploit as markets.

Branches and subsidiaries

The large-scale enterprises in Great Britain, the United States and Germany also operated subsidiaries in other national and/or overseas markets. The consequences of the railroad appeared most dramatically in the flow of goods and capital across national boundaries. Railroads crossed these borders as manufacturers and shippers sought new markets and sources of raw materials. Krupp steelworks in the Ruhr Valley in Germany depended on coal operations it owned in Spain, while fellow steel maker, August Thyssen, purchased coal in Normandy and French Lorraine. Similarly, rail and shipping lines made possible the sale of spun cotton in Lancashire, England to weavers in the Rhineland. The railroad proved a dynamic force in European national economies and in creating transnational ties that sustained many major companies and demonstrated the increasing interdependence of the emerging industrial economies.

United States firms adopted this strategy. John D. Rockefeller's Standard Oil first ventured into overseas markets in the 1880s when it began to explore British and later European outlets for the company's products. In Great Britain, Standard set up its own subsidiary whereas in Northern Europe it partnered with domestic companies in each country. Soon, it had operations in South America and Asia. Manufacturers of light machinery such as John Deere built their own factories in Germany, France and elsewhere. National Cash Register, Otis Elevator, the Baldwin Locomotive Works, among many other United States companies, all set up manufacturing and distribution outlets in other states. Henry Ford developed the assembly line that standardized production of the automobile and soon enabled him to capture both domestic and overseas markets. Ford's planning scheme, "Fordism," enjoyed great popularity in Europe where it became a model for many companies. By 1913 some 200 United States owned operations conducted business in Canada alone. The output of these operations dominated the markets in these countries for decades.

German Companies also operated overseas. The Stollwreck Company was a leader among German companies that sought out new overseas markets. Stollwreck subsidiaries appeared in several European countries such as Hungary and Belgium. In the United States Stollwreck opened up a major manufacturing site in New York City and built a repair plant in Chicago. It also incorporated the Auto Sales Gum & Chocolate Company in New York City in 1911. Stollwreck also established branches along the east and west coasts of the United States, and developed the vending machine that sold products as diverse as ready-to-eat food, gum and soft drinks.

German manufacturers of heavy industrial products such as railway machinery operated production sites in major urban centers in the United States, Imperial Russia, Hungary and Austria. These large-scale companies incorporated global sales forces that handled distribution throughout the major continental and overseas markets. German firms sold their products throughout East and South Asia, in the Middle East and in South America. This strategy, of course, depended on these companies developing a salesforce across the globe to advertise and promote their products.

Both the United States and Germany established new strategies to encourage and sustain their developing economies. Unlike Great Britain, which remained mostly a collection of medium and small-scale companies, the United States built organizational structures designed to run the emerging, large-scale companies that increasingly dominated the United States economy. These structures appeared in the railroads, the very first industry to confront scale and distance. Since Great Britain built an industrial economy before the appearance of this new transport technology, and since its domestic market remained geographically compact, the British never faced problems of distance and scale. In the United States hundreds and even thousands of miles separated raw materials from production, and markets stretched over similar distances. Railroad personnel had to deal with these issues as early as the 1840s.

The United States, Germany and Great Britain had developed the most advanced economies by 1900. These formed an emerging industrial core that stretched from Berlin in Germany and London in Great Britain to St. Louis and Richmond in the United States. To sustain the vibrant industries and growing populations in this core, all three countries needed to draw in huge volumes of raw materials and food. With the largest single economy of the three states, the United States needed to develop the most sophisticated means to extract natural resources across the globe.

Conclusion

The United States developed a full array of organizationally sophisticated and technically advanced corporations. Industries such as electrical and steel demanded both scientific knowledge and vast resources. Both experience and increasingly education provided the knowledge. Industries quickly came to depend on the scientific theory and advanced levels of technical education. The United States, with its vast population and substantial growth rates, provided a market for large-scale industry. United States corporations such as Campbell's and Heinz also developed technologies to manufacture in volume products as diverse as soap, ketchup and noodle and tomato soup. These fed the tastes and choices of United States consumers. United States companies also faced continental size domestic markets that demanded and sustained huge corporations. The United States, then, arrived at the century's end with major corporations in heavy, consumer and scientifically based industries. It benefited from its huge domestic markets.

United States corporations drew much of their scientific knowledge from men trained in German universities or professionals who worked in German research institutes. While the United States developed organizational tools, the Germans focused on scientific and mathematical assets to enhance their economic performance. Their universities developed close ties with industry and government. The combination of the three drove much of the German research so important in the newer industries, which depended on researchers with advanced degrees. United States companies took advantage of Germany's advanced education by recruiting young men who had trained there. The founder of the first long-term research laboratory at a major United States corporation, General Electric, was a German scientist, and the person charged with running it was a United States citizen educated at the Massachusetts Institute of Technology who had earned his Ph.D. in Germany.

The Germans developed a very different strategy in building their corporate bodies. The *Grossbanken*, or the universal bank, became the central institution. It did more than lend money. Banks purchased shares in industrial companies and then sat on company boards. This presence gave bankers a powerful influence in the affairs of the company. Since German banks acquired shares in most major companies across her economy, bankers also had a broad view of the economy and where companies fit into that larger picture. The Germans, unlike the United States corporate leaders, focused their energies on heavy and scientific-based industries. They depended on quality production made to specific orders. The United States companies relied on mass production that catered to large and fairly homogenous markets.

United States and German corporations also moved beyond their borders in their search for markets and to establish manufacturing sites. The United States sold its products across much of the globe, including Germany, France and Great Britain. Increasingly these products consisted of the huge range of consumer goods aimed at mass markets, reflecting the domestic strategy of the United States consumer industries. Soon, Europeans were driving United States cars and smoking United States-made cigarettes. The Germans sold products in the United States, South Asia, West Asia and North Africa. They sold heavy industrial products of high quality that mirrored the strength of their own economy. Corporations in both countries also operated major production sites overseas. Both built manufacturing and processing sites in Europe, South America and Asia. The reach of corporations now seemed limitless.

The British adopted a very different strategy. Textiles remained their chief export goods. British companies depended less on organization and science, unlike the United States and German companies, because they drew on first-generation industries. The British also placed less emphasis on technical education. British financial leaders did forge global networks for lending capital and providing services. These gave the British immense power in other parts of the world.

The United States used its vast and diverse array of corporations and industries, plus a huge domestic market, to emerge as the leading industrial power on the planet. Germany's strategy made her the second most powerful national economy while Great Britain, with sufficient resources and overseas connections, ranked third. From this point on, large-sale companies would drive the global economy and the United States stood first in this regard.

Finally, one needs to appreciate the truly revolutionary nature of corporations. They gathered knowledge on a scale and of such diversity unknown by any other institution of their day. They searched for all types of information on domestic and overseas markets, evaluating employees, developing new technologies, sustaining research laboratories, gathering cost data, determining profits, hiring lawyers to provide legal advice, recruiting accountants to monitor financial data, and countless other data. The modern corporation was a very different institution to its modest predecessors of the early industrial revolution. The United States, with its full compliment of diverse, large-scale companies, developed an unprecedented capacity to direct economic change on a global scale.

Further reading

For works that include comparative essays or analysis, see Alfred D. Chandler, Jr., *Scale and Scope: The Dynamics of Industrial Capitalism* (Cambridge, Massachusetts, 1990); Thomas K. McCraw, ed., *Creating Modern Capitalism: How Entrepreneurs, Companies, and Countries Triumphed in Three Independent Revolutions* (Cambridge, Massachusetts, 1991); Alfred D. Chandler, Jr. and Herman Daems, *Managerial Hierarchies: Comparative Perspectives on the Rise of Modern Industrial Enterprise* (Cambridge, Massachusetts, 1980); Mansel G. Blackford, *The Rise of Modern Business in Great Britain, The United States, and Japan* (Chapel Hill, 1998).

For general works that contain information on European overseas activity, see Daniel Headrick, *The Invisible Weapon: Telecommunications and International Politics 1851–1945* (New York, 1991) and *The Tentacles of Progress: Technology Transfer in the Age of Imperialism, 1850–1940* (New York, 1988); and P.J. Cain and A.G. Hopkins, *British Imperialism, 1688–2000* (Harlow, 2001).

For the United States, see Richard S. Tedlow, *Giants of Enterprise: Seven Business Innovators and the Enterprises They Built* (New York, 2001); Stuart Bruchey, *Enterprise: The Dynamic Economy of a Free People* (Cambridge, Massachusetts, 1990); Walter Licht, *Industrializing America: The Nineteenth Century* (Baltimore, 1995); D.W. Menig, *The Shaping of Transcontinental America, Volume 3* (New Haven, 1998) and *The Shaping of Continental America, Volume 2* (New Haven, 1993). Included in Richard Franklin Bensel, *The Political Economy of American Industrialization, 1877–1900* (New York, 2000) is an insightful analysis on the development of New York City.

For a study of professionalism in the United States, see Burton J. Bledstein, *The Culture of Professionalism: The Middle Class and the Development of Higher Education in America* (New York, 1978). For England, see Harold Perkin, *The Rise of Professional Society: England Since 1880* (London, 1989). See Leonard S. Reich, *The Making of American Industrial Research: Science and Business at GE and Bell, 1876–1926* (Cambridge, Massachusetts, 1985) for the inner workings of two major corporations dependent on technical knowledge and well-qualified researchers.

For a series of essays on developments in Europe, see, T.C.W. Blanning, ed., *The Oxford History of Modern Europe* (New York, 2001).

Chapter 6

Raw materials and sustaining the global economy

Introduction

The expansion of the industrial capacities of the United States, Germany, Great Britain and other European powers in the late nineteenth century created an intense demand for raw materials. These ranged from precious metals to copper, iron ore and coal, all used in manufacturing. At the same time, the surge in population and rapid urbanization in industrial states strained existing agricultural resources. To meet the new demands these states searched for regions capable of producing wheat, grains and meat in sufficient volume to feed their growing populations. Fruits, available once refrigeration appeared, joined sugar, already a longstanding export, on the dinner tables from Berlin to St. Louis.

The United States developed an increasing reliance on raw material regions. Indeed, its vast capital resources, its rapidly developing large-scale industries and its desperate need to feed its expanding population made it a major player in raw material regions. The United States had at its disposal the western part of the country, west of the Mississippi. The western region demanded the same transportation and communications systems that connected Great Britain and Germany with the undeveloped regions of Europe and areas beyond the European continent. The Trans-Mississippi region even imported capital from British investors. The vast open spaces of the plains states of the western United States held vast potential for agricultural development while the Rocky Mountains and the far west contained huge deposits of gold, silver, coal copper and other minerals. The Trans-Mississippi region also served as home to cattle and sheep that provided high protein meat products for the urban populations.

The United States also cast its net well beyond its borders. Cuba, Hawai'i, Honduras and Nicaragua came under the influence of the United States or were formally incorporated into the North American polity. Hawai'i and Cuba produced vast amounts of sugar, a central part of the diet of United States citizens. The Central American states developed into vast reservoirs of bananas and other fruits amenable to transport because of the new refrigeration technology developed in the United States in the 1880s. Coffee, too, developed into an important industry as coffee plantations began to cover the landscape of countries such as Nicaragua. Europeans showed a similar interest in these goods and quickly became part of the expanding market for tropical products.

Raw materials and European states

The United States joined other industrial states in the search for raw materials. Economies in Great Britain and Germany demanded raw materials to sustain their growth and feed their insatiable consumer and manufacturing sectors. British companies developed a close reliance on the United States South, Argentina, Egypt, Australia, New Zealand and South Africa for gold, diamonds, cotton, wheat, wool, meat and other materials. To facilitate these transfers the British expanded their merchant marine fleet, and built railroads and communications systems in many of these regions. The British gradually turned Ireland into a provider of foodstuffs for an expanding English consumer base. The shift away from manufacturing and into goods specifically intended for English domestic markets de-urbanized Ireland and commercialized its farm sector. The British also relied on their well-developed financial institutions to expand or gain access to markets, to facilitate trade and to pay for the transportation, agricultural and mining facilities. These moved food and minerals from around the globe to Great Britain. From Egyptian cotton fields in the Nile Delta to Argentinian wheat, these raw materials fueled British industrial growth.

Belgium and Portugal, too, joined the race for sources of raw materials. Belgian agents exploited the Congo. The land gave up its copper to locals forced by the Belgians to work the grueling copper mines. Often these men lived distant from the mines and only under compulsion from the Belgians did they abandon their homes for the new industrial work. The Portuguese, in a desperate effort to shore up their flagging textile industry, attempted to develop cotton plantations in their colony, Mozambique. Eventually, with force and violence, the Portuguese colonial administrators "persuaded" hundreds of thousands of Mozambique farmers to shift into cash cropping of cotton. The needs of a would-be industrial economy transformed the lives of many. The United States would pursue its interests as intensely as the Europeans.

The infrastructure of international shipping

United States companies built land and oceanic transportation adequate to ship the goods to North American markets and to facilitate exchange with export-driven economies such as Cuba and Chile. These companies also built communications systems that linked key corporations with the plantations and mining operations in Central and South America and the Caribbean. Perceived as distant and peripheral to the United States economy in 1850, these regions now played a central role in its ongoing health. The very technology that transformed the production sites and led to the rise of large-scale systems also created new agricultural regions to meet these demands.

In these new economic relationships coastal and river ports played a central role. As the chief location for the movement of imports and exports, ports had to develop effective means of accommodating both the volume of shipping and the increasing scale of the steel ships, including modern loading and unloading facilities. Screw propellers, steam engines, steel hulls and better maps of the ocean and waterways accelerated ocean crossings and increased the size of vessels and their freight loads, all of which intensified the need for modern facilities.

As major rail connections, ports linked ocean and land transportation. The ports quickly attracted rail lines eager for the shipping business. The railroads had to know the schedules of the ships since the lines arranged for the appropriate number of locomotives and rail cars to haul the goods that the ships carried to the port. The volume and range of perishable goods jumped dramatically once refrigeration and refrigerated storehouses appeared in the 1880s and the exchange of these goods demanded careful handling and co-ordination between rails and ships. Both relied on the telegraph and ocean cables to move information about arrival and departure. Both later embraced wireless communications for more effective transfers and, in the case of ships, for greater safety.

The interaction between new transportation and communications modes allowed the rapid movement of market information. This alerted manu-facturers, consumers and shippers as to prices, potential markets and other relevant information. As steam engines acquired more power and, therefore, speed, coordination assumed increasing importance. These changes reduced costs and accelerated the volume of goods shipped across long distances during the late nineteenth and early twentieth centuries. International trade skyrocketed 300 percent between 1880 and 1913.

New York City epitomized the changes that swept through major ports such as London, Buenos Aires, Montreal and Liverpool. The city's first transformation came when the Erie Canal opened in 1825. It captured the huge flow of agricultural and other products moving along the canal. New York City used its auction system to take control of the majority of United States imports before the Civil War. The auction system quickly disposed of these goods. The city handled the cotton exports on their way mostly to textile factories in Great Britain, and New York also took care of the vast majority of British textile imports. Cotton alone accounted for 50 percent of United States exports before the outbreak of the Civil War in 1861.

After the Civil War, New York again rebuilt and updated its shipyards. As the city attracted more and more corporate headquarters, law firms, financial houses and government agencies, it developed into a major information center fed by cable and telegraph. By 1900 companies such as American Tobacco ran major outlets in South and Central America, Asia and Canada from their headquarters in New York City. New York's shipyards used new technology such as elevators powered by steam to handle the volume of imports and the scale of ships that arrived daily by the score. Over half of all United States imports and around 33 percent of her exports moved through New York City by the late nineteenth century. To handle the transfer of goods to railroads or local destinations, thousands of vehicles flooded the streets. The port also hosted the largest shipbuilding operations in the United States, evidence of its importance to the national economy and international exchange. New York City stood alongside the other great Atlantic ports and even earned the name "the London of the New World" from British observers.

United States companies also developed ports in the export-driven states that supplied many of the basic metals used by American industry and the foodstuffs that met the nutritional demands of domestic consumers. In the first decades of the twentieth century, Peruvian copper and sugar were critical imports for the United States' economy. By the 1930s a desperate need existed to improve Peruvian port facilities to maintain the flow of materials to the United States. Callao, the main port, underwent extensive reconstruction by the American corporations that operated in Peru. They rebuilt piers, connected rail lines and ships and added modern loading and unloading equipment. Such innovations decreased a ship's time in port and significantly reduced the labor force, both of which meant far less costs. United States companies used the technological improvements to break the power of skilled workers running port operations.

For the United States, Great Britain and other industrial powers with overseas holdings, these developments appeared at the best possible moment. New York City, London, England, Vera Cruz, Mexico, Hamburg, Germany, Montreal, Canada and Buenos Aires in Argentina grew by leaps and bounds as goods now circulated at a volume unimaginable before these technological innovations. Hamburg ranked among the largest ports in the world, just behind the British ports of London and Liverpool and the United States port of New York. Steamships made Hamburg a key port and the expanding global trade enriched its merchants. The building of modern facilities enabled Hamburg to handle the growing volume of goods flowing in and out of Germany. Rail lines that converged on the port provided the connections between producers and steamships that docked in Hamburg. These exchanges also wove tighter the interdependence of raw material producers, manufacturers, shippers and consumers separated by thousands of miles.

Agriculture and grains

The United States Great Plains, the Canadian Prairies and the Argentine Pampas all responded to the new markets, transportation and communications ties. These regions experienced a decided transformation as landowners, migrant farmers and farm laborers moved into the vast, open spaces ideally suited to mechanized farming. With the enhanced coastal and oceanic connections, such regions could now easily feed huge, distant markets provided they developed effective strategies to exploit their local resources. In the era of new global markets, volume assumed critical importance for producers. Advantageously positioned with large empty or just emptied lands, these regions faced severe labor shortages that greatly enhanced mechanization as a strategy of production. Harvesters, tractors and other farm machinery answered the problem of labor demand and allowed for exploitation of greater land holdings than would have occurred in the absence of machinery.

Machines soon swarmed across the Great Plains in the United States, where farmers brought another 5,000,000 acres of land under cultivation. The machinery available to modest farmers through mass production and financial arrangements with big companies and local banks enabled family farmers to remain competitive and at the very center of the agricultural sector. Family farmers proved capable of meeting the demand for volume production with agricultural machinery and high quality soil. Soon they dominated the Plains states from North Dakota to Kansas. Wheat, corn and to a lesser extent other farm products filled the grain elevators and storage bins of these farmers before they were shipped to urban markets in the industrialized regions of the United States.

Behind this achievement stood a number of key personnel. Bankers provided the capital to buy land and machines. Large factories manufactured the machinery on a scale needed to meet the huge demand in the Plains states, while companies deployed outlets to provide spare parts and assist the farmers in maintaining their harvesters and reapers. Teams of managers moved raw materials from production sites to processing centers and, then, to consumers. Managers in all these operations relied on the telegraph and soon on telephone companies to move information on pricing and markets and to coordinate agricultural production. Even the federal government deployed experts to conduct scientific surveys of the west. Last, while the United States exported some of its agricultural products, the huge and rapidly growing population in the United States consumed most of the farm produce from the Great Plains.

As in the United States, the Canadian government encouraged family farms on the Prairies. The government actually preferred migrants, largely from overseas, to settle on the land. This policy reflected the underpopulation of western Canada at that time and the vast Atlantic migrations underway in the late nineteenth and early twentieth centuries. To achieve this end the Canadian authorities made land grants readily and inexpensively available to newcomers through a Homestead Act in 1872. Comparable to the United States' version, the act created a generous policy that encouraged domestic and foreign migrants to claim land. Settlers and their families flooded onto the Canadian Prairies in the 1890s and early 1900s, as they had on the Great Plains of the United States. Just as this surge created new states on the Great Plains, so too did the population explosion on the Prairies compel the federal government in Ottawa to establish two new Canadian provinces, Alberta and Saskatchewan, in 1905. The power of the federal government made equitable distribution of land a reality and one of the main reasons why family farms dominated the prairies. In both countries immigrant farmers and their families embraced their adopted nations and usually took citizenship, thereby becoming permanent assets.

The Canadian farmers, like their counterparts in the United States, deployed agricultural machinery to exploit the Prairies. In fact, farmers from the United States, who accounted for the largest share of newcomers to Canada and specifically western Canada, often brought their own reapers, harvesters and other farm machines with them.

The Canadian government also took an active role in the technical side of farming. It created the Ministry of Agriculture, which undertook genetic research on plants. In fact, Canadians developed wheat with a global reputation for quality and reliability. The Canadian government established an experimental farm system to demonstrate ways to improve the quality of the wheat and enhance its international reputation. The Ottawa-backed agents engaged in a continual dialogue with farmers on new farming "techniques" that enabled them to produce better crops in greater volume. Similarly, the United States, through the scientific bureaus of the Department of Agriculture, conducted research that led to hybrid corn, chemical pesticides and advanced machinery by the first two decades of the twentieth century. The Smith-Lever Act of 1914 created the Extension Service, staffed by county agents who passed new scientific information to farmers.

Argentina's development contrasted sharply with that of Canada and the United States. The elite in Argentina drew its members from a class of large-scale landowners who lived on the Pampas. In desperate need for labor, the members of this group of large-scale landowners wanted the country to open its doors to immigrants, most of whom came from Southern Europe. Since these newcomers arrived with few resources they ended up on the Pampas as laborers, tenants or sharecroppers owing labor or crops to the landowners. The Argentinian elite never saw these newcomers as a future cadre of landowners and family farmers dedicated to improving the country's resources. Almost none of the elite wanted a class of small-scale landowners who would undermine the power of the landowning elite. As a result a much smaller percentage of the migrants applied for citizenship in Argentina than in the United States or Canada. The migrants to the Argentine Pampas often stayed short periods, migrated from the employment of one landowner to another and generally made up a floating population of cheap labor. Rarely did they establish families or purchase property that would have placed them in the ranks of small-scale landowners and long-term contributors to the society.

The interests of the large-scale landowning classes remained in exploitation of land and not in building up a healthy population of middling farmers or urban residents. Their financial interest remained tied to the land and their influence in government merely promoted their own ends. Even railroads that connected the Pampas with the coastal port belonged to the British who, in the minds of the elite, relieved Argentina of the fiscal responsibility of constructing these links. In fact, the Argentinian landowners feared British withdrawal or domestic legislative policies that threatened British interests. In Canada the government actively intervened to insure domestic ownership of the rail system while in the United States railroads and other transportation and communications systems remained firmly in domestic corporate hands.

Newcomers created sources of cheap labor and little else, whereas in Canada, they acted as the cornerstone of the state's policy. In the United States domestic and overseas migrants filled a crucial role as permanent cultivators. Those who held financial and other power in the United States often had a direct fiscal bearing in realizing these goals. The interaction of banks, railroad owners and the farm families made for a vigorous economy in the Plains states and the Canadian Prairie that worked to everyone's advantage.

The Argentine state proved unable to give scientific and technical advice to the agricultural sector so crucial to the success in North America. Unlike Canada and the United States, where federal governments played a central role in settling and promoting the western agriculture and creating agricultural agencies, the central government in Argentina lacked comparable power or effective capabilities to develop these initiatives.

Few among the landowning class of Argentina wished for vigorous industrial development. The British served their interests and immigrants from southern Europe met their labor needs. Since British railroads, British financiers and British shipping stood behind the Argentinian *estancieros*, the large landowners, few of them saw any reason for dispensing domestic resources to encourage a cache of family farms. Dedicated to producing wheat, these would serve as competitors. Since the elite depended on export-driven agriculture, the members also staunchly supported a low-tariff policy that also allowed inexpensive manufactured goods to meet Argentine needs. As a result, foreign goods limited the potential for domestic industry. For the Argentinian elite, the free and unregulated market provided the key to success and wealth, unlike the United States, for instance, where industrial and financial elites saw high tariffs and a carefully administered market as the means to domestic prosperity. By the 1920s the United States actually accounted for more of Argentinian and Canadian industrial imports than Great Britain.

Argentinian emphasis on exports also shaped the social structure of the country. Industry as a separate enterprise never fully developed in Argentina. Major economic activity consisted of hauling agricultural goods to port for shipment mostly to British markets, and processing activities that prepared these goods for freighting. In Canada, government polices shaped by industrialists and bankers committed the country to promoting industrial activities. Manufacturing emerged in Toronto, Hamilton and Montreal while the construction of the Canadian Pacific and other railroads contributed substantially to industrial production. In the United States, a full-blown industrial economy with major corporations and huge industrial centers made the country the world leader by the twentieth century. Argentina simply chose a different path from Canada or the United States and, as a result, produced a very different agricultural sector and national economy.

Ranching and beef exports

The Argentine Pampas also differed in other ways from farm regions in North America. Unlike Canada, where the Prairies sustained a monocrop system based on wheat, the Argentinian Pampas fueled a powerful cattle industry. In Canada, climatic disasters, British regulation and United States tariffs undercut the economic viability of Canadian beef. In Argentina, cattle continued to thrive on the Pampas and provide handsome profits to members of the landowning elite.

Of course, meat producers all over the world benefited from the development of refrigerated technology in the United States. The *estancieros* proved no different. Their cattle industry prospered in the region surrounding Buenos Aires. Ranching reinforced the "aristocratic" status of the landed elite as well as demonstrating its power and the country's economic promise. For labor, the elite again depended on overseas migrants brought to Argentina by the shipping lines and railroad companies that hauled wheat and meat products to European and North American markets. Low-wage workers never saw ranching as a channel of mobility into the ranks of the propertied nor a permanent feature of their lives. These laborers differed little in their aspirations from their counterparts in agriculture.

In the United States cattle did play an important role in developing its western region. At first the burgeoning cattle industry of the 1870s and 1880s collapsed in the face of climatic disasters at the end of the 1880s. In the 1890s and early 1900s ranchers turned away from the large-scale ranches that dominated the Argentinian Pampas. Ranchers used irrigated hay and stockbreeding to produce healthier and larger cattle on smaller amounts of land and made greater profits than their predecessors on the large ranches. With the adoption of Herefords, a burly English breed that grew quicker and reached top weights in the process, the small-scale ranchers had a product that made substantial profits. A small amount of land provided a rancher with a comfortable living. These ranchers still hired the ultimate unskilled labor on the plains, the cowboy.

In smaller numbers, these laborers proved essential, yet the new ranches resembled the family farm more than they did the large ranches of novel and mythical fame. In the United States modest families handled the largest share of cattle production, unlike the Argentinian Pampas where the *estancieros* and the large-scale ranch persisted and thrived.

Minerals and precious metals

Men and women who labored in the United States certainly needed food to meet the demands of the workplace. The industries that employed workers and professionals also required minerals for production. The United States joined other industrial nations in the search for precious metals and critical minerals. From Africa to South America engineers and prospectors discovered rich veins of gold, silver and copper among other minerals. Soon, capital, rail construction materials and mining equipment followed which helped turn these sites into productive operations capable of sustaining the financial and manufacturing components of the industrial economies in Europe and North America.

The Rothschild banking houses in London and Paris played a major role in developing such mining operations around the globe. The London branch invested in gold mines in El Callao in Venezuela in the early 1880s. The Rothschild family then set up an exploration company that quickly developed into a multi-million pound operation. It acted on behalf of the Rothschilds in the South African gold boom and the discovery of gold in western Australia and in New Zealand. Both houses also invested in Spanish, Mexican and American copper mines. Rothschild money even reached New Caledonia in the Pacific, where nickel came under European exploitation.

Europeans also explored other parts of Africa in the search for minerals. They discovered rich copper deposits in central Africa that began to meet European needs after World War I when copper production in the United States slumped. Keenly aware of the United States' experiences in mining, the Europeans borrowed United States' methods of processing the copper before it moved to consumer markets. United States engineers and technical personnel dominated the upper levels of some Belgian companies since Belgium lacked adequate personnel to meet the demand.

The Pacific

Precious metal discoveries rocked the Pacific. Beginning in 1848, fortunate souls stumbled upon pieces of gold and prospectors uncovered extensive gold deposits first in California, and then southeastern Australia, followed by British Columbia in the 1870s, the Alaskan Panhandle in the 1880s and, last, the Canadian Yukon and again Alaska by 1898. The deployment of mining technology and the sudden increase in gold seekers transformed these regions, much as had occurred in South Africa during its gold boom. Temporary population surges visited all of these locations and gold seekers poured in via steamship and railroads once submarine cable and telegraphs sent the news around the world. Indigenous peoples who stood in the way of these rushes simply vanished as their land came under new ownership. Gold carried too much value not to remove these populations, and the global demand for capital only enhanced this value. The discovery of this precious metal created regions pulsating with activity, people and rising wealth for some, and hard labor for others.

The first and by far the richest discovery occurred in California in 1848 near San Francisco, then a tiny village servicing the occasional whaling ship. At first a local event, it built throughout the year and by 1849 the "Rush" was on. A hundred thousand people crowded into the once-tiny port. Hundred of ships docked and many ended up stranded as their crews jumped ships in search of wealth in the gold fields. By 1852 a quarter-of-a-million people had come to the land of gold and riches. Ships from Europe, South America and the eastern United States streamed to San Francisco, as worried captains often decided against landing for fear of losing their men. Thousands from Peru, Chile, Mexico, Hawai'i, the eastern United States, Ireland, Great Britain and Europe joined the flow of people into California. Even the Chinese arrived from distant Canton. By the early 1850s they numbered 20,000. A local event became global. Gold spoke to capitalists, miners, wealth seekers, bankers, merchants and sailors, who came from every conceivable place on the planet.

Gold turned up in Australia at roughly the same time as in California. By the 1840s pastoralists and abundant land had transformed the image of Australia from a remote landmass dedicated to convicts into a continent with opportunities for those willing to make the long journey. The majority of Europeans searching for new homes preferred Canada or the United States. Hard times in Australia and the discovery of gold in California seemed to darken Australia's future. Hundreds of gold diggers piled onto ships bound for the west coast of the United States and its gold fields. Australian miners, desperate for the wealth advertised in California, jumped any ship bound there.

Soon, the small British population feared for its future numbers as they watched their kin climb abroad the departing ships. Word of local gold strikes appeared in the Australian newspapers and soon a flood of gold seekers, once departing, now swarmed into Australia. Gold miners from California, and other United States citizens, joined this group. Very shortly, the Yankee Clipper ships took over the shipping business and carried in machinery and supplies necessary to mine for the gold. The centers of the gold, New South Wales and Victoria, saw their population rise from 265,000 to over 800,000 as the streams of gold seekers moved toward Australia. The knowledge of how to mine gold and the appropriate technology developed by Californian miners was transferred to the Australian gold fields. Surface gold proved rare and soon miners had to dig deep into the ground. Shafts, drifts and hoists powered by steam soon dominated the landscape.

News of the discovery of gold in such distant places as California and Australia moved with increasing speed to population centers in the United States and across the globe as new communications technologies developed and diversified. At first, word of mouth, mail and newspapers spread the news. Then the telegraph moved word of the gold rushes in the continental United States and to wherever the telegraph existed.

As early as the 1860s international news reached a United States citizen's home almost overnight. By the late 1890s submarine cables, telephone, and worldwide telegraphy broadcast the discovery of gold almost instantaneously to an eager public across the world. Men and women from the eastern United States, Europe, England, and on both sides of the Pacific responded with alacrity and even haste to the opportunities offered by gold in the late 1840s. But getting to the gold fields in California and Australia took a long time and often proved dangerous. Walking challenged even the hardiest. Wagons eased the burden yet improved speed only marginally. The journey across the North American continent improved considerably once the transcontinental rail lines were completed and joined the eastern, mid-western and western cities. For those who made the trip by sea, the Yankee Clipper remained the best choice, whether from Canton, New York or London.

Those in the Atlantic world sought short-cuts to the gold fields. The journey around Cape Horn took three months and often ships encountered bad weather. Shippers who provided the necessities of life and carried back the gold joined in the search for the least expensive and quickest routes. Of course reaching Australia was an immensely long voyage regardless of whether the prospector departed from Great Britain or the eastern United States.

Routes across Panama and Nicaragua stood out as the solution to these problems of space and time. Yet, these isthmian crossings lacked the infra-structure to provide effective transportation to the anticipated high volume of traffic. Once a major transshipment location for the Spanish rulers in the colonial period, the Isthmus now assumed increasing importance for the United States' government. Washington's call for mail delivery led to the incorporation of a steamer line that carried mail and passengers across the Panamanian Isthmus. The United States Steamship Company combined maritime and land transportation to establish an overland railroad across the Isthmus. The city of Panama developed into a Yankee community, which it has remained almost to the present. It also served as a satellite of New York City, from where most of the capital to support operations in Isthmus originated. The time saved when compared with sailing from the Atlantic round Cape Horn to the Pacific proved enormous and soon ships flocked to either side of the Isthmus.

Even before the Panama route was complete, Cornelius Vanderbilt sought an even shorter route via Nicaragua. He built a macadamized road that merged with bay and steamships to join the Pacific and Atlantic shores. Vanderbilt also set up steamship services between the east coast and the Caribbean coast and between the Pacific coast of Nicaragua and San Francisco. The main port on the Caribbean side, Greytown, boomed because of Vanderbilt's actions. Passengers and freight flooded through its streets, heading for the Pacific. This decision proved a huge success and greatly facilitated the journey between the goldfields and the east coast of the United States. The Commodore, as Vanderbilt was known, pulled his resources out of the Nicaraguan operation as the rail line in the Panamanian Isthmus neared completion. The Nicaraguan routes quickly declined in importance.

Soon other trading links crisscrossed the Pacific Ocean, bringing food, capital and a range of other goods for desperate populations. Coffee from Chile, Peru and Mexico woke up prospectors from Northern California to New South Wales. Australia shipped out potatoes to California. Ships carried sugar and rice purchased in south coastal China across the Pacific to San Francisco's warehouses. Australians imported goods from the same producers as California. Chinese restaurants and Chinese laundry services appeared in California and Australia. Later, goods would flow into British Columbia as thousands of miners and followers streamed north by the late 1890s.

Silver quickly joined the flow of precious metals out of the United States west. Unlike gold, found in large quantities only northern California, silver mining covered the intermountain west, the southwest and much of the western portion of Plains states. From Comstock Lode in Nevada to Park City, Utah, to Aspen and Leadville, Colorado silver mining dominated the local economy and cast a long shadow over the mining economy of the western United States. Veteran miners from California and Australia made their way into the interior of the western United States. Soon, placer mines gave out and the mining shifted to expensive shafts and drifts. Smelters to convert the ores into various metals, technical knowledge of metallurgists and other expensive equipment overtook mining operations throughout the Rocky Mountain west.

Denver emerged as the main metropolis for silver mining and the center of ore smelting. It also facilitated capital transfers into the region since mining's costs grew dramatically as silver mining spread from one location to another. San Francisco money moved throughout the region and funded silver mining operations as far east as the Black Hills in South Dakota.

Feeding a global market, silver proved sensitive to production and price changes across the planet. The closing of the British silver mint in India in 1893 plunged the silver industry and its dependent communities into a sharp depression within hours of the announcement. The news traveled with lightning speed along the new global communication system. The sharp downturn swept through the Rocky Mountain west with a fury and shut down the entire silver industry. Mining town after mining town was boarded up. Silver would recover, yet it never regained its prominence and yielded to copper mining.

Copper mining would eventually overshadow silver mining, a transformation clearly marked by the depression of 1893. In fact, as early as the 1880s the United States emerged as the world's leading producer of copper. Butte, Montana symbolized the triumph of the United States copper industry. What San Francisco investors hoped would be the richest silver mine turned into the richest copper mine in the late nineteenth century. The Anaconda claim in Butte, Montana made the Anaconda Copper Mining Company a very profitable enterprise. Copper demanded even more capital than silver, since it required a concentration and smelting plant, timber company, coal mines, and a railroad to haul ore. The copper industry supplied industrial operations in the United States and Europe with an essential metal. Much like precious metals, copper proved a vital ingredient for the capitalist world. It also drew its capital from distant metropolitan centers on the east coast of the United States and in Great Britain and Europe.

Rich copper veins attracted mining companies to Arizona in search of this industrial metal. New York City corporation Phelps Dodge eventually took control of the entire copper industry and acquired such power that the citizens of Arizona simply referred to it as the Company. Phelps Dodge controlled every aspect of the industry from the mining of copper, to its smelting, to its refining before final sale. Its large-scale production of copper sustained state coffers and, at the same time, exposed Arizona to the often wild fluctuation in global prices.

Pueblo, Colorado symbolized the power of outside ownership in the United States west. Pueblo housed the Colorado Fuel and Iron Company (CF&ICO) and stood at the juncture of several major rail lines that connected her industry with key points in the west. The CF&ICO integrated major mining operations, steel manufacturing, smelters and a host of activities. It produced the steel rails that made it possible to ship in machines, people and goods to sustain the many extractive and agricultural industries in the west. These same rails then shipped out metals, farm goods and other products of the region. The company also operated major mining companies in the west and coal production ranked as one of its main activities. By the early twentieth century CF&ICO came under the control of John D. Rockefeller, the oil titan who operated a vast economic empire headquartered in New York City.

Mexico also offered United States investors numerous opportunities in mineral exploitation. The Porfirio Diaz government ruled Mexico from the 1870s until the revolution in 1910. As part of its policy of economic liberalism, the regime encouraged foreign investments and operations to promote economic growth and industrialization. In fact, by the last days of the Diaz regime, United States companies had placed hundreds of millions of dollars in the Mexican economy. United States money, resources and engineers built the majority of the country's railroads, seen as a prerequisite for development. Mexico's rich silver and copper veins also drew the attention of capitalists from the United States. Guggenheim, Rockefeller, Morgan and many other wealthy industrialists who headed huge companies turned their sights south of the border to exploit Mexico's resources, which were increasingly needed to sustain the United States economy.

Remoteness often characterized the mineral holdings in Mexico. United States companies faced the task of building effective transportation to a distant canyon and then establishing rail connections with railroad junctions on the United States side of the border. From these junctions, such as El Paso in Texas, lines carried copper, silver and other minerals to points north and northeast.

The silver veins in the remote Batopilas in Chihuahua provide a case in point. The site contained the largest load of silver in Mexico. In 1887 United States capitalists set up a mining operation then named the Batopilas Consolidated Mining Company. With capital in excess of $5,000,000 and some 1,500 employees, the company proved an eminently successful operation. Company officers oversaw the introduction of machinery that made economies of scale a necessity to justify the investment. From the time the operation began to yield silver, over $21,000,000 worth was mined and delivered to buyers. "Bullion trains," as locals termed them, made the journey to market carrying between $60,000 to $240,000 worth of silver. Rails moved north to El Paso, Laredo, and Eagle Pass, all on the United States' border, from where the steel rails shipped precious metals to New York City banks and copper to smelters in Colorado, Missouri and Oklahoma. Similarly, the Moctezuma Copper Company produced huge amounts of copper and depended on some $3,000,000 of investments.

Railroads made El Paso a major transportation and power center along the Mexican border. El Paso acted as the junction for Southern Pacific, the Atchison–Topeka–Sante Fe, the Texas–Pacific and the Galveston–Harrisburg–San Antonio rail lines as they converged on Texas. As important, the capital that funded the activity of United States companies also passed through El Paso on its way to mining operations in Mexico. The copper veins in Chihuahua and Sonora stood as magnets for this capital and complemented the similar mineral caches in southern Arizona.

As in the case of the gold rush in northern California and in Batopilas, mining in the northern states of Mexico sparked vigorous growth. The presence of mining spurred the creation of a local cattle and agricultural industry to feed the workers and company supervisors. Also, mining machinery imported from United States factories required storage until needed in production.

Dedicated to meeting the demands of distant markets, mining operations drove local and regional development. Raw materials, and goods produced in Mexico and bound for distant markets, benefited from the completion of two transcontinental railroads through New Mexico and Arizona in the early 1880s. The southwest United States and later northern Mexico joined the larger global economy. Now capitalists from the metropolitan centers in the United States made decisions that shaped industrial operations in these regions. To power its mining operations in Sonora more efficiently, Phelps Dodge installed an electrical power plant in place of the older steam engines. The new source of power enabled the company to adopt new heavy machinery such as hoists and mechanical cages to move copper miners to and from the copper veins. The Guggenheims, through their modernized smelters, dominated the processing of ore in Mexico. The imported technology fueled Mexico's productive capacities, which remained in the hands of the United States companies.

At the same time, states such as Sonora developed a keen sensitivity to global prices since their export commodities now competed in the world markets.

The Sonoran state, for example, collected most of its revenue from foreign-owned mining operations that produced copper and silver. The introduction of Chilean copper disrupted the market for Mexican copper and led to a drop in global prices for the metal. Inevitably, this drop reverberated throughout the industry and reduced the revenue available to Sonora and its people. Sonora proved as vulnerable to global prices as Arizona.

United States' interest in metals also extended well beyond its borders and adjacent Mexico. United States corporations moved into South and Central America during the early twentieth century for the same reasons that these companies established operations in Mexico. Chilean copper and nitrate ore drew United States capital, heavy machines and engineers determined to open up new sources of raw materials. The Chilean elite welcomed these changes in the hope of reversing their declining fortunes. The elite adopted a policy of economic liberalism similar to Diaz's strategy to attract capital and resources from powerful industrialized states. United States companies eventually placed some $1 billion dollars into productive operations that ranged from huge electric power plants to drive its copper machinery to the modernization of the Chilean electricity industry. United States capital eventually took control of the profitable copper industry while United States banks provided some $90 million to the Chilean government to keep it afloat. Much of the huge investment by United States companies and banks occurred in the distant, arid deserts of northern Chile. In this region the United States capital and modernized operations took over the nitrate industry. In the process, United States companies replaced British capital and Chilean producers. Few could withstand the economic power of the United States and its desperate need for raw materials.

Similarly, American corporations established operations in the central highlands of Peru, where their machinery dug up rich copper deposits. Rail lines transported these to Callao, a port eventually updated by American capital and resources. The American corporation, Cerro de Pasco, accounted for 80 percent of Peru's copper production by the 1920s. Smelters, new reverberatory furnaces, rail lines, mechanized forms of hauling and lifting all made the company's operation efficient, productive and extremely profitable. The United States companies also created the same vertically integrated structures that typified their domestic operations. The Cerro de Pasco company put some $25 million dollars into its Peruvian sites. Of course the product of these activities helped United States economic growth.

Tropical products

The demand for tropical products also drove United States corporations to search for more productive ways to produce sugar and fruits and to exploit new locations capable of sustaining plantations. Cuba had developed into a major producer and exporter of sugar to the United States market. Central

America's climate and soil made it a storehouse of bananas and other fruits. United States companies and their employees swarmed to both sites, drawn by the tremendous profits offered by these tropical environments.

The United States had a long history of ties with Cuba. It exported technology to Cuba, specifically to develop its sugar production. By the 1830s steam power linked Havana with major United States ports such as New York and Philadelphia. The United States-built railroads moved sugar to coastal ports by the mid-nineteenth century. United States companies then introduced telegraph lines that eventually led to the creation of a sophisticated network that integrated Cuba's main cities. The International Ocean Telegraph Company of New York ran a submarine cable system that joined Cuba and the United States. United States-produced locomotives and rail cars serviced Cuban shippers and consumers. United States commercial operations and their agents claimed a major presence in the island ports and generally ranged over the entire island. They exchanged goods and services for sugar and its by-product, molasses.

This presence would expand dramatically once the United States occupation began in the wake of the Spanish-American War of 1898. United States corporate investment rose to $215 million by 1914 and an astounding $1.3 billion by the mid-twenties. The United Fruit Company and other United States-based institutions firmly established control over a substantial portion of the Cuban sugar industry. Weakened by war and subsequent debt, the Cuban planter class succumbed to the pressures of the United States corporations. United States interests even extended to the electrical industry that came under the control of General Electric during the 1920s. United States corporations also revolutionized the sugar industry, then under the technological regimes of the nineteenth century industrial revolution. United States companies such as General Sugar and Cuban Cane Sugar introduced new mechanization schemes. By the mid-1920s United States private investment dominated the Cuban sugar industry.

Honduras proved a significant challenge, since the labor force resided in the central highlands while the bananas grew best along the coast. Corporate leaders poured in some $70 million and dramatically expanded the rail network, made rivers navigable and modernized ports throughout the Honduran coast. They also set up radio stations and built telegraph lines in key urban locations. The efforts of the United States prompted the emergence of small-scale planters who relied on this transportation and communications infrastructure for their bananas to reach distant urban markets. Honduras, in fact, quickly developed into the largest banana grower across the globe. United States corporations such as United Fruit took control of thousands of acres of land, acquired through Honduran government cooperation. United Fruit actually ranked as one of the largest employers in the country.

In fact, United States corporations increasingly dominated the Central American coffee and fruit producers from Honduras to Nicaragua and Panama.

The United States companies replaced German and British interest by the end of World War I. Rail lines connected the productive interior with the coastal ports. Telegraph and telephones provided communications within the region and with the United States and other overseas markets. Transportation effectively joined distant markets and Central America, yet the rail system funneled goods directly to ports and rarely connected markets in Central America. The system reinforced the export economies and their dependence on distant markets. Coffee quickly developed into the main export of the region by the 1880s and by Word War I United States markets drew the largest share of production. The export economies survived based on the viability of coffee and, for Honduras, banana consumption, mostly in the United States.

Conclusion

The United States economy grew to the point that demand for raw materials exceeded domestic capacity. At the same time an exploding population created rich markets for basic foodstuffs and increasingly for topical tastes. These demands forced large-scale United States companies to seek raw materials overseas. In searching for these materials United States companies created a growing interdependence with economies in the Caribbean, Central and South America. To establish these links United States corporations brought tremendous economic and political changes throughout these regions. These same companies also developed sophisticated operations in the United States west where a huge reservoir of raw materials was located and, again, brought significant economic and political changes to the peoples and landscapes of the west.

Companies built sophisticated transportation and communications systems to insure the rapid movement of materials and information about production and markets. Railroads made their way across the United States plains toward the west and east coast where they connected with coal-power steam-driven ships. Railroads, telegraph and submarine cables connected raw material regions in Cuba, Mexico, Peru, Chile and other states with United States and European markets. The United States corporations remade significant portions of the economies of these countries. These companies exploited production and processing sites such as copper mines and nitrate fields in Montana and Chile, respectively. All of these sites dedicated their capacities to sustain distant markets, mostly in the United States.

The scale of these operations dwarfed all previous endeavors. Corporations shipped in huge numbers of workers or recruited locals if the sites were near population centers. Workers often came from overseas or at least from locations distant from the sites. With the aid of national governments corporations broke up communal land holdings and turned land-based peasants into day laborers. Corporations transformed economies such as those in Arizona, Sonora and Guatemala into export-producing entities geared to global markets, especially the United States. Peru furnished copper, Chile nitrate, Mexico copper, silver and oil, Cuba sugar, Montana copper, Guatemala bananas, and the Plains states wheat, grains, beef and wool. The power of United States corporations reached thousands of miles throughout the Western Hemisphere just as Europeans sought raw materials in Africa. Landscapes changed as mining operations used heavy machinery to drive deep into the earth, whether in Carson City, Nevada or in isolated Batoplias, Chihuahua. United Fruit banana plantations transformed coastal Guatemala into a highly productive region dependent on United States capital and heavy machinery.

These raw materials fed heavy industry in the United States. Steel, electrical, chemical and other industries depended on the inflow of copper and other minerals. Consumer industries saw sugar as vital to their economic well-being. Tropical fruit such as bananas created entirely new tastes and United Fruit grew into a giant enterprise based on bananas from Central America feeding domestic markets in the United States. Such new companies generated new consumer habits for millions. The new international economy made farmers dependent on consumers in New York, manufacturers in Chicago, and railroads headquartered on the east coast. Miners in Sonora received pay from companies in New York City that relied on capital backed by gold from California or Alaska. Buyers in Havana purchased electricity from General Electric Corporation that relied on German-trained chemists and engineers to produce technological innovations.

The new economic relationships and the new economies occurred throughout the world. Ranchers and wheat farmers in Argentina profited from British funded and built railroads that hauled farm and meat products to the modernized port of Buenos Aires. European shipping lines carried wheat and beef to British markets. Argentinian farmers purchased their farm machinery from United States corporations. Argentina existed as part of a broader economic network much as did Mexico and the western United States.

These new relationships called for mobile labor and in numbers previously unknown. Migration joined technology and corporations in transforming the United States and the globe.

Further reading

For general works, see Eric Hobsbawm, *The Age of Capital, 1848–1875* (New York, 1996). For a wide ranging work on finance, see Niall Ferguson, *The House of Rothschild, the World's Bankers, 1849–1999* (New York, 1998). Ivanti and Gyorgu Ranki, *The European Periphery and Industrialization 1780–1914* (New York, 1986) charts developments in Eastern Europe.

For works on United States activity in the Western Hemisphere, see John Mason Hart, *Empire and Revolution: The Americans in Mexico Since the Civil War* (Berkeley, 2002); William Robbins, *Colony and Empire: The Capitalist Transformation of the American West* (Lawrence, Kansas, 1994); Louis Perez, *On Becoming Cuban: Identity, Nationality, and Culture* (Chapel Hill, 1999); Thomas F. O'Brien, *The Revolutionary*

Mission: American Enterprise in Latin America, 1900–1950 (New York, 1996); Ralph Lee Woodward, *Central America: A Nation Divided* (New York, 1999).

For works that deal with the United States west, the Canadian Prairie and the Argentinian Pampas, see Richard White, *It's Your Misfortune and None of My Own: A New History of the American West* (Norman, Oklahoma, 1991); Jeremy Adelman, *Frontier Development: Land, Labor, and Capital on the Wheatlands of Argentina and Canada, 1890–1914* (New York, 1994); Carl Solberg, *The Prairies and the Pampas: Agrarian Policy in Canada and Argentina, 1880–1902* (Stanford, California, 1987); David B. Danborn, *Born in the Country: A History of Rural America* (Baltimore, 1995). For a survey of Australia, see David Day, *Claiming a Continent: A History of Australia* (Sydney, 1996). Arrel Morgan Gibson, *Yankees in Paradise: The Pacific Basin Frontier* (Albuquerque, New Mexico, 1993) provides thorough coverage of the United States' activities in the Pacific.

For the ports, see, L. Ray Gunn, "New York Modernizes: Economic growth and transformation," in Milton Klein, ed., *The Empire State: A History of New York* (Ithaca, 2001), pp. 307–415; Edwin G. Burrows and Mike Wallace, *Gotham: A History of New York City* (New York, 1989); Richard J. Evans, *Death in Hamburg: Society and Politics in the Cholera Years 1830–1910* (Oxford, 1987).

Chapter 7

The United States and Atlantic migration

Introduction

From the mid-nineteenth century until the 1920s, people moved across the globe in unprecedented numbers. This movement represented a massive response to the reordering of national economies precipitated by industrialization. Demands for labor reached across state borders, continents, and even oceans. Factory labor, agricultural workers, engineers, financial experts, migrants armed with virtually any type of asset from mere strength to university training sought opportunities beyond their birthplaces. In the vast majority of these cases personal and economic distress persuaded men and women to choose migration. In the mid-nineteenth century, famine compelled hundreds of thousands of people to migrate as potato blight swept over western Europe and the British Isles. Later in the century, population pressure and inadequately sized farms forced many in Eastern Europe to seek income beyond their homes. The young men and women most affected by such changes held one tremendous asset, their flexibility. The majority of these individuals voluntarily chose to migrate.

With efficient transportation to any destination and with effective information about work, these individuals moved to where demands were greatest. The industrial economies of the Atlantic world, especially the United States, demonstrated an intense, almost insatiable, demand for labor. The United States, with its huge economy, drew the largest share of the human migrations in the nineteenth and twentieth centuries. It called for workers to dig subway tunnels in the huge metropolises such as New York City, to fill the ranks of textile workers in New England or to descend the mines of Pennsylvania. The rapidly expanding economy meant the need for migrant workers never ceased. Migrants came to the United States often for short-term goals. Many did remain, while millions returned to their original homes. For the United States, short-term and long-term labor met its many diverse needs.

Yet, the United States was only one industrial economy that attracted migrants. Great Britain's economy recruited migrant workers. Germany also increasingly depended on migrant labor. This demand grew as she industrialized, particularly after 1880. Germany, like the United States, witnessed the rise of heavy industry and the demand for strong backs. It drew its labor from the eastern part of the new German state, from Austrian- and Russian-ruled Poland and from Scandinavia. Many of these migrant workers came for temporary stays to earn money, then went back to their families.

Surprisingly, other states which experienced the most intense migration were also in the Western Hemisphere. Argentina and Canada, for instance, relied on migration to fuel their economic growth. These states developed largely export-driven economies that fed the industrial populations in Britain and the continent. Argentina and Canada both witnessed the emergence of prosperous agricultural sectors that needed migrant labor. Canada preferred those who intended permanent residence while Argentina called for short-term migrants. In both cases, migrants developed their own economic strategies suited to their needs and the demands of the export economies.

Migration also constantly changed societies that sent off their young in search of work or new homes. In fact new social and familial conditions in societies where migrants originated depended on a constant stream of migrants and a return of fiscal resources from them. As important, migrants transformed their new communities. Surprisingly, migrants also helped maintain traditional families; the money they sent back enabled the family to survive. At the same time, migration created powerful personal bonds that joined societies through individuals and their families.

European population changes

Rapid population surges appeared across Europe. This meant more and more people pressed on limited resources. Europe's population increased dramatically from 187,000,000 in 1800 to 468,000,000 in 1913. Overall, some thirty-three million crossed the Atlantic from Europe and equally substantial numbers moved within Europe. European governments and elites from Germany to Scandinavia often watched with grave concern the rapid growth in their populations. For many, the increasing numbers, the shortage of land to accommodate them and the unsavory reputation of those at the bottom of the social ladder who seemed to account for this explosion persuaded state officials and national leaders to encourage out-migration. In 1840, Sweden actually made emigration a right for its citizens. The state dropped its demand for a passport. This change reflected the swing from restrictive mercantilist notions to a liberal approach that gave citizens the ability to make their own decisions.

European states also ended the serfdom that legally bound their rural populations to the land through custom and law. Beginning in 1807 and running over the next fifty years or more, governments responding to popular and market pressures ended serfdom in Prussia in 1807, in Austria in 1848 and finally in Russia in 1861. Slowly Europe witnessed the liberation of its labor force, which was eventually free to seek jobs anywhere that markets needed workers. The transformation often proved difficult and contested, yet it occurred steadily throughout the first six decades of the century.

The surging populations of western Europe collided with a major agricultural crisis that engulfed regions dependent on the potato. A blight destroyed potato crops for several consecutive years during the mid-1840s. The ensuing food shortages struck the Rhineland especially hard, and absolutely devastated Highland Scottish and Irish populations. Combined with market pressures in rural communities of western Europe, famine produced waves of out migration. The vast majority of the migrants in these waves ended up in the United States.

Ireland and migration

The tale of the Irish in the midst of this travail remains the singular most harrowing account of migration and hardship to this day. On the eve of the mid-1840s famine, Ireland stood at the end of a major demographic revolution four decades in the making. The island's population jumped from 4,500,000 in 1800 to over 8,000,000 by 1840. This explosion was in part due to the abundance of the potato crop. Small plot-holders could easily plant the potato on a few acres, where it grew in abundance and produced sufficient food for the rural families. The amazing fecundity of the potato and its capacity to flourish in most soils made it an ideal crop for the Irish farmer. As a result, a large and expanding class of small-scale tenant farmers and landless laborers emerged in pre-famine Ireland.

The famine led to a second and less celebratory demographic revolution. It relentlessly reduced the number of people through death and out-migration. The famine also transformed the structure of families that would in turn institutionalize this migration and increasingly push young people out into the world beyond Ireland, mostly to the United States. There, an abundance of jobs and ease of entry provided an outlet for the Irish Catholics seeking relief.

The departure of so many young people altered the economy of Ireland. Few men and women remained to have children. The migration also created the opportunity for landowners to shift to grains and/or grazing for cattle. Cash cropping and a market-driven cattle industry reigned supreme in an Ireland now dedicated to food production and shorn of what little industry it had in the mid-nineteenth century. Irish landowners and British consumers benefited from the changing demography of Ireland.

The Irish migration worked to the advantage of the United States, where young Irish migrants filled many of the jobs necessary to sustain the nation's industrial growth. The United States' industrializing economy demanded labor to build canals and later railroads. It also needed female labor for the textile mills that fueled New England's growth, especially as more and more mills made the industry extremely competitive and desperate for plentiful and inexpensive labor. Coal mines in eastern Pennsylvania required strong backs willing to work under dangerous and grueling conditions. In addition, the emerging middle class families called for domestics, usually young, unmarried women. Ireland provided much of this labor. In almost all cases, the Irish settled in United States industrial cities, large, medium and small. With no capital, and few of the skills demanded successfully to farm in the United States, the Irish remained in cities and quite often in the ports where they landed. Yet, their physical strength and vast numbers solved the labor needs of an economy traditionally short of workers.

Young women also took part in the Irish migration. In fact, women quickly dominated the post-famine migration, even into the 1920s. Young women faced different challenges than men, and these challenges proved formidable. Usually without family inheritance, and frequently unable to find a mate in a society where men usually migrated, women developed their own strategies.

Of course, a single woman could hope for the possibility of marriage, yet this wait usually lasted well into her twenties since men only acquired land in their late twenties or even early thirties. This decision could well end in disaster. Without a husband, young women faced a life of celibacy and one without economic opportunities. If a woman chose to marry, the decision proved an economic burden for the family, since marriages required dowries. Since a union involved property, arranged marriages quickly assumed primacy for the families. Few young women could overrule their fathers in a patriarchal society such as existed in Catholic Ireland. Either celibacy or a husband not of their own choosing faced Irish women in the wake of the famine.

Unless a woman joined one of the women's orders in the Catholic Church, and many such orders emerged from the activism of Irish nuns, migration provided a release and, at the same time, a way to preserve the family in Ireland. As important, Irish women participated in an educational system and arrived in the United States literate and prepared to fill office, department store and service jobs that expected literacy and an education. Of course, Irish women spoke English, the language of the Anglo-Irish, of official records and speech, and the one of choice for almost everyone in eastern Ireland, and increasingly so in the western provinces. Gaelic stood as a relic of the past and major impediment to those who chose to use it.

A divided yet interdependent family then developed on both sides of the Atlantic. In Ireland, the parents depended on the income their daughters sent them from the United States. The bonds of family sustained the daughter's family identity. Once in the United States most Irish women developed ties with other sisters, aunts and female members of the family already resident there. These young women wrote buoyant letters describing life in the United States and the many choices available to them. Such information brought more and more women to the western Atlantic via the emerging migration chains. Women in the United States also provided resources for other relatives or friends to make the journey from Ireland to New York City, Boston or

Philadelphia. The migration chains maintained families and friendship networks divided by an ocean.

Last, Ireland stood midway between Britain and its demands for food in one form or another, and the United States and its need for labor. The days of subsistence farming and communal life clearly had ended. The era of industrial workers laboring in the United States and commercial farmers producing food for British markets had begun. Migration literally fed one industrial economy, Great Britain, while it provided the labor to sustain the rapid growth of another, the United States. And Irish families developed strategies to survive the vast demographic and economic changes of the mid- and late nineteenth centuries.

European migration

The Irish migration demonstrated many of the characteristics of European migration. The continent, too, suffered privation during "the hungry 1840s." The west German states in particular faced severe food shortages. At the same time, land consolidation throughout western Europe squeezed out small plot holders who faced bleak futures. In Scandinavia scarce land combined with excessive crowding forced many peasants to seek their livelihoods elsewhere, quite often in the Midwestern region of the United States. Artisans in the Rhineland, Westphalia and other states in the region found they were unable to compete with British manufactured goods that arrived on the newly constructed rail lines, again courtesy of British rail technology. Their crafts endangered by industrial products, artisans joined the stream crossing the Atlantic for the United States.

Near the end of the nineteenth century, population pressure in eastern and southern Europe brought great stress to the countryside. Farms marginalized by land consolidations, noncompetitive small plots, and fierce global competition from Australia, Argentina and elsewhere set millions of young men in motion. In Russian Poland, the part of the former Polish state annexed by Russia during the partitions of the late eighteenth century, 72 percent of peasant farms amounted to dwarf holdings insufficient to support their owners. In fact a large class of rural workers unable to live solely off their land emerged in western Russia. In Austrian Poland, an identical class of rural laborers made their appearance in the late nineteenth century. By 1900, one-third to two-thirds of all peasant families in Polish territories ruled by Russia, Austria and Germany depended on money earned outside their farm and community. These wages either constituted the entire income or provided an essential addition to their family's resources. Migration provided the means to earn outside income and enabled families to survive. Millions came to the United States for precisely that purpose, to earn money in one of the many industrial jobs, save and then return home.

Hundreds of thousands of Italians came to the United States during this period. In southern Italy few peasants owned their land and most worked at the mercy of large-scale landowners who squeezed as much work from them as possible. Even among those peasants who actually owned their own land, the amount proved insufficient to meet the living standards of their families. They joined the Irish in urban construction work and carved out residential niches in industrial cities from Paterson, New Jersey to the New York City boroughs where they joined tens of thousands of migrants from eastern Europe.

Return migration

The journey of these migrants to the United States marked only one part of the complex migration process. For many, the return home completed this process, rather than taking up permanent residence in the United States. The increasingly sophisticated passenger ships that crossed the Atlantic in considerably shorter time than the older sailing ships facilitated the journey back home. Weekly vessels bound for European ports from the United States carried tens of thousands of migrants ultimately back to their villages. Some migrants made this trip on a regular basis as part of a short-term or seasonal cycle. Some Italian migrants worked in the United States from spring until late fall before returning home with the money earned while in the United States. For others the return came after several years' hard work, privation and saving before departing for their homes with sufficient resources to improve the lives of their families. This pattern of short-term stays found among many English migrants also occurred among Croatian and Slovenian migrants from southeastern Europe. Almost 60 percent of them returned to their homes. Similarly, more than 56 percent of the Slovakian migrants returned. This pattern prevailed among most migrant groups from Europe.

From 1908 when the United States began tracking return migrants until 1914 when the outbreak of World War I temporarily suspended migration, several million migrants to the United States filled passenger ships back to Europe. Some groups, notably the Irish and the Jewish migrants, rarely returned home. In the case of the Irish, few returned to an Ireland where jobs and land remained in scarce supply. For Jewish migrants a return to Imperial Russia placed them in dire jeopardy because of the pogroms the Russian government conducted against Russian Jewish communities.

Once in the United States, migrants began sending letters to their families and friends in their home communities. These letters often described the plentiful jobs and higher wages available. This information alone acted as an incentive to draw more and more peasant migrants to the United States. Letters also contained directions on how to make the journey, where to go, the cost and other similar information that facilitated the flow out of a European village. Letters also carried money to aid families or even to maintain a church. These assets enabled many families to cover insufficient income. Of course these resources moved with relative ease because of the modern communications and transportation systems and international agreements that facilitated the flow of correspondence across national borders and to far-flung destinations.

At the same time, the return of hundreds of thousands of migrants from the United States to their homes brought profound and visible changes to these communities. Returning migrants carried stories of soaring "skyscrapers," seeing United States presidents, and even encountering people of different religious affiliations, all of which amazed their fellow villagers. These tales broadened the horizons of many in peasant communities. Migrants who participated in United States politics brought back this spirit of involvement. They organized political groups and established labor unions. Almost 5 percent of all Italians had lived in the United States for some period of time by the outbreak of World War I. In the Norwegian county of Vest-Agder, 25 percent of the young men (15 years or older) had spent time in the United States, often working in industrial jobs. The United States' impact spread far beyond the money earned, saved and sent back. It touched people's understanding of a larger world beyond the confines of their homes, neighborhoods and communities.

Migration to European industrial states

Among the industrial states, Great Britain and Germany also participated in this large-scale migration. Both countries experienced steady out-migration at this time. The British, in fact, constituted the largest group of European migrants to the United States. The United States drew the lion's share of these migrants. Yet, Canada and Argentina also attracted sizable numbers of British emigrants, and after 1900 the British accounted for almost a third of all emigrants landing on Canada's shores. Most of these departures came from the ranks of working people that saw the dynamic economy of the United States as a place to earn sizable amounts of money. Canada's late nineteenth century industrialization proved irresistible to British emigrants. In fact, many more British migrants chose Canada over the United States. British migrants also made the very long journey either to New Zealand or Australia. The lure of precious metals attracted British emigrants. The gold rushes and silver veins in the United States, Canada, and Australia caught the eye of many modest British workers who hoped, as so many foolishly did, to strike a rich vein of either metal. South African gold discoveries also resulted in thousands of British migrants landing in its ports. For British emigrants who wanted land, Canada with its limitless prairie seemed more attractive than the United States, where the Census Bureau declared the frontier closed in 1890.

Great Britain also attracted migrants, mostly from Ireland. These migrants came to exploit seasonal openings in Britain's farm sectors and, increasingly, more permanent positions in her industrial and service sectors. The Irish, longsuffering under British rule, at least had the advantage of proximity and effective transportation to England and Scotland. Great Britain's economic ties with Ireland certainly facilitated migration, both short and long term. The migrants in the late nineteenth century responded to English seasonal labor needs generated by the harvest, a role that diminished over time because of mechanization or shifting to other food products. In Scotland the demand for Irish labor to harvest crops such as corn, turnips and potato suited their skills and remained high. The Irish also worked on Scottish railroad construction gangs that demanded good physical strength. In London the Irish worked in unskilled and occasionally semi-skilled job on the docks or in other sectors of the metropolitan economy. They also worked in British heavy industrial operations that benefited from the expansion of the rail system. These choices resembled those made by the Irish migrants to the United States. Irish women also found work in Great Britain. They usually ended up in domestic work and related household services such as laundry work, much as they did in the United States. Several hundred thousand Irish eventually came to live in Scotland and England. Unlike its Anglo cousin across the Atlantic, Great Britain's smaller economy and its already well-developed and ample working class reduced her need for migrant workers. In contrast, she heavily recruited the Irish to the ranks of her armies that expanded and maintained her global empire in the late nineteenth century.

Germany, too, experienced the arrival of large numbers of newcomers as well as internal migration. Much like Great Britain, Germany sent millions of her citizens across the Atlantic from the 1840s until the 1890s. The economy in western Germany developed much later than its British counterpart. As a result it lacked the capacity to absorb its exploding population of the 1830s and 1840s, especially since crop failures and an increasing scarcity of land greatly stressed peasant families in the region. At the same time, the flood of British manufactured goods undercut artisanal crafts throughout western Germany. Faced with bleak futures, many of these individuals and their families chose migration, usually to the United States. As Germany began to develop her industrial capacities in the wake of unification in 1871, she slowly gained suffi-cient volume of industrial operations to employ the overwhelming numbers of young men and women in the very late nineteenth century. In response, Germans from the country's eastern provinces and ethnic Poles under German rule flocked to the west in search of high-paying jobs in these burgeoning industries. At the same time the industrial growth virtually ended the large-scale migration to the United States.

Germany's industrial growth in the west affected her raw material region in the east, where Prussian and other landlords inaugurated sugar beet farming and processing in response to international market demands for the taste of sugar. This region provided substantial wealth to the landowners and revenues to the Prussian federal state and the national state. The departure of so many workers created an acute need for workers on both a seasonal and more permanent basis. The Poles living under Russian and Austrian rule and in search of income responded with alacrity. Soon, hundreds of thousands of Polish migrants flooded into the eastern part of the German state to provide labor in the sugar beet fields. Many of these migrant workers consisted of women, whose labor helped solve the shortages for the Prussian landowners. Many young Poles also made an even longer journey to the Ruhr valley and other industrial centers in the west. For both groups of migrants the promise of higher wages held an immense appeal.

The German government expressed concern over its eastern European workers. In particular, officials worried about the loyalty of the ethnic Poles whose ancestors had come under Prussian rule in what became eastern Germany. These ethnic Poles met their counterparts from the Russian and Austrian empires who had a more developed sense of being Polish. The incoming Polish migrants from neighboring empires certainly did bring a more articulated view of their identity, yet ethnic Poles neither embraced this identity nor abandoned their own affiliation with the German state. Still, a cautious and even paranoid German government blocked permanent settlement of Polish migrants in the state's industrial regions by forcing them to leave the country several weeks a year.

Germany also drew substantial migrations from Scandinavia, the same source that sent millions to the United States. Scandinavia experienced the same commercialization of her agricultural system in the mid- and late nineteenth century as well as a population burst that stretched the capacity of her farm sector. At the same time, the Swedish government embraced the liberal policies that encouraged Swedes to resolve their own economic plights through migration. Swedish workers, for instance, turned to agricultural and industrial regions in north Germany in search of work, either on a permanent or seasonal basis. The farm sectors of Prussia, Pomerania and other states in north Germany, encountered severe labor shortages as field hands and their families flocked to the emerging industrial regions in the west, notably the Ruhr Valley. Eventually the Swedes ended up in construction gangs that built railroads, urban structures and other similar projects, much as migrants did in the United States. They also drifted into the industrial locations in Silesia and Berlin that developed late in the nineteenth century. German companies, much as those from the United States, heavily recruited Swedish laborers for work in German factories, docks and shipyards. Swedes also moved into steel and metal operations in the Ruhr.

German companies, as with their United States counterparts, actively recruited Swedish workers through vigorous advertising campaigns. In response, Swedes came to industrial sites in north Germany where they labored in factories and mines. They also moved to ports such as Bremen, where the docks and shipyards demanded their energy to handle the vast flow of people, ships and materials engaged in the oceanic transport to North America and other destinations. In Hamburg, the Swedes actually constituted the largest migrant worker population.

Sweden also began to industrialize in the mid-nineteenth century. This produced a very different migration than normally anticipated. Swedish mechanics, skilled workers and engineers of all types made trips to Great Britain, the United States and Germany in search of new methods of production, new machinery and to engage in discussions with their counterparts in these countries. German machinery and its reputation for quality production attracted Swedish engineers and skilled workers who also participated in German training centers sponsored by the state's large firms. Swedish manufacturers acquired specific knowledge critical to the printing and chemical industries. Technically educated Swedes also brought back substantial knowledge on the building trades and manufacturing of boilers. Swedes also sought practical knowledge in pulp and other industries prominent in Germany.

The United States also contributed to the Swedish learning process. In fact, many contemporaries pointed to the Americanization of the Swedish mechanical engineering industry as an important outcome from this exchange and subsequent transfer of ideas and technical methods. Swedish engineers also developed an understanding of the emphasis on the large batch production so common in United States industry. The Swedish state, in fact, sponsored these short-term migrations hoping that United States industry would prove beneficial to the Swedish skilled and professional workers. Visiting Swedish engineers also attended industrial expositions and world fairs that displayed United States technical and industrial achievements. Industrial economies abroad contributed to the development and maturing of states as entrepreneurs, skilled workers and professional personnel brought back considerable knowledge of high-level industrial economies.

Export-driven states and migration: Canada and Argentina

In the western Atlantic, export-driven economies emerged to meet the new demands of industrial states such as Germany and the United States. Under-populated, these states desperately needed more people to make their national economies viable in the new industrial world. Export-based Argentina and Canada looked to Europe to meet their escalating labor needs. An international fleet of British, French, German and Italian carriers carried European migrants across to the Americas.

Argentina, much like other market-oriented states, depended on an increasingly international workforce to maintain its export economy based on wheat, beef and wool. Argentina conducted vigorous advertising campaigns that stressed the good pay and the high demand for workers. In 1901, the Argentine government re-instituted the practice of subsidizing migrants' voyages to South America. Under pressure from landowners, the government began to pay for the rail trip from the coast to the large-scale grain estates on the Pampas.

The Argentine government preferred young men descended from Anglo-Saxons, in the racial language of the day, or those of Germanic origin, neither of which responded. Instead, migrants from Spain and Italy came in numbers sufficient to meet the labor demands of Argentina's export-driven economy. To encourage this migration, government officials inaugurated an open door policy that included temporary quarters for migrants arriving in Buenos Aires. By the 1910s Argentina attracted the major share of the 4,000,000 Spanish migrants who crossed the Atlantic, while another 2,500,000 Italian migrants also sought work in Argentina. It stood just behind the United States in the volume of migrants received and ranked first in the proportion of the population who came from overseas. By 1914 more than 30 percent of the country's population consisted of foreign-born residents.

Population surges in Spain and Italy preceded the migration streams. These surges placed great pressure on land resources. Northern Spain in particular saw its numbers rise as fertility and life spans increased. The region around the city of Mataro and, in general, the province of Galicia provided the majority of the immigrants to Argentina. At the heart of the Spanish city, its artisans lost out to factory production supported by the surplus population which a market-driven agricultural sector had pushed out of the countryside, a common story in nineteenth-century Europe. In response to what officials perceived as a Malthusian over-population threat, they usually encouraged their fellow residents to migrate. At the same time, the commercialization of agriculture in Spain reordered labor needs and undermined remaining communal agriculture.

Population pressure and the consolidation of land ownership in northern Italy between the 1870s and the 1890s forced thousands to migrate from the region, often to Argentina. The rapid growth of industry in northern Italy significantly reduced those choosing migration as an economic strategy by the early 1900s. At this point, Italian peasants from Sicily and Calabria in the southern end of the peninsula began to replace the counterparts from the north in the migration stream to Argentina. Trapped in an agricultural system controlled by large absentee landowners such as the Roman Catholic Church or the local nobility, peasants from southern Italy opted for migration as a way to enhance their income. These migrants usually departed from Naples for New York City; significant numbers also opted for Buenos Aires.

The migrants to Argentina developed their own strategies to capitalize on the possibilities of improved wages and subsidized voyages. Italians, in particular, adopted a seasonal cycle to their migrations to the South American state, in contrast to their counterparts in the United States who often took up permanent residence. These migrants often worked in industry or construction sites, both usually in major cities where they found inexpensive accommodations. The migrants to Argentina came with only short-term intentions. One group arrived as seasonal workers attempting to capitalize on the intense labor demands of the harvest. Since the harvest seasons in South America and Europe occurred at different times of the years, this strategy enabled seasonal migrants to exploit labor in agriculture throughout a substantial portion of the year. Often workers who landed in Buenos Aires moved north to the coffee plantations in Southern Brazil once the Argentinian harvest had ended. Then they re-crossed the Atlantic into Southern Europe where agriculture needed short-term labor for its harvest cycle.

Other Italian migrants to Argentina came with a different set of expectations. They, too, hoped to capitalize on labor needs on the Pampas by working as tenant farmers under three- to five-year contracts. The rapid expansion of arable and pastoral land in the wake of victorious wars against the indigenous people whose raids limited settlement, and the emergence of new, distant, industrial markets posed an unexpected challenge to the large landowners. They took possession of tremendous amounts of land on the Pampas yet lacked sufficient labor even to break ground throughout much of their new holdings.

The migrant tenant farmer provided the answer to the labor shortage. The landowners leased out parcels of land to these tenants as a way of bringing their land into cultivation. Usually the contract included machinery to break ground, plant the crop and complete the harvest, a necessity given the lack of capital on the part of the tenant. These individuals planted wheat, most sought after by consumers in the British Isles and European industrial cities. At the end of the short-term contract, the tenant farmer planted alfalfa, the best forage crop available. Since the owners dedicated much of their land to cattle, alfalfa became a necessary crop to feed their livestock. Once the contract expired, the tenant farmer usually returned to his home in southern Italy where his newly earned profits sustained his wife and children or parents and siblings, much like his industrial counterpart in the United States who sent remittances back to his family.

The landowner benefited since the tenant farmer worked the land and grew crops that would later sell in European markets, as well as providing forage for the cattle that generated meat and meat by-products. Unlike the United States, where an internal market of urban consumers bought farm and meat products of the Plains states, Argentina lived and died by continental and British demands. Given the international character of wheat production, agriculturalists in the United States and Argentina both looked to Liverpool, where the wheat exchange set prices for this crop. Both also depended on rail and oceanic transportation, and new forms of communication, to conduct their business. Migration proved the vital ingredient to meet desperate labor needs. In the United States family farmers filled this need, while in Argentina single young men with short-term intentions met the labor shortages.

Canada leaned more toward the United States experience. Canada drew most of its migrant labor from Great Britain, the United States and the Ukraine. Canada's largest group of farmers settling the western prairie came from Ontario, just as the United States depended on westward migration of its own citizens to settle the Plains states. Certainly Scandinavians, Germans and other migrant groups joined the migration stream to the Plains states, yet citizens of the United States dominated this migration, as did Canadians in the migration stream to the western Prairie.

All three sets of farmers responded to rich urban-industrial markets. Yet, farmers in the United States and Canada carried heavy debt that rose as they expanded land under cultivation and acquired more machinery, all a necessity to remain economically. In contrast, Argentinian landowners borrowed at favorable rates from the state national bank that secured its money from overseas lenders. Short-term migrant laborers minimized their costs by renting land and borrowing machinery from landowners through annual harvests. The nature of their markets, the development policies of the government and the long- or short-term goals of the migrants shaped the future of these three groups.

Conclusion

Migration was intimately tied to economic and demographic changes in Europe. Industrialization and expanding populations sent millions on the move in the mid-nineteenth century. In the 1840s famine and hunger also played an important role, as millions of Irish were forced to seek relief outside of Ireland. Migrants from western Germany also joined this stream of unfortunates. An industrializing economy in the United States provided income and livelihoods for these migrants.

Migration based on economic choices ruled the late nineteenth and early twentieth centuries. Commercialization of farming, the introduction of industrial goods that ended crafts and part-time cottage industries compelled comparable numbers to seek income outside of their home communities. These migrations showed an amazing interdependence. The United States, with its huge economy and job opportunities, drew the lion's share of the transatlantic migrations. Migration to the United States depended on modern transportation and communication, as it did for all receiving countries. Many came to the United States with the short-term goal of earning money for their families in Europe and then returning home. Substantial numbers from eastern Europe chose to leave the United States for communities in western and eastern Europe. For these men and women, the United States remained a temporary destination and a place to accumulate resources. Of course even greater numbers remained in the United States, where they often filled jobs in construction, mining and heavy industry. Women, especially Irish Catholic women, took up work as servants in comfortable middle class homes.

Migrants from Europe also opted for destinations closer to home. Scandinavians who came to the United States also began to choose Germany in the late 1800s as her industrializing economy created a huge demand for migrant laborers and skilled workers. Poles, too, often chose Germany rather than the United States. Polish migrants filled farm labor jobs in eastern Germany and the industrial occupations in the Ruhr Valley in western

Germany. The Central European state's dynamic economy and its proximity made it a viable choice. Poles also moved in even greater numbers from the countryside to nearby industrial cities such as Warsaw. The land available to Poles, like many in eastern Europe, consisted of dwarf holdings incapable of sustaining families, and they saw their handicraft industries collapse as quality industrial goods from western and central Europe flooded the markets once dominated by household production. As Germany's economy continued to expand it also reduced to a trickle the number of Germans leaving for the United States.

Demand for labor also proved widespread in the Western Hemisphere. Admittedly the United States continued to attract millions of migrants. Yet, it remained just one of several national economies dependent on migrant laborers. Argentina built an economic strategy to sustain her wheat and beef business, which was based on migrant labor. Millions came from Italy and Spain to work the ranches and large farms on the Pampas. Their intentions, much as those of eastern Europeans who came to the United States, remained short term. The vibrant economy of Argentina that provided jobs for these young men depended on industrial markets in Great Britain and agricultural machinery largely manufactured in the United States. Economic changes worked in tandem from one end of the Atlantic world to the other.

Migration was always a two-way street. Migrants to Argentina came with specific goals that could be accomplished in a few years at most. Their needs suited the short-term demands of the landowners while enabling migrants to earn a substantial amount of money for their families in southern Europe. In the United States millions also returned home. Of course the money sent back added immensely to the wellbeing of the migrants' families. Scandinavian migrants returning from the United States also brought back political ideals that changed their home communities. Similarly, Polish migrants to Germany sent money back to their families, whose small farms failed to sustain peasant households.

Migration swept over the entire Atlantic world. Populations were uprooted and moved from one end of the industrial world to the other by choice and by necessity. The United States stood as a major destination for millions, yet a substantial number of Europeans chose other destinations.

Further reading

For a general description of the Atlantic migrations that considers all the states involved, see Walter Nugent, *Crossings: The Great Transatlantic Migration, 1870–1914* (Bloomington, Indiana, 1992). For a specific focus on return migrations from North America to Europe, see Mark Wyman, *Round-Trip to America: The Immigrant Return to Europe, 1880–1930* (Ithaca, 1997).

For an analysis of European migrants and migrations, see Dirk Hoerder, ed., *Labor Migrations in the Atlantic Economies: The European and North American Working Classes During the Period of Industrialization* (Westport, Connecticut, 1985); Leslie Moch,

Moving Europeans: Migration in Western Europe Since 1650 (Bloomington, Indiana, 2003); Klaus Bade, ed., *Population, Labour, and Migration in the 19th and 20th Century Germany* (New York, 1987); Dirk Hoerder, ed., *Distant Magnets: Expectations and Realities, 1840–1930* (New York, 1993); Kerby Miller, *Emigrants and Exiles: Ireland and the Irish Exodus to North America* (New York, 1988); Hasia R. Diner, *Erin's Daughters in America: Irish Immigrant Women in the Nineteenth Century* (Baltimore, 1984); Ewa Morawska, "Labor Migrations of Poles in the Atlantic World Economy, 1880–1914," *Comparative Studies in Society and History* 31 (1989), pp. 237–272; Colin Holmes, *John Bull's Island: Immigration and British Society, 1871–1971* (Hong Kong, 1998).

For an analysis of migration to raw material regions, see Jeremy Adelman, *Frontier Development: Land, Labor, and Capital on the Wheatlands of Argentina and Canada, 1890–1914* (New York, 1994) and Richard White, *It's Your Misfortune and None of My Own: A New History of the American West* (Norman, Oklahoma, 1991); José Moya, *Cousins and Strangers: Spanish Immigrants to Buenos Aires, 1850–1930* (Los Angeles, California, 1998).

Chapter 8

The United States and Latin America

Introduction

The economic power of the United States drew millions of migrants across both the Atlantic and Pacific Oceans. At the same time, this economic power played a major role in the United States' expansion beyond its borders. Many corporate and labor union leaders believed United States industry had saturated the country's domestic markets. They sought new avenues to resolve this vexing challenge. At the same time, some policy makers had ambitions that the United States should become a world power. For these men, power translated into a modern navy and the ability to project United States power overseas. The war with Spain in 1898 resolved the problems facing the domestic economy and the need to demonstrate the nation's power beyond its borders.

In moving beyond its borders, the United States relied on a combination of private and state resources. Typical of a state with a profound regard for the private sector, the federal government used its resources to promote the interests of large-scale corporations and investors who moved abroad in search of markets and raw materials. The United States government deployed its military might, its financial reputation and its technical expertise to facilitate the expansion of the state's major economic institutions. To accomplish these objectives the federal government developed an array of technical expertise in key industries that conducted business overseas. It also recruited men with managerial skills to build new bureaucracies capable of meeting the organizational challenges of foreign markets.

Under a series of presidents from McKinley to Woodrow Wilson the United States also developed an aggressive foreign policy. This new policy depended on United States fiscal resources, naval fleets and small contingents of United States marines. The United Sates government and its leaders generally preferred to avoid formal takeovers of polities in the Caribbean and the Americas, given the country's own republican traditions.

The central event precipitating the expansion of the United States was the Spanish-American War of 1898. Victory extended United States power into the Caribbean and into the Pacific. For the first time in its history, the United

States exercised significant power beyond its borders. In the past expansion had always been within North America and relied on the spread of United States citizens into annexed territories. In these citizens developed the land, set up governments and participated in removing indigenous peoples who had claimed the territory. Once the residents set up a functioning government and the territory reached a certain population level, the federal government admitted it to the Union as a state.

In Cuba and elsewhere, the United States had none of these resources and had to fashion new policies to govern foreign peoples. It typically sent trained administrators, who organized services and governing structures. The United States also realized the need to preserve the stability of regimes in the Caribbean to insure markets and sources of raw materials. United States companies and agents moved throughout large parts of the Caribbean and Central America pursuing such ends. In South America, these men worked closely with governments to sustain healthy economies. By the 1920s the United States had established its power throughout Latin America.

The professional-managerial capacity of the federal government

The capacity of the federal government to expand the power of the United States overseas depended on its growing technical and organizational abilities. The professional-managerial capacities of the private sector convinced many in government of the need to develop similar skills to promote United States interests overseas. Well aware of the deficiencies of the federal government in comparison with the organizationally and technically sophisticated corporations, President Theodore Roosevelt supported measures designed to enhance such capacities. In 1906 the Lodge Bill and a formal order written by Roosevelt transformed the consular service. These actions created a service based on merit and promotion among consular employees. The government also raised the salaries of the consular personnel. These measures were clearly intended to upgrade the professional status of federal bureaucrats who dealt with foreign trade. Previously these positions provided sinecures for individuals seeking patronage jobs. Merit and achievement played a small role in their appointments.

The government also empowered its diplomats to work closely with business interests. This policy accommodated a foreign policy designed to promote business initiatives overseas and, in fact, allowed private agencies to take the lead in developing relationships with other states. Congress also ordered its personnel to collect data on global markets that consumed United States-produced goods. United States overseas agents increasingly demonstrated the same abilities and technical expertise found in multinational corporations such as the United Fruit Company.

Roosevelt's successor, William Howard Taft, continued the policy of professionalizing the diplomatic corps and enhancing its expertise. Taft's first assistant secretary of state, Francis Huntington Wilson, expanded the State Department's personnel to include Latin American specialists. Assignments based on training, experience and knowledge led to such appointments and gave the State Department capabilities it previously lacked in a region central to United States prosperity. Taft's successor, Woodrow Wilson, developed systems of collecting information to evaluate the increasing volume of data flowing into the State Department from these regions.

During the post-World War I era the federal bureaucracy continued to develop its professional ethos and expertise. Under President Calvin Coolidge Congress passed the Rodgers Act in 1924, which increased the salaries of diplomats and consular employees. The Act also emphasized professional achievement and created the U.S. Foreign Service out of the diplomatic and consular corps. The Bureau of Foreign and Domestic Commerce positioned its attachés in the major urban centers across the globe. The agency also designated its qualified personnel to collect information on the automobile and paper industries to assist their managers in marketing and selling U.S.-made goods. In keeping with the theme of private corporations realizing the government goal of promoting economic expansion, this research provided businesses with critical information dealing with their markets and foreign competitors. Government even stepped in to provide private enterprise with data on the post-World War I global economic landscape.

The United States Congress also contributed to the competitiveness of United States overseas corporations and investors. The Federal Reserve Act of 1913 enabled banks to set up branches in foreign markets. United States corporations such as heavy manufacturing behemoth U.S. Steel agreed to run their financial affairs through United States overseas banking branches. First National City Bank took the lead in this effort. By 1920 the New York City Bank counted some 120 overseas outlets compared to a handful at the outbreak of World War I. Congress also passed an act to allow banks to purchase shares in corporations that conducted business abroad. United States companies now enjoyed a full range of services and support from both public and private institutions. These companies also benefited directly from World War I, which pinched off the flow of goods and capital from European producers and enabled the United States banks and corporations to displace Great Britain, the dominant European power in Latin America, and Imperial Germany, which had exercised considerable economic muscle in Central America.

Recognizing the advantages that competing foreign companies enjoyed through overseas cartels, Congress passed the Webb-Crone Act in 1918 that empowered United States companies operating overseas to form cartels, outlawed within the continental United States. While contrary to United States political traditions, policy makers knew full well that overseas competitors used such tactics in their attempt to extend economic influence.

The Spanish–American War and the expansion of the United States

The United States began its overseas expansion into Latin America with the Spanish–American War of 1898. Unlike European powers, the United States proved reluctant to annex Cuba. Its leaders saw that the defeat of Spain, a declining European imperial power, and the subsequent liberation of Cuba hardly justified making the island a colony. Within the United States many in positions of power opposed a colonial venture due to their own republican tradition of self-government. In keeping with this tradition, opponents of the war persuaded President William McKinley to accept the Teller Amendment (April, 1898) that Cuba would remain free and independent once the United States defeated Spain.

Yet, almost in contradistinction, the United States later declared its right to intervene in Cuban affairs in the Platt Amendment. This measure intended to protect the property rights and expanding ownership of land by United States companies and investors. This policy enabled United States private interests to control crops, labor and, ultimately, markets. The Platt Amendment legitimized the deployment of United States troops to secure property rights and safeguard United States citizens and residents of Cuba. United States troops moved into the island state several times after 1903 to insure political stability and to protect the property of United States interests. As important, United States government-backed agents brokered loans from United States banks for Cuba that sustained its solvency. These made Cuba financially dependent on the United States while diminishing the possibility of public debt, banned under the Platt Amendment.

In this regard the United States differed little from Great Britain, which used its diplomatic and financial personnel to establish a financial protectorate over Egypt. The North African state ended up fiscally subservient to British interests while the state's sugar- and cotton-bearing land came under British control. London also deployed colonial troops to secure political stability and the rights of British companies and investors. In fact, Roosevelt praised the British success in North Africa. As the United States expanded its presence in the Caribbean it also sent its financial experts to Egypt to study British methods.

The United States entered a Cuba already engaged in a rebellion. This uprising promised a social and political revolution once the Cubans removed the Spanish bourgeoisie and Spanish administrators, the face of the colonial state. The United States' intrusion derailed the uprising and preserved Cuba's Spanish bourgeoisie. In doing so, the United States enabled the Spanish bourgeoisie to maintain its position in Cuban society.

In fact, the United States urged the members of Spanish bourgeoisie to remain in Cuba rather than return to the Iberian Peninsula. The *Peninsulares*, as the bourgeoisie were known, benefited from the United States presence. At the same time, the United States also encouraged migration from Spain to bolster the Spanish-born community. The *Peninsulares* openly embraced the United States and anticipated lavish patronage in return for their support. The island's leaders realized the United States could provide protection against the Cuban revolutionaries, the *Independentistia*. Of course the *Peninsulares* rarely generated enthusiasm among those who fought the Spanish colonial authorities and simply could never build a majority sufficient to win elections, despite United States backing. Unable to rely on the *Peninsulares*, the United States resorted to the Platt Amendment as a more secure way to shape Cuban affairs.

From the beginning of the occupation, the United States' policies anticipated the North American state's goals in Cuba. Led by Governor Leonard Wood, occupation officials attempted to create a modern social order that surprisingly complemented the modern corporate society. Wood made every effort to provide safeguards for property ownership and to make private property unassailable. His refusal to extend suspension on debt obligations of Cuban planters facilitated the transfer of substantial amounts of land to large United States owned companies. Foreclosures that occurred on a large scale crippled the Cuban sugar planters as a group. He also ordered the creation of special courts designed to break up villages based on communal ownership, inimical to commercial sugar production. Such a transformation typified states such as the Mexican republic, where traditional landholding conflicted with export-driven agriculture. In fact, modern industrial states pushed the capitalist notion of private property over communal systems wherever the possibility existed for modern agricultural enterprise.

The impact of United States corporations on Cuba

United States investments flooded into Cuba in during the occupation. United States capital revived the island's main export industry, sugar, and restored its prominence among producers throughout the world. United States companies took advantage of the desperate state of the Cuban sugar producers, whose land and sugar-processing facilities lay in ruin in the wake of the turmoil of the mid- and late 1890s. Faced with debt and no capital reserves Cuban sugar producers sold out largely to United States buyers. Yields in the mid-1890s, amounted to roughly $50,000,000 and sunk to new lows by the early 1900s. By the outbreak of World War I, this total exceeded $200,000,000. United States companies also merged sugar-processing sites under legal holding companies in an attempt to make the enterprise more efficient. The introduction of new technology from the United States increased dramatically the output among sugar estates on the island.

In fact, United States engineers and technical expertise made the processing of sugar a machine-driven enterprise in perpetual motion that reduced the time involved and increased the volume. Virtually every aspect of milling underwent significant change because of new machinery and more efficient management of resources. United States engineers and chemists would come to dominate the technical fields of the industry. These professionals and United States managers rationalized and made the work site far less personable and more professional. By the mid-1920s United States companies had invested some $750,000,000 into the Cuban sugar industry. Major corporations dependent on sugar, notably Hershey, a chocolate producer, and Coca Cola and Charles Hires, soda manufacturers, placed substantial amounts of money in Cuban sugar plantations and sugar processing refineries.

Of course, a tide of United States citizens came with these companies and the military occupation. Engineers, skilled workers, professionals, office workers, soldiers and many others entered Cuba in the wake of the United States victory. In fact, so many plumbers arrived that their numbers justified the formation of a Labor Union situated in Havana. The presence of so many of these highly skilled craftsmen also demonstrated the extensive infrastructure rebuilding undertaken by United States companies. In general the United States restored much of the economy that had suffered during the rebellion of the 1890s and the war of 1898.

Education, too, assumed a vital role in shaping the perceptions of Cuban youth. United States textbooks served as the medium of instruction. Students learned United States history and acquired an understanding of North American-style civics. United States officials also adopted a New York City program encouraging Cubans to embrace the values of United States society. The United States also developed programs at its universities to train Cuban teachers. Hundreds of Cuban teachers spent summers at Harvard enhancing their knowledge and classroom techniques under the direction of the North American faculty. Other institutions of higher learning in the United States developed their own programs to enhance Cuban pedagogic abilities.

Occupation governor, General Leonard Wood, saw education as a means to imprint United States culture on the Cuban young, and through exchange programs on their teachers. Wood saw a future Cuba as a version of the United States and even imagined Cuba to be of Anglo-Saxon origin. Later, United States corporations picked up the task of attempting to transform Cuba and its people, though often with less success. These cultural exchanges persisted beyond the diplomatic and martial actions of the United States and, in many ways, previewed the expansion of United States' consumer culture across the globe in the late twentieth century.

North American communities, usually founded by United States corporations operating in Cuba, stood as the most visible and often inflammatory sign of the expanding United States presence. North American corporate employees and their supervisors carried their own material expectations. Companies such as General Electric and Bethlehem Steel more than met these expectations. Residential infrastructure included basics from water to electricity while amenities such as trees, shaded sidewalks, tennis courts and golf courses appeared in these towns. Corporate employees introduced United States' holidays and ritual to Cuban life. Christmas (December 25) replaced King's Day (January 6). Fourth of July celebrations and Thanksgiving Day feasts created a social calendar distinctly North American and involved Cubans as guests, servants or workers. Cubans who attended or sustained these events through their labors spoke English. Many in the Cuban world expressed anger over the material distinctions between their towns and those of the North Americans, known among Cubans as *la zona Americana* or *el barrio Americano*.

The reaction of Cubans to United States corporations

With so many United States corporations operating in Cuba, many Cubans worked for these companies. The United States corporations brought their cultural forms with them and expected Cubans to live up to their demands. Negotiations played no role in the thinking of United States managers. Unlike consumer goods or English fluency, which were desired by many Cubans, workplace discipline United States-style often provoked anger, resentment and often resistance, much as it did in North America. Even the small-scale island businessmen and the Cuban middle class complained bitterly about the dominance of the United States.

In the face of labor opposition, United States corporations turned to foreign workers as a solution. Assuming the lead, United States sugar corporations successfully pressured the government in 1912 to allow migration from Haiti and Jamaica. By the end of the 1920s, the workforce in the sugar industry drew a third of its number from these two islands. In response Cuban workers called for "preferential" hiring for their peers over foreign-born laborers with little or no success.

Such tensions accelerated strikes throughout the 1920s. These focused on control of the workplace and, inevitably, wages. Communities threw their support behind the Cuban workers since the companies usually operated under United States ownership. A national sentiment permeated the discussions of labor and capital in Cuba. Migrant workers, the increasing ability of United States engineers to direct work, and mechanization undermined the Cuban efforts.

United States corporate culture stood at both ends of the debate. It produced the novel goods that symbolized modernity while demanding that Cubans produce more goods for their markets. The corporations created a multiethnic workforce that affected both Cuba and the other island societies in the Caribbean and Central America. These same issues filled the debates between capital and labor in the United States and throughout South America wherever United States corporations set up shop.

The United States and Central America

Under Theodore Roosevelt, who succeeded the assassinated William McKinley as President in 1901, the United States developed a far more aggressive policy toward her neighbors to the south beyond Cuba. Roosevelt issued his famous Corollary to the Monroe Doctrine in 1904. It changed fundamentally the thrust of the Monroe Doctrine that intended to preserve the sovereignty of states in the Americas. The Corollary sanctioned United States intervention when it deemed such action necessary to prevent financial and political collapse. Roosevelt focused on two polities central to United States policies in the Americas, the Panama Canal and the Dominican Republic. The canal provided critical economic and strategic advantages. United States policy makers saw it as essential for sustaining the state's expanding global reach.

An isthmian canal stood at the center of Roosevelt's vision of the United States as a major power. The canal was intended to provide the United States with a far shorter and infinitely less dangerous route from the Atlantic basin to the Pacific coast and the resources of coastal states such as Chile and Peru. The canal would also facilitate the movements of goods from one economic region to another. Certainly, such an ambition enjoyed a vigorous life during the gold rushes of the nineteenth century. Financial backers in New York City invested their resources in constructing a railroad across the Panamanian isthmus, and from that moment onward the United States dominated the region. The canal, once built, would also give the United States a tremendous strategic advantage since its navy could easily shift resources between the oceans.

The United States worked closely with the men who engineered the revolution that created an independent Panama. Once the Panamanian state achieved independence, Roosevelt's representatives negotiated a treaty for the right to build a canal from Colón on the Caribbean coast to Panama City on the Pacific coast. The Hay-Bunau-Varilla Treaty gave the United States unlimited power in the Canal Zone, in effect a sovereign territory within the new state of Panama. Colombians expressed outrage over United States actions, while Panamanian leaders remained angry over the absence of their representatives, yet the United States occupation remained uncontested until the late twentieth century. The six-mile-wide Canal Zone opened countless possibilities for the United States. With troops stationed in the Canal Zone and construction completed in 1914, the United States connected the vibrant economies of the east coast and the Caribbean with those of the eastern Pacific.

The United States put its stamp on the isthmian zone in other ways. Her sophisticated machinery and her public health and medical capacities made the construction of the canal a reality by overcoming natural and biological obstacles. A project of almost unimaginable dimensions, the canal demanded machinery of immense capacity to excavate hundreds of tons of earth and to build double locks large enough to accommodate ocean-going ships. The

United States also brought professional expertise, in this case medical doctors and public health specialists who accompanied the many engineers and hydraulic specialists who directed the building of the canal. Their knowledge diminished considerably the deadly diseases such as malaria and yellow fever that threatened the entire project.

Once completed, the canal facilitated the movement of mass produced goods, raw materials and foodstuffs between the Caribbean and Atlantic basins to the Pacific basin. The canal also greatly enhanced the movement of information, freight and passengers. The canal, combined with the networks of United States naval bases, harbors and protectorates, gave its fleets access to all regions of the Atlantic and Pacific in a fairly short time. The Panama Canal met both the economic and the strategic goals of United States policy makers and corporate leaders.

Roosevelt's vision of an unchallenged United States in the Western Hemisphere faced its main opposition in the isthmian states from Germany. Imperial Germany acted as a major economic force in Central America. In tandem with Great Britain, Germany was a source of major investments in the region. By the earlier decades of the twentieth century, German companies had carved out niches in Guatemala and elsewhere in Central America. German capital also sustained economic activities in the region, while Germany provided rich markets for Guatemalan, Costa Rican, Nicaraguan and El Salvadorian coffee. Much like their United States counterparts in late nineteenth-century Mexico, German businessmen built transportation and communications infrastructures in states that bordered the Atlantic Gulf coast. Railroads, telegraph and port services all resulted from these efforts that intended to facilitate the export of coffee, the main commodity of region.

United States planning for the Panama Canal made policy makers aware of the presence of Germany as a force in the region. The quality and suitability of United States machinery, its more efficient business practices, and the growing power of its corporations facilitated the ascendancy of the North American state among the isthmian states after 1900. United States corporations made significant headway in states such as Guatemala and Honduras, and dramatically so after 1914. Competition with Great Britain and the outbreak of World War I drew almost all German resources from Central America. The United States, already positioned by the actions of its corporations, quickly moved into Central America as the Germans vacated their holdings in the region. Great Britain, too, faced United States assaults on its position in the region, even aside from the disruption of World War I. Typically, these appeared in the form of United States corporations, most notably United Fruit. As the dominant United States company in Central America, United Fruit carried substantial economic and political clout, and turned British Honduras into an economic dependency of the United States. Ruled by a small resident elite of British nationals, largely merchants, British Honduras depended on mahogany exports. The colony's banana producing potential eventually drew the attention of United States companies, particularly United Fruit, based in Boston. United Fruit moved into British Honduras in order to buy up land and consolidate landholdings.

As the largest producer of bananas in Central America and with control over the shipping lanes, United Fruit presented one choice to British officials in British Honduras: work with the United States company. British administrators, eager to develop available agricultural export industry, willingly joined forces with United Fruit. Eventually, London raised the money to build a major rail line that greatly facilitated the emerging banana industry. By 1910, United Fruit bought up land in a number of banana producing areas of British Honduras. World War I crippled the mahogany markets while the banana consumer market in the United States soared. Those in British Honduras who favored United Fruit came to dominate the legislative body by 1920. Resistance by local mahogany producers failed to overcome the enormous power of United Fruit. By World War II, British Honduras, formally a British colonial possession of Great Britain, in reality existed as an economic dependency of the United States, its corporations and its rich markets for tropical fruit.

The United States and the Dominican Republic

The Dominican Republic posed another challenge to Roosevelt in his efforts to make the United States the dominant power in the Western Hemisphere. The island state faced a growing debt crisis and the potential instability associated with bankruptcy, the very combination Roosevelt warned Latin American states to avoid. Roosevelt vigorously responded to the debt crisis that engulfed the Dominican Republic. While the name 'dollar diplomacy' is attached to William Howard Taft, Roosevelt actually developed the basic policy of using financial loans provided by private United States Banks to debtor states in Latin America during his years as president.

Much of what constituted this approach grew out of United States business practices among large-scale banks and companies in the late nineteenth century. Jay Cook pioneered loans to the federal government. He financed much of the Civil War loans through bonds. He subsequently persuaded a number of major financial houses to guarantee Pennsylvania Railroad bonds issued in the year 1870. This investment in major economic institutions yielded huge profits and created the basis for other banks to follow suit. Eventually investment banking concentrated in New York City, the major transportation and financial hub in the northeast. Large, sophisticated banks assumed the funding of railroads, the largest enterprises in the world. Investment banks then developed the sophistication to handle large-scale, complicated loans. At the same time, financial advisors who brokered these loans developed their own degree of professionalism. The financial skills built up during the late nineteenth century, the sophistication of the financial advisors, and the capacity of the major investment banks to assemble large amounts of capital and monitor subsequent loans provided the very foundation for the dollar diplomacy of the twentieth century.

As in the case of so many new professions, financial specialists acquired their first credentials in the universities that developed legitimizing curricula for the practitioners of new empirical disciplines. Economics as a major field appeared in United States universities during the late 1800s, and by the 1920s a new subfield, international economics, developed. One of the leading financial advisors of the era, Edward Kemmerer, who brokered loans to financially troubled states, held the inaugural chair in International Economics at Princeton in the late 1920s. Such developments gave authority to the new field and carried substantial weight when these financial advisors brought their new scientific knowledge to states such as the Dominican Republic. Professional associations such as the American Economics Association and the American Institute of Accountants greatly enhanced the reputation of financial advisors. Demands for quality and specific training, along with restricted access to the profession, validated these men and their careers. The financial experts acted as the new symbols of authority backed by scientific knowledge and an array of credentials.

Roosevelt and his successors incorporated financial experts as the centerpiece in executing their policies toward other Latin American states. These financial advisors assisted in reorganizing a state's fiscal affairs and in adopting the gold standard as part of the reforms intended to restore financial stability to troubled states. The advisors also worked out loan arrangements with a major United States bank that would provide the capital in the form of a loan. The State Department provided a list of approved banks and in the case of what contemporaries labeled the 'controlled loan' installed a qualified individual to run the customs house, the main source of revenue for the borrowing country. In all cases, the troubled states depended on an export crop or commodity intended for United States markets and imports from the United States to help sustain the economy. The presence of the United States government as a guarantor for these loans encouraged private banks to participate. In cases where neither a customs supervisor nor the military appeared, banks depended on the State Department's approval of the loan and the presence of a United States trained financial expert to demonstrate the future creditworthiness of the debtor state.

Roosevelt used this approach in dealing with the debt crisis of the Dominican Republic. In 1904 the Dominican Republic faced European creditors demanding repayment and backing this demand with warships. The island republic also housed a superb harbor and stood astride the water route to the Panama Canal. This location meant the Dominican Republic held substantial strategic advantages the United States wanted to claim and certainly wanted to keep out of the hands of European powers.

For Roosevelt the Dominican crisis sternly tested his corollary. It also embodied the twin threats of fiscal mismanagement and the ensuing political disorder, neither of which Roosevelt would tolerate. Worried over alleged opposition to the strong-arm methods used to make Cuba a protectorate, Roosevelt and his advisors adopted a dependency scheme based on financial control of the Dominican economy. Eventually, this scheme incorporated the financial advisor skilled in international finance, the private bank secure in the knowledge of government participation to minimize risk and the activist government relying on a private agency to realize foreign policy goals. The receiver general recommended by Roosevelt and paid by the Dominican Republic took control of the island's customs house. The receiver general monitored the Republic's revenues while the investment-banking house of Kuhn, Loeb and Company provided the loan to bail out the Republic. United States bankers agreed to participate because of the presence of the United States government. A financial advisor who specialized in international banking negotiated the controlled loan.

The loan satisfied the aims of United States policy makers. It also met the needs of Dominican leaders. They fully anticipated that United States involvement would rescue them from certain bankruptcy and would protect them from European creditors. The loan also stabilized the export sector, consisting mainly of sugar, and fended off internal opposition. For both parties, the controlled loan of 1907 met expectations.

William Howard Taft, Roosevelt's immediate successor, and secretary of his Treasury, Frank Knox, continued Roosevelt's policies of a political loan. They actually coined the term dollar diplomacy. For them it also meant substituting money for bullets and diminishing the role of the military, so prominent in Cuba. Dollar diplomacy also acted as an adjunct to Roosevelt's corollary since it used United States bankers to remove Europeans from the fiscal affairs of the debtor state. The resulting stability and tax incentives for sugar producers on the island and importers on the North American mainland drew a legion of investors and entrepreneurs to the Republic.

Under Taft and his presidential successors United States leaders forcibly repeated Roosevelt's notion that the nation's prosperity relied on an economically healthy world system, a position consonant with Roosevelt's view of the domestic and the larger economy. Taft and his administration pursued every angle to promote loans by private banks as a means of moving capital to countries where United States companies hoped to sell their goods. Such a policy reflected the United States' expanding role as the major global creditor and the largest holder of gold in the world. By moving capital to potential markets, the United States and its private agencies, the investment bankers, created new consumers and stable regimes, both essential for prosperous capitalist exchanges. The State Department gave its approval that provided assurances to private lenders and, at the same time, minimized the role of the federal government.

Dollar diplomacy in various forms prospered through the administrations of Presidents Wilson, Harding, Coolidge and Hoover. Under Wilson the United

States added force to dollar diplomacy and expanded it to regimes such as Haiti and Nicaragua. He also installed teams of highly specialized professionals who oversaw every aspect of the Dominican economy from taxes to budgets. Ironically, the United States sent marine contingents to insure order in the Republic. Despite the open pacific intent of dollar diplomacy, marines remained a bulwark in the Dominican Republic through the early 1920s, and into the 1930s for Haiti and Nicaragua where troops restored order and/or suppressed opposition to United States policies. The combination of force, technical experts, and controlled loans, the same assets used by the British to build their influence, expanded and sustained United States power in Latin America.

The United States and financial protectorates

The United States used another approach to deal with many states in South America. The United States continued to rely on the financial advisor and the private bank, in fact to the exclusion of troops and appointed customs directors. The government still operated through a network of financial advisors approved by the State Department. Yet, these advisors operated outside of official United States approval. They carried the official stamp of the government and used their expertise to recommend solutions to fiscal problems states confronted. As anticipated, states under financial duress enlisted the aid of these unofficial government experts to resolve fiscal difficulties that threatened the solvency of regimes in South America. Their successes rescued troubled governments such as Peru and Colombia throughout Latin America. Stable governments and healthy markets proved central to United States interests in South America as elsewhere in the Western Hemisphere. This approach avoided the introduction of troops and resources at a time when government officials worried over accusations of imperialism.

Edward Kemmerer stood as the leading figure among the network of financial advisors who, in effect, conducted United States foreign policy. He played a major role in developing dollar diplomacy. He also recruited and trained a number of acolytes who carried his approach to numerous states. University trained and employed, Kemmerer acquired substantial experience working in financial affairs in the United States colonial government in the Philippines. There he successfully reformed the currency so vital to United States interests.

The United States government then sent him to Egypt as a special commissioner to investigate the banking reforms the British intended to implement to improve the fiscal state of its protectorate. Egypt served as a model for the United States in its efforts to build financial protectorates such as in the Dominican Republic. It also provided valuable information for Kemmerer and others who established United States informal presence in states where the United States preferred to avoid the formal protectorate. Neither Kemmerer nor policy makers chose to ignore such a valuable experience as they drew up their own fiscal policies.

Kemmerer advertised himself as a scientific expert capable of transforming national economies. He claimed his policies could restore financial stability and reputation to a state in demanding fiscal circumstances. Once restored, states could then attract foreign investments to jumpstart their economies to the benefit of all. His successes in the 1920s seemed to validate his claims for scientific knowledge as a way to resolve fiscal troubles. The credentials of financial advisors from university positions to professional associations impressed potential borrowers and grew in importance as states such as Peru seemed to benefit from his insight.

At the center of the largest network of financial advisors who worked with governments in Latin America, Kemmerer and his disciples saw stability as their overall aim, the same outcome the United States government intended. The Kemmerer voluntary loan lacked the sting of the controlled loan and the United States recommended a receiver who, in effect, governed the economy of the borrowing country. The voluntary character of the Kemmerer loans and the absence of the United States government removed the possibility of nationalistic opposition to United States selected receivers. Yet, Kemmerer's success facilitated the expansion of United States economic and political leverage throughout the region.

Conclusion

The expansion of the United States into the Western Hemisphere gave it economic and often political power equivalent to that which the Europeans exercised in Africa. Yet, the United States eschewed imperial ambitions. Instead it worked with private corporations to achieve economic hegemony in the hemisphere. Presidents such as Theodore Roosevelt understood the need to build agencies capable of working with powerful private bureaucracies that ran the country's huge corporations. Federal organizational power and expertise grew dramatically in the early twentieth century and acquired capabilities unimaginable in the late nineteenth century. By the 1910s and 1920s public and private agencies intersected in many arenas, from data collection to economic evaluations of overseas markets. The United States expansion reflected its own political traditions and economic assets.

United States power depended critically on the sophistication of its investment banks and financial experts. These provided the means to create fiscal protectorates that gave the United States the ability to insure political stability throughout the Caribbean and much of Latin America. This stability, then, produced viable markets for United States corporations, and sources of critical raw materials. Instability opened up the possibility of European intrusion as well as civil unrest, neither of which promoted United States interests. Financial loans from United States banks created fiscal dependencies in the Western Hemisphere while financial experts introduced policies designed to preserve sound finances. These policies also aimed at creating fiscal capacities to repay the loans.

The financial juggernaut paved the way for United States corporations in island states such as Cuba and Central American polities including Nicaragua. United States power once confined to the continental North America moved with a speed equal to any European power. The United States and its private corporations moved the Germans out of Central America and eventually displaced the British in South America. The United States political power now complimented its economic interdependence with polities in Latin America. No power would dispute or challenge United States hegemony in the Western Hemisphere.

Further reading

For a general discussion of imperialism and its European context, see Timothy Mitchell, *The Rule of Experts: Egypt, Techno-Politics, Modernity* (Berkeley, 2002); Bernard Waites, *Europe and the Third World: From Colonialism to Decolonisation c. 1500–1998* (New York, 1999); Timothy Mitchell, *Colonising Egypt* (Berkeley, 1991). For the impact of the professional-managerial ethos on foreign policy, on the federal government of the United States and on Latin America, see Stephen Skowronek, *Building the New American State: The Expansion of National Administrative Capacities 1877–1820* (New York, 1986); Thomas F. O'Brien, *The Revolutionary Mission: American Enterprise in Latin America, 1900–1945* (New York, 1996); Emily Rosenberg, *Financial Missionaries to the World: The Politics and Culture of Dollar Diplomacy 1900–1930* (Durham, 2003) and *Spreading the American Dream: American Economic and Cultural Expansion, 1890–1945* (New York, 1982).

For a recent work connecting United States overseas expansion with continental expansion, see Fred Anderson and Andrew Cayton, *The Dominion of War: Empire and Liberty in North America, 1500–2000* (New York, 2005) and "American Wars of Liberty and Power," *The Chronicle of Higher Education* (December 6, 2004), B6–B9.

For an analysis of the United States' occupation of Haiti, see Hans Schmidt, *The United States' Occupation of Haiti, 1915–1934* (New Brunswick, 1971); Mary Renda, *Taking Haiti: Military Occupation and the Culture of U.S. Imperialism, 1915–1940* (Chapel Hill, 2001). For the United States' relationship with Cuba, see the wide-ranging and incisive Louis Perez, Jr. *On Becoming Cuban: Identity, Nationality, and Culture* (Chapel Hill, 1999) and his *Cuba Under the Platt Amendment 1920–1934* (Pittsburgh, 1986).

For the impact of the war of 1898, see Thomas Schoonover, *The War of 1898* (Baton Rouge, 2000). For a work that deals with the United States and Latin America in the twentieth century, see Mark T. Gilderhus, *The Second Century: U.S.–Latin American Relations Since 1889* (New York, 1999).

For collections of essays that cover many topics from cultural exchange to advertising, see Steve Striffer and Mark Moberg, eds., *Banana Wars: Power, Production, and History in the Americas* (Durham, 2003); Gilbert M. Joseph, Catherine LeGrand and Ricardo Salvatore, eds., *Close Encounters of Empire: Writing the Cultural History of U.S.-Latin American Relations* (Durham, 1999).

Chapter 9

The United States and the Pacific

Introduction

By the 1890s United States economic power far exceeded that of the other leading industrial powers. However, the overseas presence of industrial states such as Great Britain still dwarfed that of the United States. Near the end of the decade the United States embarked on a series of outward thrusts that made it a major player in the Pacific and increasingly in East Asia. The nation's military power opened the way, as it had in the Caribbean. Professionals and experts would follow in the wake of generals and soldiers.

The victory in the Spanish–American War of 1898 precipitated this expansion. At the end of hostilities the United States acquired the Philippines, its first formal colony. The United States saw the island chain as an opportunity to introduce democratic practices, in keeping with her own political world. The colonial administration set about establishing elections and improving the infrastructure of the Philippines. The United States' interest in the Philippines proved more strategic than economic. The assets of the island chain had limited value for the North American state, whereas the Filipinos saw the United States as a rich market for their goods.

The United States' commitment to these goals challenged policies of Imperial Japan, a new power ascendant in the Pacific and mainland Asia. In Japan the United States encountered an industrial power with ambitions very different to those it held. While the United States pursued its ambitions of trade in the Pacific and in China, Japan too was fashioning expansionist plans in Northeast Asia and commercial opportunities in China. Japan's rulers pursued their ambitions to build an empire in Northeast Asia. These men believed it imperative to acquire an empire to vindicate Japan's standing as a major power equal to Britain, France and other powers. As with their European counterparts, the Japanese saw colonies as sources of raw materials and potential markets for Japan's export-oriented industries.

The two states also developed competing policies toward China, where Japanese manufacturers and policy makers saw Japan's economic future. Japan operated in a geography where competitors, namely China and Russia, presented serious threats to her plans for empire. Ultimately, Japan and the United States collided over such issues and resolution came only through a brutal war (1941–1945) that decided which power would prevail.

The war of 1898 and the Philippines

The war of 1898 transformed the United States into a colonial power, even if a well-intended one. United States leaders such as naval officer Alfred T. Mahan, assistant secretary of the Navy, and future vice president and president, Theodore Roosevelt, among others saw the triumph as part of the country's grand destiny. Senator Albert Beveridge from Indiana even claimed that the United States held the right to govern the island chain. He further argued that the United States' racial destiny legitimized its capacity to rule an inferior people such as the Filipinos. Beveridge, Mahan and leaders with strategic concerns saw the Philippines as the "Gibraltar of the Pacific," essential for United States defensive concerns. None of this group proved eager to surrender their new possession.

As they secured their hold on the Pacific island chain, United States policy makers engaged in fierce debates about issues such as governance and political stability. Even as naval and ground forces took possession of their Filipino colony, national leaders argued vigorously over such an act, one out of keeping with the nation's republican traditions. United States policy makers also understood full well that the seizure of the Philippines placed the United States in the imperial club. To counter this association, the United States introduced elections and full citizenship to all Filipinos. The United States president and administrators in Washington announced their intentions to give the Filipinos the capacity of self-governance denied them for so long by their former Spanish rulers. The United States even banned the use of the word colonial from its records and it placed the Philippines under the Office of Insular Affairs rather creating a formal colonial office, the normal practice among European powers.

Some Filipinos objected and took up arms to demonstrate their opposition to United States rule. This act provoked a furious response by the United States. Fully 126,000 troops confronted Filipino rebels in a vicious conflict that lasted three years, 1899–1902, and left over 200,000 Filipinos dead, an even greater number wounded and much of the Filipino countryside devastated. The United States officials also relocated villagers to what the United States Army deemed secure areas. Sporadic resistance continued in Muslim-dominated Mindanao until 1913, yet, for all practical purposes, the national movement ended by 1902. The United States showed its determination to defeat all resistance to its rule.

Governing a colony

The United States relied on its own political traditions in devising schemes to administer its new colonial possession. Two styles of governing accompanied

United States administrators. One system depended on decentralized rule that typified the United States in the nineteenth century. In this scheme, political bosses carried the weight of governing through networks of lieutenants who remained in close contact with the voting constituencies. In exchange for support, bosses and their political machines used their resources to satisfy the needs of their supporters. Of course in return, their supporters delivered votes and hopefully victories to the bosses and their political parties.

The progressive movement in the United States embodied the other method of governance. The professional-managerial advocates who drove this approach drew their inspiration from technical and knowledge-based corporations and professional associations. Progressives intended to remove the patronage-oriented political machines that ignored rationality and efficiency as a means of governing. They sought to restructure government along the lines of the private sector corporations that privileged expertise and professional competency in administering public services, not favoritism and partisanship that marked the political machines and bosses. Disinterest, performance and quality outcomes characterized the domestic progressives. Elected officials, too, won office based on their professional and business qualifications and not on party or personal loyalty. Colonial administrators who embraced the progressive spirit and ideas built public executive agencies that incorporated the power of decision making and the expertise and disinterest quality that guided the true progressive on the mainland.

William Howard Taft symbolized the tension between the patronage scheme and the professional-managerial approach. He assumed direction of the Philippines in 1902. As a veteran of Cincinnati and Ohio politics, Taft knew well how political machines functioned at every level. Urban political bosses such as George Cox of Cincinnati and state politicos, notably Joseph Foraker and his supporters, backed Taft's programs and policies in the United States Congress. Relying on the machine-style politics in developing relations with the Filipino leaders, Taft established close ties with Filipino leaders drawn from the landowning *Mestizo* class that had begun appear after the 1750s. These ties attached the landowners to the colonial administration through mutual interests and exchanges of political favors. Taft even donated money to the island colony's first political party, the *Federalistas*; an organization Taft believed could promote Americanization. He also gave the party members privileged access to jobs that he officially reserved for Filipinos. Some 200,000 recruits flocked to party banners in hopes of securing the benefits of the United States' patronage of the *Federalistas*. "Pork barrel" legislation that grew out of this patronage system developed into a hallmark of Filipino politics much as it did in the United States. From this association the landowners developed into a national oligarchy that thrived under United States patronage.

Yet, Taft acted as a good progressive in his capacity as governor general of the colony. He saw the Philippines as an arena where colonial administrators could realize progressive ideas such as efficiency in government. Under his direction, bureaucrats charged with running the colony introduced notions of expertise and knowledge-based, professionally run agencies that developed policies in the interest of all Filipinos rather than specific constituencies. For example, the Executive Bureau created standardized means of managing government at all levels throughout the island chain. This included finance, taxation and handling local affairs. To accomplish these ends the Bureau centralized decision making and ordered careful monitoring of agencies and individuals under its purview in the same fashion as occurred in large-scale corporations. It remained avowedly nonpartisan and acted in the best interests of the governed. Other offices, notably that of the Insular Auditor who reviewed all expenses of government in the Philippines, operated on the same principles. The calculating mentality of the United States professional and managerial groups made its mark on Filipino governmental affairs.

United States administrators also set up a civil service that recruited on the basis of talent and competency. The civil service stood as one of the progressive movement's outstanding achievements in the United States. In 1913, the United States replaced the majority of its civil service personnel with Filipinos, demonstrating the effectiveness of training young and able Filipinos for responsible positions. Recruited on merit, they continued to perform at high levels until the United States turned over complete control of the civil service to Filipinos in 1920. The civil service stood as one of the visible results of the United States reforms.

The occupation also created an educational system that drew its students from the rising sons of the middle and even lower class families. English provided the medium for education and helped prepare rising talent for careers in the Filipino bureaucracy that relied on English. Introducing English marked a colonial decision and compelled educated Filipinos, among others, to master a foreign language and to conduct business in this tongue. The United States also added institutions of higher learning; again instruction and reading occurred in English. Occupation officials established quality universities modeled after those in the United States. Unlike the French, for example, that recruited able young men who attended university in France, United States personnel built the University of the Philippines in Manila. It gave its students a substantive education and content-based professional degrees. This outcome reflected the egalitarian and democratic ethos of the United States colonial administration. At the same time it created a cadre of managers and professionals able to deliver quality services distinct from the landed elites who filled the patronage networks.

Colonial administrators' plans for reshaping Filipino society in part through mass education of the population never fully materialized. The administrators counted on revenues from sugar production. Yet the United States Congress refused to extend relatively light duties on Filipino sugar entering the United States in the 1902 Tariff and this decision radically reduced the money flow into the islands. It also discouraged United States investors from placing money in the island economy. Congress even placed limits on the amount of land a company could own.

As a result, United States officials faced the prospects of working through the landowning *Mestizo* class favored by Taft. Local leadership groups monopolized office holding in the first decade, a pattern that would hold for decades into the future. United States administrators had to work with the willing collaborators among the elite. They could provide the resources absent in the United States camp and knew full well how to maintain their hold on the island economy and society.

The United States and the Filipino infrastructure

The United States also deployed its physical resources to improve the infrastructure of the Philippines, much as it did in Cuba and elsewhere in the Caribbean and Central America. In fact, European powers engaged in such activities for several decades before the United States took up such tasks. In an effort to provide fiscal stability, a policy almost universal in Latin America for the United States, fiscal advisors reformed the island colony's currency. Its engineers modernized port facilities in Manila and in other Philippine ports to facilitate handling the large, sophisticated ships that carried freight across the Pacific. The United States administrators also oversaw the construction of a major road system throughout the island chain. The roads accelerated the shift from subsistence to commercial farming as sugar, tobacco, hemp and coconuts replaced rice, corn and other food crops. Since the United States lowered the duties for Filipino products in the 1909 Tariff and provided the majority of imports, the island economy developed an almost permanent attachment to the United States economy. Of course, United States-made products considerably dampened local efforts to develop domestic industry and created dependencies at all levels of the Filipino economy and society.

Along with growing ties between their economies, United States consumer industries began to promote and sell personal items closely identified with tastes and fashion in the United States. Elite Filipinos, and even ordinary Filipinos with sufficient money, embraced United States styles in clothing and behavior. United States popular songs accompanied the widespread adoption of the English language. Popular culture clearly made its way into Filipino consumer choices and manners, as had occurred in Cuba. Dependency at a personal level marked Filipino society within a decade of United States occupation and colonial rule.

Race and the Filipino colony

The United States personnel also brought their racial codes with them. These flourished in United States occupations in Cuba, Puerto Rico, Haiti, the Dominican Republic and, in fact, in any location where white officials encountered people of color. Just as interracial marriage stigmatized the white person in a United States protectorate in the Caribbean so, too, did it mark those white men who chose Filipino women as wives. This decision earned grooms the nickname "Squaw Man." Clubs such as those in Manila also banned Filipinos on the basis of color. Locals could work as servants in United States clubs but never appear as members.

United States residents even built a secluded community two hundred miles distant from the heat and diversity of Manila. Comparable to the British hideaway towns in India such as Darjeeling, the mountain community of Baguio housed North American families in United States-style housing. Large gabled houses surrounded by green lawns provided United States residents with the familiarity of home in a climate drier than that found along the coast. Social practices and racial codes that governed the United States proved every bit as powerful as the democratic ethos United States officials wished to establish among the Filipinos.

Learning from other colonial powers

United States officials discovered that their lack of experience in governing a colonial population posed a serious challenge. Since administrators in other colonial settings confronted these problems, United States administrators increasingly turned to them for advice. United States officials and colonial experts visited European colonies to develop a better understanding of the issues facing them in the Philippines.

Modern transportation greatly facilitated these excursions. Steamship lines serviced all the key ports in Southeast and East Asia and made such journeys relatively short and comfortable. United States officials departing from Manila could reach Hong Kong in three days by the end of the nineteenth century. The British India Steamship Company made the trip from Manila to Calcutta every twenty-one days. The same technology that facilitated the movement of goods and passengers across the Pacific and the Atlantic oceans also made possible the professional and diplomatic exchanges within Asian waters.

Capitalizing on these resources, United States officials traveled all over Southeast Asia, with frequent stops at places such as Dutch-controlled Java and the British-ruled Straits settlements of Malaya. United States colonial officials and experts met with their counterparts to discuss a broad array of topics such as public health and farming. For example, a prominent member of the United States Philippine Commission sailed to the British colony of Northern Borneo to learn what techniques the British employed to rule colonial peoples as the United States faced in the Philippines. Similarly, United States officials toured Singapore's plantations that sustained the city's rubber and tapioca driven economy. United States officials clearly hoped to acquire as much knowledge as possible about running plantation economies in the tropics.

These officials also attended inter-imperial conferences that featured talks on common problems of governing and maintaining colonial populations and sustaining their economies. The Belgians and Portuguese also worked with British and French officials in developing knowledge about military strategies for subduing the colonial population and upholding colonial authority. Such information aided colonial powers, including the United States, in effectively running their colonies.

Decision makers and those who carried out their policies also spent a good deal of time studying the topic of colonial governance. These men clearly understood the broader imperial world and the importance of carefully investigating the experiences of Europeans and their interactions with colonial populations. In his book, *The Administration of Dependencies*, Alpheus Snow urged policy makers to study the governing tactics Europeans employed throughout the colonial world and to provide a guide for United States administrators. Similarly, Senator Henry Cabot Lodge of Massachusetts authored a critical bibliography on colonial rule intended to assist United States colonial administrators in their tasks. These accounts formed part of a larger literature available to United States policy makers. Clearly, these efforts demonstrated that United States colonial officials recognized the larger imperial world and the returns available from a careful consideration of European experiences.

The treaty system and the Chinese market

The Philippines made the United States a major player in the western Pacific. It also provided a launching pad for those constituencies that eagerly looked to the Chinese market. The allure of the rich markets in China proved irresistible to many in the United States. China operated under a British installed treaty system that forced the Chinese to open up their major ports to European traders in the wake of her defeat in the Opium Wars (1839–1842, 1856–1859). Great Britain's negotiators opened up more ports for her merchants and industrialists to sell their goods. Essentially, Great Britain established a free trade system under the treaty arrangements. Assured of her edge in competition with other industrial states, Great Britain lodged no objection to competitors such as the United States that subsequently signed similar treaties with Imperial China. As a result, the North American state reaped the same commercial benefits enjoyed by the British. Admittedly the British continued to dominate Chinese markets until World War I, but United States companies operated on the same playing fields as the British and other Europeans.

China and the open door

To the distress of the United States and Great Britain, the loss suffered by China in the Sino-Japanese War (1894–1895) precipitated a series of concessionary grabs by European powers. These consisted of giving foreign powers a virtual monopoly over specified geographic regions such as the Shangtung Peninsula and clearly threatened the free trade scheme embraced by the British and the United States. The response of the United States to the compromising of Chinese sovereignty via concessions appeared in the "open door" statement of Secretary of State John Hay. He proposed that a free trade policy prevail throughout China in both the spheres of influence under foreign control and in all other markets. The "open door" notes presumed that no persuasion would convince the imperial powers to abandon their respective spheres. Hay intended that all powers engaged in the sphere strategy would respect previous agreements that maintained open markets and that none would impose monopoly in their respective spheres or any discriminatory barriers. In fact, Hay wrote the notes at the urging of the British, who clearly shared the United States' interest in free markets. The open door policy brought the United States and Japan into direct contact, since both deemed China to be part of their export markets.

Japan, the United States and the open door policy in the Chinese market

The Japanese pursued a sphere of influence in China north of the Great Wall in Manchuria. To the south, Japanese policy makers complied with the British notions of free trade even during the concessionary period. After the United States issued the "open door" notes, the Japanese observed the intent and temper of Secretary Hay's policy statement. The Japanese understood full well the costs of installing a colonial administration on an unwilling population, and realized at this point that the scale of China's large and growing people vastly exceeded their capacity. They also believed the potential consumer markets held vast profits, a notion shared by Japanese manufacturers who worked closely with government officials.

World War I and new directions for Japan and the United States

World War I transformed the China situation. As a decade-long British ally, the Japanese declared war against Germany. The Japanese actually held little interest in the outcome of the European war. They did, however, hold a keen interest in the Asian theater. Taking advantage of Germany's commitment to Europe, the Japanese seized the German sphere of influence, the Shangtung Peninsula, occupied by German troops and government officials. The Japanese also took over the German-held Marshall, Caroline and Marianna Island chains in Pacific Micronesia. The Japanese knew full well the vast distance between Europe and East Asia effectively blocked German action. The war also opened up opportunities for the Japanese to expand their presence in China and, with the fall of Imperial Russia, to capitalize on the absence of Russian power in the

Far East. The United States remained committed to free markets while Japan only conditionally chose this option. While both states enjoyed cooperative relations in the 1920s, they increasingly diverged in their policies in the 1930s.

By December 1941 these tensions compelled the Japanese to launch an attack on the United States. War and its enmities colored mutual attitudes toward each other. The resolution of that conflict made the United States the dominant power in the Pacific and a major force in Asian affairs until the present day. The allied victory in western Europe, coupled with the defeat of Japan, made the United States a superpower. Its capacity to affect global affairs grew dramatically over the next half a century. Even Soviet Russia, its chief rival in the Cold War (1946–1989), proved unable to match the United States in either military or economic strength.

Conclusion

War brought the United States and Japan colonial possessions. War also made both states powers in the Pacific and Asia. Their presence would shape events in Asia for many years to come. The United States acquired the Philippines as her first and only colonial possession. She introduced democratic practices, encouraged self-government within limits and made election a central part of the local governing systems. The United States also had to used force to persuade Filipino leaders to accept their island chain's status as a colonial possession.

Despite the United States' avowed goal of self-government in the Philippines, she also deployed colonial administrators and experts, common in all colonial systems including Japanese and European. Her administrators participated in conferences on governing colonial peoples and visited European colonies to observe and learn from their experiences. In essence, the United States developed its own style of colonial rule that merged both democratic ethos and colonial-style rule driven by expertise. The Filipino economy also developed a close commercial relationship with the United States markets yet the island chain remained marginal to the economic fortunes of the North American state.

In China difference and similarities between the policies of the two powers emerged with crystal clarity. Japan, in contrast to the United States' rejection of territorial aggrandizement, developed a sphere of influence in Southern Manchuria via the South Manchurian Rail Line. In China, south of the Great Wall, the Japanese embraced the British treaty system that rejected territorial influence. The declaration of the United States open door policy in 1899 was a reassertion of this practice in the face of expanding spheres of influence by other European powers. Japan acquiesced, since she realized the impossibility of installing a colonial system capable of controlling the huge population of China south of the Great Wall. For the United States, the open door policy represented its commitment to free markets and economic competition.

Both powers had developed the resources to exercise power beyond their borders, and both often drove events in the Pacific and East Asia. For the United States, her growing power in Asia complimented her massive presence in Latin America. Her corporations, her navy and her array of experts and organizational personnel in the private sector and government gave her unprecedented capacities to precipitate change and to challenge Japan's empire. By 1945 the United States had defeated Japan in a brutal war and established her position as a leading power in Asia.

Further reading

For a general discussion of imperialism and its European context, see Timothy Mitchell, *The Rule of Experts: Egypt, Techno-Politics, Modernity* (Berkeley, 2002); Bernard Waites, *Europe and the Third World: From Colonialism to Decolonisation c. 1500–1998* (New York, 1999); Timothy Mitchell, *Colonising Egypt* (Berkeley, 1991); Bruce Berman and John Lonsdale, *Unhappy Valley: Conflict in Kenya and Africa* (Athens, Ohio, 1992).

For a valuable collection of essays on the Philippines, see Julian Go and Anne L. Foster, eds., *The American Colonial State in the Philippines: Global Perspectives* (Durham, 2003). For an in-depth examination of Filipino life and its relationship with colonizing powers, see Vincente L. Rafael, *White Love and Other Events in Filipino History* (Durham, 2000). Two general works that cover the colonial period in Filipino history, are H.W. Brands, *Bound to Empire: The United States and the Philippines* (New York, 1997) and Stanley Karnow, *In Our Image: American Empire in the Philippines* (New York, 1989).

For general works on Japan, see Carl Mosk, *Japanese Industrial History* (New York, 2001); Peter Duus, *Modern Japan* (New York, 1998); James L. McClain, *A Modern History* (New York, 2002); Tessa Morris-Suzuki, *The Technological Transformation of Japan: From the Seventeenth Century to the Twenty-First Century* (New York, 1994). For works that deal with the Japanese imperial experience, see Ramon H. Myers and Mark Peattie, eds., *The Japanese Colonial Empire, 1895–1945* (Princeton, 1984); W.G. Beasley, *Japanese Imperialism 1895–1945* (Oxford, 1987); Peter Duus, Ramon H. Myers and Mark P. Peattie, eds., *The Japanese Informal Empire in China, 1895–1937* (Princeton, 1989); Yoshihisa Tak Matsusaka, *The Making of Japanese Manchuria, 1904–1932* (Cambridge, Massachusetts, 2001). For an award winning account of the tensions between Japan and the United States, see Walter LaFeber, *The Clash: U.S.– Japanese Relations Throughout History* (New York, 1997).

Chapter 10

The United States and the world, 1945–2005

Introduction

In 1945 the United States possessed a level of immense power that would have been unimaginable at its founding. Unlike earlier decades of the twentieth century, when its corporations and government agencies focused their efforts on Latin America and the Pacific, the victory over Nazi Germany and ultranationalist Japan in 1945 enabled the United States to exercise its power throughout the globe. The United States faced the twin tasks of rebuilding Western Europe and Japan, and confronting an increasingly hostile Soviet Union. By the late 1940s the tension between the United States and the Union of Soviet Socialist Republics (U.S.S.R.). erupted into the Cold War.

For the United States re-establishing prosperous economies also greatly enhanced its ability to deal with the Soviet Union. A healthy Germany and Japan would stand as bastions against Soviet expansion. At the same time, United States corporations in co-ordination with the federal government moved into European markets. The United States persuaded Western European governments that free trade and relatively unobstructed markets served their interests. The efforts to contain the Soviet Union overlapped with the policy of sustaining recovery throughout Western Europe and promoting United States-style capitalism.

During the post World War II era, the United States exploited its techno-logical edge in industries dependent on consumer products, communications and transportation. It pioneered satellite communications and developed revolutionary computer and Internet systems that changed the face of the global market. It also developed new transportation technologies that altered the economic landscape of the globe. These technologies fueled the global reach of United States corporations and increasingly undermined the efforts of the U.S.S.R. to maintain even equality with the United States in standard of living.

The United States remained closely involved in Latin American states and economies. These provided essential markets and continued sources of raw materials. Here, too, the United States remained vigilant in preventing pro-communist regimes or even progressive governments that promoted social policies such as land redistribution that worked against the policies of free trade and markets.

In Asia the United States rebuilt Japan for the same reasons it had restored a shattered Germany. United States policy makers saw an economically vibrant Japan as a bulwark against the expansion of communism. Japan benefited directly from the United States wars in Northeast and Southeast Asia, Korea (1950–1953) and Vietnam (1964–1975) since she supplied many industrial goods to the United States military. The United States also gave Japan relatively free access to its own domestic markets. Japan modernized its economy, developed startling new management techniques, and by the 1980s seriously challenged United States corporations in North America.

United States cultural and consumer industries made their way into notoriously closed Japanese markets. These same industries also moved into other Asian markets. Fast food, Hollywood movies, rap music, and consumer goods appealed to audiences in Japan and East Asia in general.

Last, the United States engaged in a fierce arms race with the Soviet Union, one that included developing and enhancing the capacity of nuclear weapons. The United States also fought wars, but these were in Asia and against communist powers other than the U.S.S.R. In both the Korean War (1950–1953) and the Vietnam War (1963–1975) the military relied on conscription for manpower. Neither conflict ended in victory. By the 1970s, and particularly after the United States' defeat in Vietnam, the United States military turned away from draft and to a volunteer army. This decision truly professionalized the military, since men now signed up out of choice rather than compulsion and often saw the military as a long-term proposition. At the same time, technological changes transformed the way the military fought and defeated its enemies. The two Gulf Wars (1991 and 2003) showed the superior assets of the new military unmatched by other military systems (see Epilogue). By 2005, the United States military occupied military bases and installations across the entire globe. The combination of vast economic strength and military power gave the United States immense capacity to drive economic and political changes across the planet.

The Cold War

As World War II wound down, the United States pursued organizational strategies to create an economic world governed by free trade, open markets and financial and political stability. In the summer of 1944 the United States and its allies accepted the Bretton Wood Accords. These led to the establishment of the International Monetary Fund (IMF) and the International Bank for Reconstruction and Development, later known as the World Bank. The IMF originally assumed responsibility for currency stability and convertibility among national economies. It also intended to act as an agency that lent money as a "last resort" to states in need of revenue. The economic world as it evolved in the postwar era created a very different function for the IMF. It now lends money to financially troubled states in the developing world. The authors of the World Bank foresaw its role as giving major loans to developing economies. Both institutions operated from headquarters in Washington, D.C. and both came under the influence of the United States Treasury and its director. The massive problems facing Europe and Asia far exceeded the capacities of either institution to rebuild their shattered economies. That charge fell to the United States, the only polity with sufficient resources to accomplish this end.

The United States faced an even bigger challenge as events in Europe led to the outbreak of the Cold War, a battle of political wills between the United States and the Soviet Union over the economic and political future of Europe and even the entire globe. Policy makers in Washington, D.C. decided during the period from 1946 into early 1947 that the Soviet Union posed an imminent danger to the United States and its allies.

The Greek Civil War in 1946, which pitted a royalist Greek regime against communist insurgents, brought the United States into the fray. In fact, its commitment to the anti-communist regime actually led to the Marshall Plan that sped up the rebuilding of much of Western Europe. The declaration of the Truman Doctrine of Containment in March 1947 signaled the formal start of the Cold War. The installation of communist regimes in Poland and elsewhere in Eastern Europe and the division of Germany between the Western powers and the Soviet Union also marked the Cold War's opening rounds.

The tensions hardened by the late 1940s. In 1949 the United States and the Western European powers established the North Atlantic Treaty Organization as a defensive pact against Soviet aggression. The victory of the Chinese communists in 1949, along with the Soviets detonating an atomic bomb, increased tensions between the United States and the Soviet Union. By 1950 the United States engaged in an all-out war in the Korean peninsula against the North Korean Communist regime and its major ally, the People's Republic of China. The war ended in a stalemate.

In the midst of these dramatic events the United States turned its attention to the desperate situation in Western Europe. Foreign-policy makers faced the challenge of creating an economically viable Western Europe. The United States used the Marshall Plan, implemented by the Economic Co-operative Administration (ECA), to achieve this vast goal. The Marshall Plan assumed that economic misery created a fertile ground for communism, and promoting economic recovery thwarted such conditions.

The approach embedded in the Marshall Plan reflected United States' thinking on markets. Its ideological origins derived from the Four Freedoms articulated during World War II. The freedom from want was directly tied to the standard of living that Truman and other United States officials saw as crucial in Western Europe. United States officials also assumed that a prosperous economy would foster democratic behavior of the kind that flourished in North America. So, United States officials saw consumer freedom as a crucial outcome of the Marshall Plan. The rising standard of living would pose the greatest challenge to the Soviet Union and those trapped behind the Iron Curtain.

The United States also intended to introduce its style of capitalism, or elements of it, to Western Europe. This meant an emphasis on efficiency, mass production and eventually mass consumption once the European economies recovered and wages rose substantially. United States economic advisors urged minimal government intervention in the economy, in line with the United States free market philosophy. United States policy makers also wanted the power of unions severely circumscribed and left-wing parties marginalized throughout Western Europe. With such political sentiments suppressed, reigning governments presumably had little incentive for expansive social programs that ran counter to the free market ethos of the United States.

World War II also ended the older pattern of consumption that stressed scarcity and status as determinants of purchasing goods. The United States offered an egalitarian model built on free access for all and unlimited production coupled with high wages. United States companies had been exporting consumer goods to Europe since the late nineteenth century and knew well the advantages of operating in this market. An economically vibrant, postwar Western Europe that embraced free trade offered United States corporations a substantial market for their goods. In this regard the merging of foreign policy interests with those of the private sector corporations made the United States a formidable agent in European economic life.

The ECA also vigorously promoted these ideas through mass marketing techniques. The full-lunch-pale motif appeared in many guises during this campaign. The film unit of ECA produced some 200 documentaries featuring these themes for Western Europeans. While the elites in European societies, especially in France, saw the United States' efforts as culturally imperialistic, ordinary Europeans looked favorably on the United States' reputation for economic opportunity and the array of consumer good becoming available in the 1950s.

The United States encouraged the creation of a larger European economy free of trade barriers. Policy makers and their business allies saw the resulting larger economy as a huge market for United States goods and capital investments. In 1947, the European states, the United States and Great Britain signed the General Agreement on Tariffs and Trade. It reduced customs duties and removed discriminatory trade measures. The conditions of immediate postwar Europe delayed these efforts but eventually trade would move with minimum duties. The United States continually promoted the integration of the European economy. The Europeans established the Organization for European Economic Cooperation, the European Payments Plan and the European Coal and Steel Community, all of which further merged the separate economies of Western Europe. Eventually, the sentiments embodied in these measures led to the European Economic Community in 1957, or the Common Market. For the United States these measures resulted in a larger economy geared to free trade and capital investments. For Europe these measures were revolutionary given the past history of competitive national economies.

The United States also showed its concern for the revival of a democratic political system in Germany. United States officials wisely decided to rebuild self-government in Germany based on the German state's own parliamentary institutions. As crucial, the United States excluded from public life those men who had participated in the Nazi regime. While the purges proved incomplete they opened up avenues for new political leaders and parties that began the actual process of representation. Germany would no longer act as a force for war and belligerency. Integrated into the larger European community, prosperous and democratically governed, West Germany served as an example for people living under Soviet control.

The United States also relied on its eminently successful visual media to advertise its achievements to Europeans. Hollywood had moved into European markets in the 1920s and drew large audiences for its movies. Of course the tensions of the late 1930s and World War II temporarily halted Hollywood's successes. United States movie companies saw the Cold War as a major opportunity to resume their presence in European markets. Hollywood's representatives convinced the State Department that United States movies could play an important role in keeping the allegiance of Europeans and persuading them of the economic and political advantages the United States had to offer over the Soviet Union. The movie studios capitalized on the access to European markets provided by the United States, in particular to West Germany. Hollywood movies showed Europeans scenes of prospering families and material abundance. Movies also conveyed positively United States values and traditions. These served United States' interests well in its struggle with the Soviet Union.

Hollywood's near monopoly of the film industry in Europe enhanced its value to the United States cause. It simply overwhelmed the West German market. In France, where substantial opposition emerged to importing United States movies, a desperately needed loan from the United States persuaded the French to drop their quota on Hollywood movies. The French government resorted to a limited quota in 1948; yet French-made films continued to decline in number. United States films showed in movie theaters throughout the continent. In fact, by 1951 Hollywood-produced films comprised 61 percent of all movies released in Western Europe. As the domestic market slowed for Hollywood studios, European markets accounted for a growing share of their profits. Last, most governments in Europe, including Great Britain, blocked studios from converting their profits into dollars. A sympathetic Congress passed a measure that reimbursed the studios for the revenue trapped overseas.

The Soviet Union hardly stood by in this battle of ideas and goods. It conducted a cultural and diplomatic offensive against the United States.

During the late 1940s Moscow pursued a major peace offensive. Aware of the substantial fears over nuclear weapons, Moscow called for nuclear disarmament and asked the United States to abandon its atomic weapons. The Soviet Union also awarded Stalin Prizes to individuals who worked for disarmament. At the same time, the Soviets issued the Stockholm Peace Appeal aimed at Western Europe, where fears of nuclear war gathered widespread support for such measures. The Soviet Union stepped up its cultural assault on the United States through a vigorous exchange program designed to bring leading intellectuals, students and union leaders from Western Europe to the U.S.S.R. The Soviets released numerous publications designed to win support of Western Europeans while sponsoring ballet troupes and symphonic productions throughout Western Europe.

The United States also pursued a cultural and psychological campaign against the U.S.S.R. Combined with the eminently successful Standard of Living campaign, the United States possessed ample resources to cope with challenges from the U.S.S.R. The United States now used its technological capacity to reach populations deep in Eastern Europe. It set up émigré-run Radio Free Europe and Radio Liberty to reach the populations living behind the Iron Curtain, a novel use of United States resources and a direct result of its new global power.

The United States cultural offensive included dance, music, art and learning. In the late 1940s the United States government launched the Fulbright Exchange Program, named after Senator William J. Fulbright of Arkansas. It facilitated faculty and student exchanges between the United States and European countries in an effort to promote a better understanding between the societies. In the tense environment of the Cold War, the program served political objectives as much as cultural ends. At the same time the United States Congress passed the Smith-Mundt Act in 1948 that called upon the federal government to use all its cultural and educational resources in the confrontation with the U.S.S.R. The United States government now played an active role in promoting the mutual understanding that it perceived as important in the era of the Cold War.

In response to many Foreign Service complaints about the shrill of anti-communist tirades, the State Department and the United States Information Agency sponsored tours of orchestral ensembles, prominent soloists such as Isaac Stern, and theater groups that staged plays of prominent writers such as Tennessee Williams. The State Department of the United States federal government also sent jazz musicians, notably Louis Armstrong and Dizzy Gillespie, on tours of Europe. Such events were intended to persuade Europeans that the United States enjoyed a sophisticated culture, one that measured up to the quality of its vast array of consumer goods. These programs spread the presence of the United States cultural forms throughout Europe. They also served to counterbalance Soviet attempts to convince Western Europeans of the superiority of the communist system.

The United States also established the Congress of Cultural Freedom in 1950. It, too, represented an effort to battle the Soviets on cultural grounds. In 1952 it sponsored in Paris a festival dedicated to artistic accomplishments. The Congress sent musical groups from the United States and made sure that famous Russian émigrés, such as Sergei Prokofiev whose works the Soviets banned, played before European audiences. The Congress also published a major journal, *Encounter*, which relied on pieces by famous British and European writers and reached a subscribers base of 16,000.

The United States also capitalized on the success of its abstract impressionist painters, such as modernist Jackson Pollock. They developed their own style of painting, one that challenged every norm of painting and won audiences all over Europe. Modernism thrived, commentators argued, only in a free society and nowhere else. It served as an advertisement in the Cold War while contributing to New York City's ascendancy as the cultural capital of the Atlantic world. In the absence of federal funds to promote this style of painting and the artists who produced it, private agencies stepped in to provide the resources. The Museum of Modern Art in New York City repeatedly sponsored exhibitions in Europe.

The United States policies and private sector programs enhanced the image and influence of the North American state in ways the Soviets could never replicate. The Marshall Plan incorporated Mrs. Consumer, mother, wife and penultimate consumer in the United States. Europeans saw United States wives as tall, stylish, middle class women, well coiffured and fashionably dressed. These women duly impressed Europeans. The "new woman" in the United States enjoyed liberation from many of the backbreaking chores of the household, yet epitomized domesticity. She often appeared in Europe with her husband, who came to attend international conventions such as those held by the Rotary. European women's magazines adopted the United States model. Around 200 of these magazines circulated in Europe and acted as the main source of information on living standards for European women. They described the new household conveniences and their role in making life comfortable for the housewife and her family.

By 1960 the middle class had achieved the consumer goals outlined twenty years before and within a decade the working classes arrived at the same point. Western Europe had by all measures of modernity and comfort become a mass consumer society. For Europeans the notion that certain goods defined the minimum standard of living for comfort acquired a near universal recognition.

By the early 1960s the United States had made its presence felt in numerous ways in the Atlantic world. It successfully challenged the U.S.S.R. through a western alliance and through its role in facilitating the rebuilding of shattered European societies, which had by now regained their prosperity. The United States had also persuaded leaders in these societies, especially in West Germany, to embrace its formula of free trade, open markets and integrated regional economies. The Marshall Plan succeeded beyond expectations. United States consumer goods moved into European markets as the United States policy makers had intended. The United States had also convinced parts of West German industry to adopt the mass production and marketing techniques that ruled the United States industrial economy. Western Germans and Europeans in general enjoyed rising wages and full employment that seemed to insure economic security rare in earlier times. The notion of consumer freedom that dominated much of the United States rhetoric had taken hold in West Germany and Western Europe. These achievements diminished the Soviet-style economies in Eastern Europe, always poorer by comparison. In the realm of consumer and cultural competition the United States had clearly outshone the U.S.S.R.

In the meantime, United States technology made significant advances in the late 1950s through the 1970s. These gave it an immense edge over the Soviet Union, which simply lacked the capacity ever to catch up with the United States. The technological changes also gave the United States important assets in developing its economic reach across the globe. During these years United States researchers, often lodged in the military, developed phone services across the United States and the Atlantic and satellite communications. Congress established the National Aeronautic and Space Administration (1958) to run the United States Space Program, a response to early Soviet successes. Along with the National Defense Education Act that enabled the federal government to fund scientific research, NASA eventually pushed the United States far ahead of the Soviet Union.

At the same time, technical innovations transformed the private sector. In that realm, jet airliners eventually replaced prop planes and greatly added carrying capacity and speed. Boeing Corporation in Seattle developed jets capable of carrying 300 passengers, which reduced airfares for regular passengers. Innovations such as AT&T's microwave amplification techniques reduced operating costs in oceanic phone calls. With such a reduction in prices, major corporations embraced the telephone as the primary means of moving information across the Atlantic. This truly created the basis for global communications at instant speeds. Together, these technological innovations created the basis for a much more tightly integrated global market. These innovations diminished the impact of distances and time as transportation and communications changes had done so often in the past.

The major development, the computer, grew out of military needs but moved with great speed into the private sector. The International Business Machine Corporation (IBM) pioneered computers. At first the United States military provided the major market for IBM products. By the 1960s the company had developed computers for domestic markets in the United States. Its computers also moved quickly into the European markets, where the company gained a lion's share of sales. Of course the low tariffs, free trade and access gave IBM important advantages. Airports, phones and eventually computer terminals joined ports and railroad stations as means of moving information and/or people and cargo across national boundaries.

By the 1960s satellite capacity developed rapidly. AT&T introduced Telstar and later Intelsat satellite systems. These enabled the company to transmit television programs across the Atlantic and Indian Oceans. By 1971, the International Telecommunications Satellite Consortium incorporated nineteen countries committed to setting up a satellite communications system. It relied on the Communications Satellite Corporation set up by Congress in 1962 as its "operating arm." Eventually it developed the capacity to serve the entire globe. The refusal of the Soviet Union to participate only reflected its marginal position in space technology. The United States now occupied a major position in global communications, a far cry from a government reluctant to enter the international community after World War I.

Such technological changes simply overran the capacity of the Soviet Union to approach the United States capacity. President Ronald Reagan took decisive steps to bring down the U.S.S.R. First, he blocked Soviet access to the United States technology that had fueled so much growth in the west and gave the North American state leadership in this realm. He then forced the Soviet Union into an expensive arms race well beyond its financial capability. He also persuaded the western powers and Japan to abandon energy exploration in the U.S.S.R. while convincing the Saudis to increase their oil production in a successful effort to drive down the price of oil, the chief export of the U.S.S.R. The cost of a barrel of oil plummeted from a high of $30.00 per barrel down to $12.00.

President Reagan took other steps. He ordered that ground-to-air, hand-held missiles be sent to resistance fighters in Afghanistan, which Soviet troops began occupying in 1980. The occupation proved costly and ended in a Soviet withdrawal. Similarly, he supported groups opposing communist regimes in Africa and Central America. As a former filmstar and keenly aware of the power of visuals, President Reagan used satellite television networks to send images of the prosperity of the United States to the U.S.S.R. These contrasted with the stark reality of Soviet life, materially poor and with little hope of change. Such images helped sparked dissent in Russia. Last, his promotion of the Strategic Defense Initiative was a key bargaining tool in discussions with the Soviets, who realized they lacked the resources to match this expensive program.

In November 1989 the Berlin Wall, the symbol of Soviet strength in Europe, came down. The Soviet empire in Eastern Europe quickly unraveled and by 1991 the U.S.S.R. ceased to exist. The Cold War ended. The impact of Reagan's policies played a key role. The technology certainly made a crucial difference in realizing Reagan's stated aim of toppling the U.S.S.R. The United States also effectively used its status as the premier consumer society to good effect. Even as early as the famous Kitchen debate between Vice President Nixon and Soviet Premier Khrushchev in 1959, the United States' decided edge in this realm was obvious to all. By 1991, the Soviet Union was a shell of its once greatness while the United States stood as the leading economic and cultural power in the world.

United States technology and service industries

In the last stages of the Cold War and into the 1990s, United States technological capacity continued to accelerate. By the 1980s, news services created global networks. These moved information on a twenty-four hour basis to ordinary individuals. Ted Turner's CNN symbolized this revolution in information exchange. Headquartered in Atlanta, Georgia it broadcast news, weather, business, scientific, entertainment and any type of information to viewers throughout the United States and Canada. Eventually he developed CNN International, which used the globe as its market with regional outlets fashioning news and information to local customers. Entrepreneurs such as Turner consistently demonstrated innovative approaches in new technology and industries, and flexibility in keeping and expanding their audiences.

As this technology developed, United States service companies began expanding their presence in overseas markets. The expansion of McDonald's began in 1967 when it opened up an outlet in Canada. By 1980 it operated 1,000 outlets abroad. Before the end of the decade, McDonald's 10,000 restaurants in forty-seven countries served 20,000,000 people a day. By 2001 it ran more outlets in Europe than in the United States. It even ran successful outlets in Moscow, the onetime capital of the leading communist state in the world.

McDonald's also understood what United States corporations realized earlier in the century, the need to accommodate local cultural concerns. In accommodating these concerns, McDonald's in France hired only French citizens, used the French language and relied on local ingredients for its products. The company sold franchises only to French business persons. In fact, McDonald's success in France and elsewhere on the continent persuaded European food entrepreneurs to use the United States fast food giant as a model for their own operations as they jumped into the competitive arena. At roughly the same time, fast food giants in the United States, notably Kentucky Fried Chicken and Burger King, moved into European markets.

United States companies also took a commanding position in capital markets. As technology acquired more and more sophistication, prices for gathering financial information dropped while the costs of doing business, notably daily transactions, also fell dramatically. The VISA credit card stood out as one of the companies that benefited from the transnational markets. Started in 1970, it provided full financial payment services for cardholders in the domestic markets. By the early twenty-first century, its service network range across the planet and the number of customers grew from 30,000,000 to 1,000,000,000, with business transactions totaling over $2,000,000,000,000,000. The company depended on computer terminals and phone lines for its basic technology and updated via the Internet in the 1990s. The time for each transaction plummeted from five minutes to fewer than five seconds. It eventually accounted for 57 percent of the global market in credit card exchanges and its brand name enjoys universal recognition around the planet.

The Internet revolutionized communications in the 1990s. It grew out of the military's concerns over the ability of the Soviets to conduct an assault against its centralized communications system. With the ability to move information erased, the military knew full well its capacity to react to other Soviet attacks would decline sharply. As a result it sought a network approach that decentralized communications, making it impervious to Soviet weapons. The new system, developed by the major defense entity, Rand Corporation, wedded with the personal computers available by the 1980s from Apple, IBM and other manufacturers.

Once the Internet scheme moved into the public domain during the 1990s it immediately transformed communications. Emails quickly became the normal means of reaching colleagues, friends and distant associates. Sending messages costs very little, while the transmission rate approached lighting speed. The Internet served many clients, from business and military people to diplomatic personnel and ordinary individuals.

The overseas presence of the entertainment industry as well as its capacity to draw foreign visitors to the United States demonstrated the persistent cultural power of the United States. Its theme park in Orlando drew visitors from all over the United States and Europe. In fact, Disney World in Orlando drew 28 million visitors in 1990, more than the whole of Great Britain attracted in the same year. It ranked after France, Spain and the United States as the major tourist attraction in the world. Disney sold $1,500,000,000 in trinkets and gifts in Tokyo Disney in one year.

Walt Disney Studios opened up a Disney theme park in Paris in 1990. The location gave the Disney businessmen a site accessible for much of Europe; over 300,000 people lived within a two-hour car or plane ride of the park. The park encountered problems in its early years and had to adapt fares, hotel accommodation and food to European tastes and resources, and even changed some of the themes built into Disney parks. Disney even relented on the ban on alcohol sales. Critics lambasted Disney, yet the company enjoyed rising profit levels after these changes were instituted. United States theme parks became a part of European vacation plans. United States themes adapted to the culture of France much as United States consumer and cultural industries successfully did in Mexico in the 1920s and 1930s.

Hollywood-made films also continued to flourish in European markets. After a brief downturn in the late 1960s though the 1980s, when European stars and movies caught the attention of United States audiences, Hollywood regained its dominant position. Quality movies and superb directors in the 1970s and 1980s enabled Hollywood to re-establish its prominence. Hollywood's blockbuster movies in the 1980s and 1990s captured huge audiences in the

United States and Europe and began to marginalize European films. These plummeted by 25 percent during the 1980s.

Technology accelerated this dominance in the last decades of the twentieth century. Video players and videotapes, and theaters with multiple screens all created more opportunities for European audiences to see Hollywood movies. By the early twenty-first century, DVDs and DVD players increased the number of United States films in European households. By 1995, Hollywood films made up 81 percent of all movies shown in Europe. Even in France, where a film industry still prospers, Hollywood movies still comprise 61 percent of all films shown.

Television, too, moved in the same direction. Technology played an important role. Film proved easy and inexpensive to transport. European television studios also discovered that purchasing United States-made programs costs far less than if domestically manufactured. United States companies also showed sensitivity to audiences in designing their programs, much as Hollywood producers and studios did. The television series "Baywatch," with physically attractive stars and their often-revealing outfits proved a major success in European markets. By 1995, United States television programs made up three-quarters of all programs aired throughout the entire continent of Europe and Great Britain.

United States corporations such as General Electric and General Foods used their huge scale of production to crush their competitors. As early as the 1960s General Electric Corporation sold 200,000 separate products, well beyond the capacity of any comparable manufacturer on the continent. The mammoth United States Corporation, General Foods, could undercut any French candy manufacturer by simply reducing the prices on its sweet goods by a few percent. Chrysler Corporation alone manufactured more cars than all French automakers combined. The New York Exchange dwarfed its French counterpart. Gaullists in France expressed hostility toward the United States, yet the French continued to buy United States products.

By the 1990s, the United States' economic and cultural presence in European markets added another asset, namely the English language. The majority of young Europeans spoke English. It had also served as the basic language in diplomatic and business affairs, in scientific and media discourse and many other areas of exchange. The use of United States English facilitated the movement of United States goods and culture across borders and oceans as well as enhancing the influence of the United States.

Latin America

The United States expanded its presence in Latin America in the wake of World War II. In part, the growth of United States influence grew out of its consumer export industries. These had already claimed a beachhead in the prewar years in states such as Mexico and Cuba. United States policy makers also worried over the presence of pro-communist regimes and even left-of-center regimes, as they had in Europe. Both ideology and the economic policies that originated in socialist thought threatened the economic viability of United States investments and operations in Latin America. These carried considerable force for the men who conducted United States policy and ran its business operations in the region. The United States had already established a history of intervention in the region earlier in the twentieth century. In the postwar era, the United States continued this policy. In Guatemala, for example, a progressive left of center government under Jacobo Arbenz came to power during the 1950s. Arbenz's associations with prominent communist party members in Guatemala worried United States leaders, including President Dwight Eisenhower. As a result, in 1954 the C.I.A. organized and backed the counter-revolutionary group that overthrew Arbenz.

The United States again faced a similar challenge in Castro's Cuba in the wake of the 1959 revolution against Fulgencio Batista, a onetime United States-backed ruler. Castro's policies realized the fears of United States policy makers and private investors. His agricultural policies removed the large landholdings of United States corporations even as he moved to nationalize the island's economy. In the process he established a highly centralized state that ran the national economy and an authoritarian regime that rejected the democratic notions so important to the United States. The command economy failed and this forced a decentralized approach by 1970. For a few years the Cuban economy flourished as sugar, still the main export, thrived in the international markets. Castro used the revenue to purchase new technology and other goods available on the global markets. He eventually outran the island's income. By the mid-1980s Castro placed a moratorium on debt repayment and ended the decade carrying $6,000,000,000 in debt. Foreign banks and lenders avoided Cuban calls for more loans.

Cuba ironically developed a dependent relationship with the U.S.S.R. and relied on its heavy subsidies to survive. Cuba's failure to achieve a higher standard of living became apparent at the end of the 1970s as relatives who had fled to the United States returned with goods of a quality and variety simply absent on the island. No doubt this contributed to the flood of Cubans who bolted the island nation in 1980, with the government's begrudging approval, for the United States.

Opposition either to the United States or elites backed by the United States occurred frequently in Latin America yet such opposition, unlike Cuba's faltering survival, rarely succeeded in the long run. The United States fiercely resisted pro-communist or communist regimes in Latin America because of their socialist economic policies and authoritarian approach to governing. Regimes such as the Sandinista in Nicaragua, for example, used state power to redistribute resources and rejected free trade. Above all, the United States wanted stable regimes that safeguarded foreign investments and acted as a magnet for capital investment, similar to policies dating back to the early twentieth century. So in the process of battling hostile pro-communists forces either directly or indirectly, or supporting coalitions hostile to these forces, the United States attempted to insure stability and remove the possibility of governments inimical to its interests.

The United States had always pressed for free trade and access to markets in the region. The liberal regimes of the nineteenth and early twentieth centuries had accommodated United States wishes since these governments saw this strategy as an important way to modernize. Beginning in the late 1930s and lasting for several decades, Latin American leaders embraced import substituting industrialization (ISI) as a way to promote domestic industry and shield it from competition from more powerful United States industries. This policy involved high tariffs, giving out government contracts to local manufacturers, and establishing publicly owned companies. The states assumed the major role in industrializing national economies.

Of course, this choice ran counter to United States free trade policies. ISI also encountered other problems that set it on a self-destructive course. Major capital goods arrived only as imports from the United States or other major industrial economies. In effect, the very dependency ISI intended to end just re-surfaced in a new guise. At the same time, prices for many of the staple exports that Latin American states sold began to drop, reducing the amount of revenue states such as Chile and Argentina had available to buy capital goods. Limited domestic markets for goods produced by the state supported industries placed limits on productivity. ISI also promoted capital-intensive industries that provided limited employment for domestic workers. Unemployment became a serious problem by the 1960s. As economies stumbled and even collapsed ISI lost favor, to be replaced by new policies. These favored rejoining the global markets, inviting back large multinational corporations such as IBM and reworking fiscal obligations with major United States and European financial institutions.

By the 1980s and 1990s, these states faced a catastrophic debt crisis. The United States, for instance, accumulated huge amounts of dollars invested by Middle Eastern oil magnates benefiting from the oil price rises of the 1970s. United States banks lent this money to faltering governments in Latin America. This led to a major debt crisis by the 1980s and 1990s. States such as Mexico survived only on more loans from the United States. The United States and agencies such as the International Monetary Fund, really an agency under the United States Treasury, imposed severe fiscal regimes on these states. Essentially these new regimes imposed "neoliberal" policies on debtor states. This involved state withdrawal from the private sector and a sharp reduction in states' subsidies to various domestic constituents. The measure also called for open markets and free trade policies. Mexico's agreement to join GATT demonstrated the sharp reversal in its government's policies. The most visible act in this radical shift in policies was Mexico's signing of the North American Free Trade Agreement in 1991.

Quite often the men who fashioned these new policies acquired their college and graduate economics education at major United States universities. In Chile the men who developed the state's economic policies trained at the University of Chicago, noted for its free market policies. From the late 1970s these United States-trained economists fashioned a free market economy in Chile, one that prospered. Ironically, the military regime under General Augusto Pinochet used their success to justify its continued rule. Eventually, a democratically elected government replaced Pinochet's brutal regime near the end of the 1980s. The United States supported the elections, yet domestic dissent and building opposition led to the actual change.

United States companies that manufactured consumer goods continued to enjoy success in Latin American markets, much as they did before World War II. Goods as diverse as Coca Cola, pickup trucks and automobiles thrived in Latin American markets into the twenty-first century. Equally as important in the eyes of Latin American consumers, United States goods held a significantly higher status than those locally made by hand. Even products made in joint partnerships used foreign design, foreign machinery to manufacture and foreign capital to fund the operation.

By the late 1970s new United States service corporations greatly expanded their operations in Latin American markets. Burger King, McDonald's, Kentucky Fried Chicken and other fast food companies breached markets where national cuisines prevailed. In Argentina, where people enjoyed eating out, many in the middle and working classes turned to McDonald's as an inexpensive choice when the economy declined in the late 1980s. Yet in most of Latin America McDonald's feeds a more upscale market. In Mexico City on its first day of business in the mid-1980s McDonald's sold around 10,000 hamburgers to a fashionable clientele. Sales in Latin America proved so healthy that McDonald's planned huge investments in the late 1990s to increase dramatically the number of outlets. In part, this decision grew out of declining sales in the North American markets. Essentially, a United States inspired diet vigorously competed with customary local menus.

The 1990s saw shopping malls come to Latin America. Architects adopted United States models while United States manufactured goods appeared on shelves throughout the region. Even the English phrase "go shopping" entered into local expression. In Mexico City, one outlet of the United States corporation Wal-Mart sold $1,000,000 of largely United States goods in one day.

Coca Cola also thrived in the markets of Latin America. The company had a long history in states such as Mexico even before World War II. By the 1940s it operated bottling plants in Guatemala, Honduras and Colombia. Coca Cola also prospered as a marketable commodity. By the 1990s it dominated the Brazilian market and in Peru the company bought half the shares of their main competition, a Peruvian company. In Mexico Coca Cola enjoyed tremendous sales among an audience that consumed yearly over 400 bottles per person.

With the removal of tax barriers instituted by the North American Free Trade Association (NAFTA), the North American corporation took control of more than 60 per cent of the country's market. Coca Cola symbolized modernity for Latin American customers. Intense marketing and advertising insinuated Coca Cola into every aspect of social life, from dances to family evenings.

These sales benefited from the neoliberal policies of Latin American states that took center stage as ISI faded from memory. Either voluntarily or through the IMF, governments in Latin America removed tariff barriers, opened up domestic markets and allowed goods or services to flow unimpeded across their borders. The debt crisis of the late 1980s and the 1990s ushered in these policies that worked to the advantage of United States industries. The IMF imposed budgetary restraints on debtor states and limited their scope of action.

East Asia

The United States became a major power in East Asia as a result of World War II. Japan surrendered to United States military forces by September 1945 and for the first time in its history faced an occupying army. As the Cold War unfolded, United States policy makers decided an economically weak Japan would endangers its anti-communist policies in East Asia. A vibrant Japan under United States tutelage would provide the stability Washington believed essential in the region. They also saw a revived Japan as a cornerstone of a healthy Asian economy and a network of anti-communist states that stretched from South Korea to the Philippines.

As important, the United States saw integrating Japan into North American markets as an effective way of sustaining its recovery and then promoting subsequent growth. The United States government hastened the transfer of technologies such as electronics to Japanese manufacturers. This policy lasted for decades and proved crucial both in Japan's recovery and its surge to becoming one of the leading economic powers in the world.

The United States also gave Japan access to its North American domestic market, one of the richest consumer states in the world. Japanese competitiveness had steadily grown over the decades and by the 1980s had seriously undermined or threatened many United States industries, such as semi-conductors and car manufacturing. In the automobile industry, Japanese manufacturers barely produced 100,000 cars a year in the late 1950s yet by the twenty-first century its fuel efficient, high quality and stylish cars captured a significant share of the United States domestic market. Japanese manufacturers even moved into the high-end range with their Lexis and Acura brands. In fact, the Japanese Automobile Corporation Subaru persuaded the daughter of an ex-United States president to film an advertisement for its products.

Presidents such as Richard Nixon had expressed a reluctance to force the Japanese to open their markets to the same extent as had the United States for Japan. The United States depended on naval and army bases in Japan and its general role in the United States Cold War policies. Despite various agreements with the Japanese government in the 1990s, the United States never enjoyed the access to the island nation's domestic markets that it did in Europe and Latin America. Profitable economic activities such as telecommunications and finance remained beyond the reach of United States companies. Japan, then, developed a very different relationship with the United States than occurred in Latin America.

Yet, United States products often made their way into Japan and East Asia in general. McDonald's, the premier United States fast food corporation, captured a substantial share of Japanese hamburger sales. It operated 3,000 restaurants in Japan. The Japanese see McDonald's as a safe place for their children and a location where women can meet, because it serves no alcohol. In fact many Japanese enjoy conversation and social exchanges at a McDonald's. The South Koreans also see McDonald's as much as a social place as an eating establishment. In the People's Republic of China McDonald's operates over 230 outlets, an outcome of Deng Xiao Ping's economic liberalization policies the 1980s. Chinese tourists in Beijing frequently stop at a McDonald's to enjoy the "taste" of the United States. The Beijing outlets proved so popular that student efforts to boycott McDonald's in the wake of United States' bombings in Belgrade in 1999 simply collapsed as customers continued to use the restaurants. In Hong Kong, McDonald's has also acquired a reputation as a good place to celebrate children's birthdays.

Kentucky Fried Chicken joined McDonald's in capitalizing on the Chinese market. Its Qiamen restaurant fed troops from the People's Army during their occupation of Tiananmen Square in the wake of the 1989 crushing of the student uprising. The managers of Kentucky Fried Chicken knew well the importance of adapting to the local customer base, a lesson learned in Mexico and elsewhere decades earlier. Their outlets feature *Qiqi*, or Chicky in English, who sports a United States baseball cap. While the company downplays its traditional symbol, customers in Beijing still have their pictures taken in front of the statue of Colonel Sanders.

Starbucks Coffee, the Seattle chain, operates profitable outlets in Japan, the republic of South Korea, Malaysia, China and elsewhere in East Asia. In fact, the Starbucks shop in the Tokyo District of Shibuya remains the busiest outlet in the world for the company.

United States popular culture captivated Japanese audiences as much as it did European and Latin American audiences. Its music, from jazz to rock-and-roll consistently drew Japanese listeners. Today, Sumo wrestlers attempt to master rap music, a style originating in the African American neighborhoods of United States cities. Every weekend hundreds of thousands of Japanese youth sit eagerly in front of their television to watch the satellite channel broadcasting *Soullook: Seize the Night*, shown live from New York City's famous Cheetah Club. Japanese youth sport United States-style blue jeans and drink the ubiquitous Coca Cola.

Hollywood movies consistently draw Japanese viewers. The style of dress, clothing and behavior featured in these films has appealed to the Japanese since United States occupation forces began showing these movies. The success of Whoopi Goldberg's 1998 movie, *Sister Act*, shows their consistent popularity. The movie proved so compelling to the Japanese that many came to Harlem in New York City to attend a workshop on singing gospel music. The Japanese in general see the United States as far more energetic than any European counterpart. United States goods, popular culture and consumer services spread across the entire planet in ways unimaginable at its founding. These goods and services have moved into people's lives, encouraged new personal habits, and added a degree of comfort and high entertainment value to their daily routines.

Conclusion

The Cold War erupted almost immediately after the end of World War II. Moscow and Washington clashed over their vast ideological differences, ideas of governing and economic systems. In the long run the capacity of the United States successfully to promote and realize a high standard of living among its allies and to achieve technological advances beyond Soviet abilities played a crucial role in the demise of the Soviet Union.

In the process of promoting prosperity and anti-communist regimes in Western Europe and elsewhere in the world to defeat the Soviet Union, the United States also persuaded these governments to accept free trade, free markets and convertible currencies to make prosperity possible. The United States encouraged the creation of an integrated West European economy through GATT, the Common Market and other agreements that facilitated the flow of goods through low tariffs.

The United States also used its resources to insure anti-communist governments in Latin America. In an effort to develop economic independence from the United States and other industrialized states, South American governments developed the economic strategy of ISI. The strategy never fully realized its ends and South American states proved unable to break their dependent relationship with the United States. This dependency hardened during the debt crisis that raged in many states during the 1980s and into the 1990s. The fiscal regime the IMF imposed for its loans insured open markets, low tariffs, and reduction of state social expenditures and, in the end, facilitated the rise of neoliberal governments in much of South America. Yet, few of the Latin American states have been able to escape the crushing weight of debt repayment.

United States industries capitalized on the free trade and open markets promoted by their government in the post-World War II era. United States-made consumer products moved into Europe during the late 1940s, accelerating in quantity in the 1950s and 1960s. The large, integrated market in Western Europe created by treaties and agreements benefited the United

States even as economies in the region began to prosper. By the 1970s and the 1980s Western European economies had developed as consumer driven, very much like the United States economy. Thus sustaining a growing prosperity not only demonstrated the superiority of the United States consumer strategy over the far weaker Soviet economy, it also opened up the rich continental and British markets. United States cultural industries (film, TV), fast food and fiscal services blanket Latin America and Western Europe. These speak of the widespread influence of United States popular culture throughout the globe.

The United States also developed new technologies, partly from the space race with the Soviet Union, partly from the military competition and partly from private sector developments. Satellites, satellite communications, computers, ocean phone services and other communications technology greatly enhanced the United States' strategic and economic assets. These technologies marginalized the Soviet Union, already irrevocably behind in its people's standard of living and, at the same time, greatly enhanced the United States companies in overseas markets.

The United States' capacity to project its values and material life overseas grew dramatically as Hollywood and television captured European markets. By the 1990s these two visual media reigned supreme throughout Europe and Great Britain. These media joined in giving the United States almost unmatched capability of projecting its popular and business cultures overseas, including Latin America.

The United States faced a different situation in Japan. Strategic necessities compelled the United States to rebuild Japan. United States policy makers realized an economically vibrant Japan would stand as a bulwark against the spread of communism, much as a prospering West Germany would in Europe. To sustain Japan's recovery and its growth, United States policy makers gave Japan access to its huge domestic market. By the 1980s the Japanese had developed a formidable industrial sector that challenged the United States in many essential industries. The United States now found Japan was an economic competitor.

Yet, United States service corporations and popular culture made their way into Japanese markets and successfully penetrated markets in Asia. McDonald's and Kentucky Fried Chicken sold their products to families in Japan and Taiwan. Soldiers of the People's Republic of China even lunched at the Kentucky Fried Chicken outlet on Tiananmen Square in Beijing. The busiest outlet for Seattle's Starbuck's coffee chain is in the Shibuya District of Tokyo. Rap music and Hollywood films also captivated audiences in Japan and Asia. The United States cultural and economic reach now stretched around the globe.

In the end the United States had moved a long way from its early days as a small and weak republic. Its technological capacity, its vast global markets and its military prowess marked it as a superpower with the capacity to influence markets and regimes around the globe.

Further reading

For a reference source for the twentieth century in general, see Joel Krieger, ed., *The Oxford Companion to Politics of the World* (New York, 1993). For an analysis of the United States and its place in the process of globalization, see Alfred E. Eckes, Jr. and Thomas W. Zeiler, *Globalization and the American Century* (New York, 2003). An overview of United States efforts at promoting democracy across the globe can be found in Tony Smith, *America's Mission: The United States and the Worldwide Struggle for Democracy in the Twentieth Century* (Princeton, 1994).

For works that deal with consumerism, see Victoria de Grazia, *Irresistible Empire: America's Advance through 20th-Century Europe* (Cambridge, Massachusetts, 2005); Richard Pells, *Not Like Us: How Europeans have Loved, Hated and Transformed American Culture since World War II* (New York, 1997); Warren I. Cohen, *The Asian American Century* (Cambridge, Massachusetts, 2002); Arnold J. Bauer, *Goods, Power, History: Latin America's Material Culture* (New York, 2001).

For a work that deals with multinational corporations, see Richard J. Barnet and John Cavanagh, *Global Dreams: Imperial Corporations and the New World Order* (New York, 1994). For an overview of Latin America, see Frederick Stirton Weave, *Latin America in the World Economy* (Boulder, Colorado, 2000); Thomas E. Skidmore and Peter H. Smith, *Modern Latin America* (New York, 1992).

Epilogue
Toward the future

The end of the Cold War and the terrorist strike against the United States on September 11, 2001 marked important events in the spread of the global economy embodied by the United States. The collapse of the Soviet Union and an end to its empire in Europe brought Eastern European states such as Poland into the global economy. The strike against the World Trade Towers and the Pentagon signaled the determination of the Islamic radicals to remove the United States from the Islamic world.

In the case of Al-Qaeda and its leader, Osama bin Laden, the United States, its power, its wealth and its capacity to project its culture throughout the world threatened Islam. In effect, men such as Bin Laden want to create an Islamic-ruled zone that barred goods and services from the United States and other western industrial countries. They come from countries that are marginal to the global economy yet have experienced its impact.

The issue remains less the specific grievances, than the willingness to remain outside the emerging global economy and the efforts to disrupt it. At the same time, rogue states such as Iraq under Saddam Hussein also threatened the stability of the global economy since they ignored the rules governing this system when it suited their purposes. The United States, with its immense investment in free markets and free trade as well as its commitment to a global economy where goods and people move unhindered, see terrorist groups such as Al-Qaeda and states such as Iraq as dangers to its economic ideals, even aside from the imminent danger they may pose to the North American state.

In this emerging system the United States military has assumed a critical role. The military's role in providing security for the United States and, ultimately, the stability necessary for a global economy has become paramount. The invasion and occupation of Afghanistan and Iraq underscore this role. The Asian states housed Al-Qaeda training centers and headquarters while Iraq's dictator, Saddam Hussein, posed a threat to stability in the Middle East, a vital oil producing region.

To achieve these goals the United States relies on its unmatched military. Its leaders had transformed the military from services dependent on the draft for manpower to an all-volunteer force. This dramatic change gave the military a professional character at all levels, one well suited to the increasing technological and tactical demands of fighting in the twenty-first century. Smart bombs, new stealth aircraft, and startling innovation in battlefield communications made the United States military unbeatable in inter-state wars.

Of course the challenges of dealing with non-state entities such as Al-Qaeda demanded a far more complicated scheme. This involved the Treasury Department, bankers, customs agents and attorneys all crucial to stopping flow of capital to such networks. The military had to work closely with law enforcement agencies in tracking terrorists and with the State Department in follow-ups once a state such as Iraq was defeated. The military now operates in a more complex environment, greatly enhanced by technology and new players all dedicated to protecting United States interests and the stability of the global economy. It remains an important cog in the globally oriented United States, one that insures political and economic stability. The challenge of the next century for the United States will be its capacity to maintain this stability so vital for its overall interests.

Further reading

For works that address the United States military and its development in the past few decades, see Williamson Murray and Major General Robert H. Scales, Jr., *The Iraq War: A Military History* (New York, 2003); Bruce Berkowitz, *The New Face of War: How War Will Be Fought in the Twenty-First Century* (New York, 2003) and a critical commentary, Chalmers Johnson, *The Sorrows of Empire: Militarism, Secrecy, and the End of the Republic* (New York, 2004). On a broader approach to the place of the military in an array of United States institutions, and the new international environment, see Thomas P.M. Barnett, *The Pentagon's New Map: War and Peace in the Twenty-first Century* (New York, 2004) and for an overall view of the global economic landscape, see Thomas L. Friedman, *The World Is Flat: A Brief History Of The Twenty-First Century* (New York, 2005), especially chapter 11, "The Unflat World", pp. 371–413.

Conclusion

The calls for the internationalizing of United States history owe much of their energy to what many scholarly critics argue is the narrow focus of United States historians. Equally as important, internationalizing the United States past demands a reconsideration of the "Exceptionalist paradigm" that influences public and academic thinking alike. Scholars argue that the United States' commitment to liberty, equality of opportunity and minimal government separated the nation from other polities. These ideas stretch deep into the country's history, from its founding documents to its current policies. George Bancroft, the most noted popular historian of the late nineteenth century, embraced the notion of divine providence as a moving force in shaping the United States. His ideas were greeted by an enthusiastic national audience.

Over the last century historians have raised many serious and often unassailable critiques of "Exceptionalism." Race, class and gender studies have pointed out the limitations of liberty, self-government and economic opportunity. Scholars have also expressed reservations over the altruistic nature of United States foreign policy.

Within the past decade many United States historians have begun to pursue comparative history and research that connects the United States' experiences with that of other countries. In many ways, this turn recaptures the concerns of an earlier generation of historians who did ask questions about the larger context. Textbooks have begun to incorporate some of the materials uncovered in this research. Still, a field dedicated to the United States in the broader arena has yet fully to develop. At the same time, debates over Exceptionalism persist and the advent of the Internet has spurred even more discussion from both supporters and opponents of Exceptionalism. The paradigm still enjoys a healthy existence.

Recently world historians have argued that the United States needs to be seen in the context of a larger world, one where global processes and broader human communities played crucial roles in shaping the national experience. What appears exceptional to United States citizens reflected the country's own inward focus without understanding the reach of migration, commercial capitalism, revolution, the professional-managerial ethos and the corporation, or other phenomena that touched human communities across the globe.

The preceding chapters address this concern among world historians. Some chapters relied heavily on comparisons. As important, the book raises the interactive nature of the United States' relationship with larger contexts. The United States projected power, popular culture, and its political system abroad. Such phenomena occurred with other polities. States such as Great Britain, with strength and institutions sufficient to reach beyond their borders, precipitated change in many societies across the globe. The cases of language and popular culture explain why Indians and Filipinos speak English, or why the British drive Ford automobiles. Similarly, the power of German education makes clear why scientists who worked in United States corporate research labs earned their doctorates in Germany. The point remains, whether initiating such changes or participating in changes with multiple origins, the United States participated in larger human communities.

The British North American colonies, later the United States, provided such an example. They developed a complex set of economic relationships that reached well beyond their Atlantic coast. The Caribbean islands, West African polities, Scotland and Ireland among other centers of population and major economic activity provided the colonies with markets for its products and sources of goods. As important, distant societies in West Africa also supplied human beings who made the Southern colonies in North America eminently prosperous. Their labor and knowledge produced the goods that sustained British investors, colonial planters in North America and the Caribbean wealthy. Commoners, including men of African origin, worked the ocean-going ships that provided the glue that held all the disparate parts of the British commercial empire together. The construction and maintenance of those ships sustained a flourishing New England economy dedicated to maritime activities across the breadth of the Pan-British world.

North Americans also drew their plantation labor from Africa to sustain agricultural staples such as tobacco, rice, cotton, sugar and indigo. Distant markets sustained the plantation economies and the slave labor system of South Carolina or Georgia into the nineteenth century. Industrial markets created the basis for the settlement of Alabama, Mississippi and other Deep South states.

This larger economic context continued to shape the United States into the twentieth century. Its economy depended on mineral deposits in Northern Mexico, Peru and Chile, to name a few locations. It also drew sugar from Cuba and Hawaii. Even the Philippines sent small batches of tropical fruits and products to United States consumers. Labor from the Caribbean worked United States-owned plantations in Cuba and Honduras. In many of these states the political leadership worked closely with United States corporations, intending to capitalize on the industrial sites these companies constructed, the port they improved and/or the railroads they built.

The national narrative always incorporates immigration as one of the distinguishing characteristics of the nation. Such discussions generally isolated the United States' experiences from the broader movement of peoples across the globe. Migration, the term scholars prefer to use, has always characterized human societies. Scottish and Scottish-Irish migrants quite often chose the British North American colonies in the eighteenth century. Yet, Scots also moved to London and to Canada in great numbers. Scottish-Irish people migrated to Scotland and to England as well as to Nova Scotia. In the late nineteenth century, British migrants came to the United States in large numbers. Many also moved to Canada, Australia, South Africa and New Zealand. Others chose imperial colonies in Africa and some even moved to South America.

In the Atlantic world, the United States drew the largest number of migrants. It also had the largest economy. Yet, Argentina proportionally attracted more migrants than the United States. Brazil and Argentina also served as the main destinations for the vast majority of Iberian migrants who crossed the Atlantic in search of work and homes. Canada actually counted more British migrants than the United States. Among the millions of migrants who sought work and residences in the United States, many came with only short-term goals in mind.

Industrial states also attracted labor. The Irish moved to Great Britain both during and in the decades after the famine. Some moved farther north to Scotland. Poles and Germans in the eastern reaches of the German states moved to west Germany to fill the ranks of industrial labor. The Ruhr Valley offered high-paying and steady jobs to hundreds of thousands of migrant workers. At the same time, an equally larger number of Poles from Austrian and Russian controlled Poland replaced the departing workers in east Germany, where they labored in agriculture and mining. In an earlier period, Scottish and Scottish-Irish migrants also journeyed across the ocean, mostly in search of land. They ended in places as diverse as the British colonies in North America, Nova Scotia in Canada, and the Caribbean islands. Scottish-Irish migrants also moved back to Scotland for many different reasons and, of course, many headed for England. The British colonies certainly drew the lion's share of this Scottish-Irish diaspora, yet many chose other destinations. Migration represented a constant process that shaped and reshaped societies and economies across the globe. The process never ceases and the United States' participation remained as prominent in 1900 as it did in 1770.

Those who returned to their home communities carried the influence of the United States well beyond its borders. Politics in Scandinavia changed because of the experiences of their citizens who lived in the United States and acquired many of its political habits. These men and women served as counterparts to migrants from Germany, Russia and Eastern Europe, who reinvigorated socialist politics and union activities in the United States. Architecture in Southern Italy resembled a style prominent in the United States because of Italian migrants who spent time in North America.

The United States consciously exported its political culture based on representative government, a written constitution and rule of law. United States officials demanded elections and choice. Such decisions rarely worked out as imagined in the policy making rooms of Washington. In the Philippines the United States colonial administration did turn over substantial autonomy to an elected government. Its members had achieved public office through the electoral process and this tradition would persist. At the same time, members of the *Mestizo* landowning elite controlled government. The United States officials ended up working through the landowners because of their power, their extensive ties within communities and their capacity to see through government operations. Representative government also existed side by side with a fierce racial code the United States brought to the Philippines. Last, colonial administration remained distinct in installing a representative system. Yet, it also borrowed from European colonial systems in Asia and Africa. Its administrators also participated in imperial conferences on governing colonies.

The professional-managerial groups appeared in all industrial societies. The United States relied on them to build large corporations, to move its industrial infrastructures to sites close to and distant from the national borders. British engineers built railroads across the globe while German industrialists operated plants throughout Europe. Experts in many disciplines shared information necessary to governing colonial populations. United States colonial administrators, usually with sophisticated educational backgrounds, frequently engaged in such exchanges.

In the post-World War II era, the United States assumed increasing global power. It faced a hostile Soviet Union in a protracted struggle that lasted until the early 1990s. These powers faced each other in a divided Europe and spent decades in an arms race. Ironically, the United States fought its wars in Asia and never won. It did triumph in the contest over standards of living, in communications technology, in the space race and in popular culture by the late twentieth century. The Soviet Union could never produce consumer goods, movies, television programs or fast food as United States corporations did during the Cold War. The reach of the United States extended dramatically as her military acquired better technology, expanded its military bases across the globe and opted for a professional force rather than draft recruiting. By the early twentieth century, no other power could equal the United States in terms of the assets it held.

These chapters will not decide whether the exceptionalist paradigm prevails or succumbs. The intent is to contribute to efforts to reconsider the United States' place in the world community. Engaging the broader world suggests different ways of understanding the United States experience.

Further reading

For discussions of Exceptionalism, see Dorothy Ross, *The Origins of American Social Science* (New York, 1992), especially chapters 2 and 3. See also Dorothy Ross, "Historical Consciousness in Nineteenth-Century America," *The American Historical*

Review 89 (1984), pp. 909–928 and Ian Tyrrell, "American Exceptionalism in an Age of International History," *The American Historical Review* 96 (1991), pp. 1031–1055. For a response to Tyrrell's article and his counter, see Michael McGerr, "The Price of the 'New Transnational History,'" *The American Historical Review* 96 (1991), pp. 1056–1072. For an early call to broaden approaches to history, see Akira Iriye's Presidential Address in *The American Historical Review* 94 (1989), pp. 1–10. For a thoughtful and provocative examination of world history and its implications for the discipline, see Michael Geyer and Charles Bright, "World History in a Global Age," *The American Historical Review* 100 (1995), pp. 1036–1060.

For a discussion of United States history and the need to widen the scope of research, see David Thelen, "Of Audiences, Borderlands, and Comparisons: Toward the internationalization of American history," *The Journal of American History* 79 (1992), pp. 432–462 and Joyce Appleby, "Recovering America's Historic Diversity: Beyond exceptionalism," *The Journal of American History* 79 (1992), pp. 419–431.

For a random sample of websites where American exceptionalism is discussed and debated, see http://enwikipedia.org/wiki/American_Exceptionalism; http://www.wwnorton.com/catalog/spring97/american.html; http://www.economist.com/printedition/ displayStory.cfm?Story_ID=2172066; http://www.answers.com/topic/exceptionalism.

Index

Routledge History

The Routledge Atlas of American History, 5th Edition
Martin Gilbert

'. . . especially clear and helpful…well laid out and useful
for quick reference'
The Economist

This new edition of *The Routledge Atlas of American History* presents a series
of 157 clear and detailed maps, accompanied by informative captions, facts
and figures. Updated with additional maps and text and including significant
recent events, the complete history of America is unravelled through vivid
representations of all the significant landmarks, including:

- politics – from the annexation of Texas to the battle for black voting
  rights and the results of the 2004 Presidential election
- military events – from the War of Independence and America's standing
  in two world wars to the conflicts in Korea, Vietnam and the Gulf,
  includes new maps covering the war in Iraq, the American campaign in
  Afghanistan and the War on Terror
- social history – from the abolition of slavery to the growth of female
  emancipation
- transport – from nineteenth-century railroads and canals to recent
  ventures into space
- economics – from early farming and industry to the state of America
  today.

The history of North America from early settlement to the present day is
presented to students and enthusiasts of the subject in this fundamental reference
book.

ISBN10: 0-415-35902-3 (hbk)
ISBN10: 0-415-35903-1 (pbk)

ISBN13: 978-0-415-35902-3 (hbk)
ISBN13: 978-0-415-35903-X (pbk)

Available at all good bookshops
For ordering and further information please visit:
www.routledge.com

Routledge History

American Cultural Studies

Neil C. Campbell and Alasdair Kean

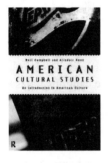

'Something of a godsend . . . as a teaching resource this book is second to none ... achieves levels of multiplicity rarely, if ever, reached by others.'

Borderlines: Studies in American Culture

American Cultural Studies is an interdisciplinary introduction to American culture for those taking American Studies. This textbook:

- introduces the full range and variety of American culture including issues of race, gender and youth
- provides a truly interdisciplinary methodology
- suggests and discusses a variety of approaches to study
- highlights American distinctiveness
- draws on literature, art, film, theatre, architecture, music and more
- challenges orthodox paradigms of American Studies.

ISBN10: 0-415-12797-1 (hbk)
ISBN10: 0-415-12798-X (pbk)

ISBN13: 978-0-415-12797-4 (hbk)
ISBN13: 978-0-415-12798-1 (pbk)

Available at all good bookshops
For ordering and further information please visit:
www.routledge.com

Routledge History

The United States and Latin America: A History of American Diplomacy 1776-2000

Joseph Smith

Providing a concise, balanced and incisive analysis of US diplomatic relations with Latin America from 1776 to the end of the twentieth century, this timely work explores central themes such as the structure of international relations, and the pursuit of American national interest by the use of diplomacy, cultural imperialism and economic and military power. Joseph Smith examines:

- the rise of the USA as an independent power
- its policy towards Latin-American movements for independence
- the evolution of the Monroe Doctrine
- pan-Americanism
- dollar diplomacy
- the challenge of communism.

Highlighting Latin American responses to US policy over a significant time span, the study documents the development of a complex historical relationship in which the United States has claimed a pre-eminent role, arousing as much resentment as acquiescence from its southern neighbours. Including a timely discussion of the current issues of debt, trade and narcotics control, this unique and valuable study will be of interest to all those with an interest in US and Latin-American international relations.

ISBN10: 0-415-35834-5 (hbk)
ISBN10: 0-415-35835-3 (pbk)

ISBN13: 978-0-415-35834-7 (hbk)
ISBN13: 978-0-415-35835-5 (pbk)

Available at all good bookshops
For ordering and further information please visit:
www.routledge.com

Routledge History

Martin Luther King, Jr

Peter J. Ling

'Peter Ling's *Martin Luther King, Jr* is a thoughtful, perceptive and thoroughly well-informed work of scholarship. It is an excellent treatment of n impressive and inspiring human being.'
David J. Garrow, author of the Pulitzer Prize-winning
Bearing the Cross

'Peter Ling's biography of Martin Luther King, Jr is a singular accomplishment. What other distinguished scholars have written in mammoth volumes. Ling has carefully and succinctly presented in a highly readable and perceptive brief book.'
Stephen Lawson, Rutgers University

Drawing on recent scholarship on the Civil Rights Movement, this volume condenses research previously available only in the larger literature. Peter Ling's crisp and fluent style captures the drama, irony, and pathos of King's life and provides an excellent introduction for both students and general readers.

ISBN10: 0-415-21664-8 (hbk)
ISBN10: 0-415-21665-6 (pbk)

ISBN13: 978-0-415-21664-7 (hbk)
ISBN13: 978-0-415-21665-4 (pbk)

Available at all good bookshops
For ordering and further information please visit:
www.routledge.com

Routledge History

Gender in World History
2nd Edition
Peter N. Stearns

'A comparative history of immense ambition . . . [It] will be profitably
consulted by gender historians. It successfully demonstrates that gender
is a historical construct that is rebuilt by each generation and varies
from culture to culture.'
Journal of Contemporary History

From classical times to the twenty-first century, *Gender in World History* is a
fascinating exploration of what happens to established ideas about men and
women, and their roles, when different cultural systems come into contact. This
book breaks new ground to facilitate a consistent approach to gender in a world
history context.

This second edition is completely updated, including:

- expanded introductions to each chronological section

- extensive discussion of the twentieth century bringing it right up to
  date

- new chapters on international influences in the first half of the
  twentieth century and globalization in the latter part of the twentieth
  century

- engagement with the recent work done on gender history and theory.

Coming right up to the present day, *Gender in World History* is essential reading
for students of world history.

ISBN10: 0-415-39588-7 (hbk)
ISBN10: 0-415-39589-5 (pbk)

ISBN13: 978-0-415-39588-5 (hbk)
ISBN13: 978-0-415-39589-2 (pbk)

Available at all good bookshops
For ordering and further information please visit:
www.routledge.com

Routledge History

Migration in World History
Patrick Manning

From the spread of *Homo sapiens* onward, migration has been a major factor in human development. This wide-ranging survey traces the connections among regions brought about by the movements of people, diseases, crops, technology and ideas.

Drawing on examples from a wide range of geographical regions and thematic areas, Manning presents a useful overview, including:

- earliest human migrations and the first domestication of major plants and animals;

- the rise and spread of major language groups such as Indo-European, Afro-Asiatic, Niger-Congo, Indo-Pacific, Sino-Tibetan, Altaic, and Amerindian;

- trade patterns including the early Silk Road and maritime trade in the Mediterranean and Indian Ocean;

- the increasing impact of maritime and overland migrations on areas of life such as religion and family;

- the effect of migration on empire and industry between 1700 and 1900;

- the resurgence of migration in the later twentieth century, including movement to cities, refugees and diasporas.

ISBN10: 0-415-31148-9 (hbk)
ISBN10: 0-415-31147-0 (pbk)

ISBN13: 978-0-415-31148-9 (hbk)
ISBN13: 978-0-415-31147-2 (pbk)

Routledge History

Childhood in World History
Peter N. Stearns

Childhood exists in all societies, though there is huge variation in the way it is socially constructed across time and place. Studying childhood historically greatly advances our understanding of what childhood is about and a world history focus permits some of the broadest questions to be asked.

In *Childhood in World History* Peter N. Stearns focuses on childhood in several ways:

- childhood across change - the shift from hunting and gathering to an agricultural society and the impact of civilization and the emergence of major religions;
- new and old debates about the distinctive features of Western childhood, including child labour;
- the emergence of a modern, industrial pattern of childhood in the West, Japan and communist societies, including a focus on education and economic dependence;
- globalization and the spread of child-centred consumerism.

This historical perspective highlights the gains but also the divisions and losses for children across the millennia.

ISBN10: 0-415-35232-0 (hbk)
ISBN10: 0-415-35233-9 (pbk)

ISBN13: 978-0-415-35232-1 (hbk)
ISBN13: 978-0-415-35233-8 (pbk)

Available at all good bookshops
For ordering and further information please visit:
www.routledge.com

Routledge History

Religion in World History

John C. Super and Briane K. Turley

Individuals and groups have long found identity and meaning through religion and its collective expression. In *Religion and World History*, John C. Super and Briane K. Turley examine the value of religion for interpreting the human experience in the past and present. This study explores those elements of religion that best connect it with cultural and political dynamics that have influenced history.

Working within this general framework, Super and Turley bring out three unifying themes:

- the relationship between formal and informal religious beliefs, how these change through time, and how they are reflected in different cultures;
- the relationship between church and state, from theocracies to the repression of religion;
- the ongoing search for spiritual certainty, and the consequent splintering of core religious beliefs and the development of new ones.

The book's unique approach helps the reader grasp the many and complex ways that religion acts upon and reacts to broader global processes.

ISBN10: 0-415-31457-7 (hbk)
ISBN10: 0-415-31458-5 (pbk)

ISBN13: 978-0-415-31457-2 (hbk)
ISBN13: 978-0-415-31458-9 (pbk)

Available at all good bookshops
For ordering and further information please visit:
www.routledge.com